Through the Looking Glass

Observations in the Early Childhood Classroom

Sheryl Nicolson
Saddleback College

Susan G. Shipstead
California State University, Fullerton

Merrill, an imprint of
Macmillan Publishing Company
New York

Maxwell Macmillan Canada
Toronto

Maxwell Macmillan International
New York   Oxford   Singapore   Sydney

Cover photo: Zephyr Pictures © Melanie Carr
Editor: Linda A. Sullivan
Production Editor: Linda Hillis Bayma
Art Coordinators: Peter A. Robison, Vincent A. Smith
Photo Editor: Anne Vega
Cover Designer: Thomas Mack
Production Buyer: Jeff Smith
Artist: Jane Lopez
Electronic Text Management: Ben Ko, Marilyn Wilson Phelps

This book was set in New Baskerville by Macmillan Publishing Company and was printed and bound by R. R. Donnelley & Sons Company. The cover was printed by Phoenix Color Corp.

Macmillan Publishing Company
866 Third Avenue
New York, NY 10022

Macmillan Publishing Company is part of the
Maxwell Communication Group of Companies.

Maxwell Macmillan Canada, Inc.
1200 Eglinton Avenue East, Suite 200
Don Mills, Ontario M3C 3N1

Library of Congress Cataloging-in Publication Data
Nicolson, Sheryl.
    Through the looking glass : observations in the early childhood
classroom / Sheryl Nicolson, Susan G. Shipstead.
        p.   cm.
    Includes bibliographical references and index.
    ISBN 0-02-387491-0
    1. Observation (Educational method) 2. Early childhood education.
3.   Child development. I. Shipstead, Susan G. II. Title.
LB1027.28.N53 1994
372.21'072—dc20   93-15479
                                                            CIP

Printing: 1 2 3 4 5 6 7 8 9   Year: 4 5 6 7

Photo credits: All photos copyrighted by individuals or companies listed. Brian Cummings, pp. 11, 16, 56, 60, 90, 99 (middle), 103, 124, 139 (right), 157, 178, 184, 194 (bottom), 280, 297 (bottom), 302; Susan G. Shipstead, pp. 2, 7, 13, 25, 34, 53, 58, 65, 77, 83, 92, 99 (top and bottom), 106, 112, 117, 126, 130, 134, 139 (left), 142, 146, 147, 154, 166, 170, 194 (top), 212, 219, 227, 234, 244, 249, 256, 259, 282, 289, 291, 297 (top), 312.

Dedication . . . _____

To my husband Norm, who endlessly
supports and encourages my
dreams and ambitions.

—S. N.

In my life I am blessed with a great love, Patrick,
Two treasured children, Matthew and Maggie,
And the anchor of my dear dad, Erwin.
To you four, I dedicate this work.

—S. G. S.

Preface

In the fall of 1988, we taught a course on observation in the early childhood class-room, and therein we sowed the seeds of this text. The book you hold in your hands is the product of nearly 3 years of our commitment to write an observation text that unites solid methodological instruction with a broad understanding of children's development. We have found that if students learn *how* to observe while also paying close attention to *what* to observe, they are able to use their skills to full potential. This text maintains a close relationship between observing, understanding what one observes, and improving the educational program and environment.

Because our goal in *Through the Looking Glass* is to integrate observation and child development, we have included several helpful features. Chapters 2 and 3, which describe highlights of development during the preschool and primary grade years, establish a common ground of information for knowledgeable and novice readers in the field of child development. Our Growth Indicators of child development are concrete guides for *what* to observe. In each chapter presenting an observational method, we have offered two detailed examples, one from preschool and one from the primary grades, to show how educators effectively study issues in classrooms, interpret the data, and initiate follow-through plans. We have arranged the chapters to build on the reader's expanding understanding of observation, and the Think About sections at the end of each chapter ask the reader to ponder a question or problem that anticipates the content of the next chapter. The Think About sections serve as consistent reminders that educators draw on observational methods to respond to critical issues in their early child-hood classrooms. Finally, the Student Activities and Action Projects provide abundant opportunities to involve the reader in the observational process.

Upon completion of the manuscript, we flipped a coin to determine which of us would be the first author. We hope our readers remember that the order was set by chance and that teamwork produced this text.

Special Acknowledgments

I send my heartfelt appreciation to my Mom and Dad for believing in me; to my sister, Linda, for her wise counsel and thoughtful suggestions; to Janece Kline for facilitating my transition from elementary to preschool teaching; and to the many children and college students I have had the privilege of working with—they have been my true teachers!

—*Sheryl Nicolson*

Many of my contributions to *Through the Looking Glass* have direct threads running to significant people of my past. I am indebted to Courtney Cazden for a masterful class on observation at Harvard. My work at High/Scope Educational Research Foundation was enhanced by experiences with Dave Weikart, Clay Shouse, Carole Thomson, Joanna Phinney, Mary Hohmann, Linda Rogers, and Bernie Banet; I salute one and all. I thank my Stanford heroes, John Flavell and Dick Snow, for their exemplary instruction, guidance, and fine human nature. Finally, I send global appreciation to the many children, teachers, directors, and students with whom I have had the good fortune to work for helping me know in my heart what I learned in my head.

—*Susan G. Shipstead*

Collective Acknowledgments

We wish to thank our friends and colleagues who took precious time to read portions of our manuscript and offer advice, especially Pat Dumas and the Saddleback College students who pilot tested the manuscript in the fall of 1992, Ellen Grangaard, Sherrie King, Stephen McClelland, Judith Ramirez, Carole Raylin, and Annette Unten.

We extend our gratitude to the many educators who welcomed us into their classrooms, with special recognition to the following: Amy Ambellan, Ingrid Andrews, Ellen Grangaard, Kim Graves, Gail Harrison, Jeff Herdman, Marilyn Johnson, Carol Johnston, Jan Miner, Kathy Moon, Jody Parsons, Terry Peterson, David Rover, Linda Sabic, Laurie Santamaura, Sandra Senn, Lillan Smith, Grace Van Thillo, and Cathy Weitstock.

We'd also like to thank Ingrid Andrews, Pauline Dinger, Paige Sessions, and Georgie Tiernan for contributing specific observations. The library staffs at Saddleback College and California State University, Fullerton offered time-saving help, and they, too, have our thanks.

Writing the manuscript is only half of the tremendous task of creating a new text. We would like to express our appreciation to those who have carried out the publishing half, the fine staff at Merrill. In particular we thank our editor Linda Sullivan, production editor Linda Bayma, copy editor Laurie Endicott Thomas, photo editor Anne Vega, and marketing manager David Faherty.

The reviewers of our text have offered important suggestions, insights, and information. Their various regional perspectives, backgrounds, and experiences were invaluable to us as we worked to write a text that would meet the needs of all observation students. Your contributions were most helpful, and we thank you! Our reviewers included Anita Brehm, East Carolina University; Barry Bussewitz, Solano Community College; Jeri Carroll, Wichita State University; Richard Fiene, Pennsylvania State University at Harrisburg; Russ Firlik, Sacred Heart University; Barbara Foulks, SUNY Geneseo; Carol Gestwicki, Central Piedmont Community College; Barbara Graham, Norfolk State University; Berta Harris, San Diego City College; Adrienne Herrell, California State University, Fresno; Janice A. Meyer, Roger Williams College; Lillian Oxtoby, Borough of Manhattan Community College; Colleen Randel, University of Texas at Tyler; and Wayne Reinhardt, Edmonds Community College.

Brief Contents

Contents

CHAPTER 3

Highlights of Development During the Primary Grade Years   *56*

PART I

Preparing the Looking Glass

CHAPTER 1

Toward an Educational Approach

Imagine you are an early childhood educator in a preschool classroom. This morning, you are standing outside near the swings. Out of the corner of your eye, as you turn your head, you catch a glimpse of Annie whisking the yellow road grader away from Tajima.

- What are your initial thoughts?
- What details do your senses absorb?
- Do you smell the first hints of lunch about to be served, which might have reminded the youngster of a fleeting opportunity to get the beloved toy?
- What do you see the child do?
- What do you hear the child say?
- Did the child have the toy first and simply reclaim it?
- Or had the child been wandering around the play yard when she grabbed the toy in an unprovoked act?

Even in such an ordinary situation as this, you may accurately or inaccurately appraise the situation and respond appropriately or inappropriately. Your skills as an observer make a difference in your guidance and education of this young child.

Continuing on this flight of fantasy, consider what you might know about the child and this behavior.

- Is this the first time you have seen this child grab a toy from another, or has this deed been a frequent classroom headache?
- Have you noticed a pattern of preceding events that predictably prompt this act, such as rejection by other children?
- What circumstances or expectations outside of school might have promoted this seizure? For example, is the child dreadfully lonely now that a beloved sibling has gone off to college? Or is grabbing ignored in the home so that it has become the child's common strategy to procure a desired object?

Stop and think for a moment about what else you want to know about this child and the episode before you decide how to respond. What major piece of this puzzle is not yet in place? What information is crucial to your thoughtful and appropriate response?

Your understanding of the child's developmental level is essential to the selection of a supportive response. If the child is a young 2-year-old whose energies have advanced gross motor skills more than language, you would evaluate the event and respond differently than if the child is a 5- or 6-year-old. One of your jobs as an educator of young children is to understand child development in enough detail that your responses are individually based and ensure future growth.

For those who have studied child development and early childhood education, the classroom provides opportunities to apply useful theories. By understanding the milestones of physical, cognitive, psychosocial, and creative development and by applying a variety of observational methods, students can enter the field of early childhood education equipped with the ability to plan activities, experiences, and environments that enhance children's growth. Well-trained teachers can select materials that challenge individual children at opportune moments. They can suggest and organize activities that encourage children to think differently about familiar experiences. They can respond to problem behaviors with flexible strategies. They can view children's similarities and differences with a broad perspective. They can improve their own teaching effectiveness. They can guide children's social growth. The list goes on and on.

You can be a good early childhood educator if you provide developmentally appropriate materials and experiences for children; *developmentally appropriate* means that the selection is based on the age and individual needs of the children in the program (Bredekamp, 1987). Set your sights higher. You can be a remarkable teacher if you understand child development and are able to provide materials and experiences that optimize each child's total development. The key is observation.

Ambitions of This Book

In the beginning of this chapter, you imagined a preschool scenario and engaged your mind in thoughtful considerations. Learning is not passive. One of your jobs as a reader is to stop and think about the points, examples, and questions raised in this book. Make the information your own by reflecting on how it relates to your unique store of knowledge and experience. Expect to answer questions in the text and raise more of your own.

Beyond working as an active reader, you will be asked to participate in student activities and apply what you have learned. Search for additional opportunities to explore topics and ideas new to you. Look, listen, and watch the young children around you—at the movies, in shopping malls, and in your own and friends' homes. Plan field trips to observe model early childhood education centers. Willingly participate in class discussions, and learn from your classmates as well as from your instructor. Integrate your new knowledge with your own experience base. How does it fit? What questions do you have? Are there inconsistencies? Explore these ideas. Then, at the end of each chapter, take time to grapple with the problems and questions in the Think About sections; your ideas will provide a transition into the topic of the next chapter.

The focus of this book is on observation for early childhood educators, specifically those who work with preschool and primary grade children. The purpose of this book is to teach the application of an array of observational methods within a child-development framework. A strong foundation in child development is a must for observation. Therefore, the beginning chapters of this book highlight the general growth patterns of preschool (ages 2 to 5) and primary grade (ages 5 to 8) children, drawing on developmental theory and research. Continued emphasis on the comprehensive development of preschool and primary grade children is intertwined throughout the examples, applications, and interpretations of observations in each chapter.

Throughout this book, the aim is to present the methodological tools to tackle questions and concerns in early childhood classrooms with skill. Competence is gained in observational skills by studying each method's definition, appropriate applications, strengths, and limitations and by practicing the construction and use of each. *Through the Looking Glass* will guide you in achieving this competence.

The text will emphasize that one observational method is not inherently superior to another. Understanding observational methodology allows the educational practitioner to select a method on the basis of its appropriateness in a particular situation. Further, developing an ability to use a variety of methods promotes a view of the subject (child, teacher, or interactions) through different windows. Just as your appreciation and understanding of a statue is limited if you only stand in front of it or to the side, so is the grasp of people and their relationships confined by relying on a single method of study.

The organization of this book addresses the importance of keeping the subject (child, teacher, and interactions) as the focus of observations. This book begins by presenting highlights of child development and introducing observational methods appropriate to the study of individual children and related conditions. Then the looking glass expands to include teachers and teacher–child interactions. The integration of child-development theory and the application of observational skills in working with young children are stressed; a multitude of examples will help you keep real classrooms and real people in mind. Learning how to apply observational methods will increase the joys of teaching and further the progress in becoming a remarkable teacher.

The Road to Sound Observation

Now the journey of this text begins. You will take the first step on the road to sound observation by examining reasons for observing and exploring topics suitable for classroom study. Next, you will review guidelines for effective and unobtrusive observation in the early childhood classroom. Finally in this chapter, you will consider the crucial differences between objective and subjective observation and develop objective observational skills. Let us begin.

Reasons for Observing.   In vibrant classrooms the observational process occurs daily and is the foundation for rich learning experiences. Box 1.1 lists reasons for observing in the early childhood classroom. Observing allows teachers to assess the progress and problems of the children and teachers in the classroom; they can then make adjustments to promote growth. On a daily basis, teachers document small developmental steps in children and plan supporting experiences. Weekly, they supplement the curriculum and learning environment on the basis of the assessed needs of individual children. They also use their observational skills to choose appropriate responses to behavioral difficulties, such as a preschool child grabbing a toy from another child or a primary grade child using fists to solve a playground problem. Teachers use the well-drawn details gleaned from classroom observations to measure and record each child's developmental growth over the entire year in an individual portfolio. (A portfolio is a collection of observational records and work samples for one child, usually kept for a period of one year.)

"Assessment of children's development, learning, and interests should be an integral part of all early childhood programs" (Schweinhart & McNair, 1991). Observations of children's growth and development facilitate short-term and

---

Box 1.1
Reasons for Observing in the Early Childhood Classroom

- Chart developmental growth (physical, cognitive, psychosocial, and creative) for each child.

- Evaluate each child's strengths and limitations from a realistic perspective.

- Analyze specific problems.

- Plan appropriate curriculum, materials, responses, strategies, and interactions based on individual needs.

- Plan responsive environments indoors and outdoors.

- Maintain records for study teams, conferences, and ongoing feedback to parents.

- Arrive at a comprehensive understanding of each child or a teacher through the application of several observational methods.

- Appraise teacher practices, and design staff development.

The early childhood classroom provides diverse and abundant opportunities for observation.

long-term classroom planning and are the basis for parent conferences and record keeping. Further, teachers use observations to evaluate how they are teaching. For example, a teacher could assess whether the questions most frequently posed to children stimulate thinking and conversation or if they request one-word responses.

What to Observe.   Look at the above photos of a classroom filled with busy children. Examine what the teacher and children are doing. What materials are they using? What activities are in progress? How are the children interacting?

Now stop for a moment and compile your ideas about what you might observe in this classroom; list the topics in Student Activity 1.1. You may want to add primary grade examples and other ideas not suggested by the photos. Think about examples of children's developmental growth, the influences of the environment, developmentally appropriate practices, and effective teaching strategies.

Student Activity 1.1 ———————————————————————————

Topics of Observation

List topics to observe in an early childhood classroom.

Examples:

- Types of roles enacted in the dramatic play area
- Frequency of on-task behaviors

1.

2.

3.

4.

5.

6.

———————————————————————————————————————

The following is a typical list of observational topics brainstormed by students interested in preschool and primary classrooms. It is based on their own experiences.

Students' Topics of Observation
1. Listening and learning
2. Frequency of aggressive behavior outside
3. Classification skills
4. Block building
5. Types of teacher questions
6. Reading comprehension
7. Clarity of speech
8. Motor skills
9. Teacher responses to cultural diversity

10. Interaction patterns with peers

11. Eye contact between teachers and children

12. Ability to follow directions

13. Promoting self-esteem

14. Kindergarten readiness

15. Active role of teacher

16. Evidence of anti-bias curriculum

17. Separation and independence

18. Length of attention span during specific times

Look at Student Activity 1.1 and compare your ideas with the above list. Are there similarities? Did you think of items not on this list? Now reread both lists carefully while thinking about how each topic could be observed in a classroom.

All the items on the student list are concerns teachers may have, but not all are directly observable. Some are too general and some too vague. Observation is most useful when we can pinpoint exactly what it is we are looking for and what it is we want to see. For example, "frequency of aggressive behavior outside" could be categorized and accurately observed, but "listening and learning" is too complex to specify exactly what behaviors we would be looking for. "Listening and learning" is too general and too vague. Narrowing the topic to state a specific act of listening, such as listening during story time, suggests a manageable focus to the teacher. Now turn your attention to Student Activity 1.2 for practice in evaluating topics to observe.

Student Activity 1.2

Evaluation of Topics of Observation

Using your list from Student Activity 1.1 and the Students' Topics of Observation list, read each item carefully and determine if it is an appropriate topic of observation or too general and vague. Place each item in the proper column below.

Appropriate Topic
Example: Frequency of
aggressive behavior outside

Too General/Too Vague
Example: Listening
and learning

You are on the road to sound observation when you can identify topics that are specific and observable. If you found that in Student Activity 1.1 you listed some vague or general items, see if you can now revise them to be more explicit or delete them if they are not workable. As a teacher, you will conduct a variety of observations on many different topics. Continue to practice selecting appropriate behaviors to observe; use all available opportunities.

Guidelines for Observation. As you learn to become a competent observer, you will be spending time in classrooms practicing various methods. Reasonable preparations for a classroom observation will help you get off to a good start and maximize the amount of information you will be able to gather. The following helpful suggestions are applicable to any observational method you select and may also be used in your own classroom with some modifications.

1. Clarify the purpose of your observation. Spend time before the observation to examine its purpose. What is the assignment? Do you understand the method you plan to use? Focus on the "big picture" of your observation.

2. Schedule your visit if you are observing in a classroom other than your own. No teacher will appreciate being surprised by your arrival. Phone about a week ahead to arrange the date, time, and length of your observation. Generally explain the purpose of your observation; for example, you might say that you will observe teacher–child interactions. If you describe your observation question in minute detail (e.g., What are the types and frequencies of the questions teachers ask children?), you risk prompting atypical behavior. Leave your phone number in case the teacher needs to contact you before your visit.

3. Come equipped with the necessary materials and a warm smile. For most assignments you will need paper or your observation form, pencils or pens, and something firm to write on. Check in with the school administrator (bring your college ID card for identification), and greet each adult in the classroom. Some normal anxiety about being observed can be alleviated by being friendly and acknowledging each adult individually.

4. Select a position from which to observe. Look around the classroom to note your options. You want to be as inconspicuous as possible; thus, you should sit down and keep to the outskirts of activities in progress. You will increase your viewing range if you sit with your back to the wall. You want to find the fine line that will allow you to hear and see what's going on without interfering in or detracting from the activity.

5. Note the "lay of the land." If you are not acquainted with the classroom, spend about 10 minutes becoming familiar with the layout of the classroom, the materials accessible to the children, and what is going on. During this time you want to satisfy your curiosity about general matters so you can then turn your attention to the specifics of your observation. Drawing a rough map of the room is helpful.

6. Check your own emotional responses to the children, teachers, and classroom. Clear away any biases or judgments that may cloud your focus, such as the labeling of a child (e.g., spoiled, bossy, or stressed) or reactions to a situation that resembles an unpleasant personal experience.

7. Respond in a natural way to children's inquiries about your presence. If a child asks why you are there or what you are doing, respond with "I'm just visiting to see what preschool (or first grade or whatever) is like." This is usually enough to satisfy and reassure the child as you continue to observe.

8. Include a heading on your recording form. Be sure to report the following information and any other that is requested on your form or necessary for your observation.

Center or School/Grade:
Date: Time:
Observer: Child or Group Observed/Age:

Objective Versus Subjective Observation.   The material that follows defines the most fundamental skill necessary to sound observation. Consider this scenario. Two college observation students visited a kindergarten playground.

Observations may be collected inside and outside the classroom or, as this student is doing, through a one-way mirror.

They watched the same boy, Cyd, who is 5 years and 1 month old (5;1), as part of their assignment to spend 5 minutes recording one child's activity.

Student A wrote the following observation:

The boy I am observing (Cyd, 5;1) is playing all alone with a dinosaur in the sand. He doesn't seem to have any friends. He plays with just one dinosaur all by himself for a while. Then he gets bored and goes to get some other dinosaurs at the end of the sand area. He demands the teacher's attention, probably the only person who will listen to him. He tells her that the biggest dinosaur is the boss, probably what he wants to be all of the time. No wonder he is playing alone.

Student B wrote the following observation:

The boy (Cyd, 5;1) is sitting in the middle of the sand area, his left foot tucked under his right knee, and reaches into the toy bin and grasps a small plastic dinosaur in his right hand. He stands, leaning on his left hand to push his body upward. Holding the dinosaur, he walks slowly to the edge of the sand area and places the dinosaur to the left of two other plastic dinosaurs lined up on the wood outlining the sand area. In a loud voice he exclaims, "Now you're all here." He spins around to the teacher and announces as he points to them in lined order, "Tyrannosaurus is the boss 'cause he's the biggest. The stegosaurus is the next boss 'cause he's the next biggest. The dimetrodon is the baby. He's not very big."

Both observers watched the same child, at the same time, engaging in the same activity. Yet the accounts are very different. Go back and reread the two paragraphs. What are the specific elements that differentiate the two passages?

Student A's observation is based on personal impressions and feelings about the child. Consequently, this student has recorded an observation that is influenced by biases and preconceptions. This type of observing is called *subjective observation*.

On the other hand, Student B impartially recorded only the facts and events. This observer has left out evaluations, judgments, impressions, and personal speculations. This observation is not, then, a personal interpretation. This type of observing is called *objective observation*. The observation can be useful, in this instance, to keep records of the child's developmental growth. The trained teacher would not miss the opportunity to note and record Cyd's display of seriation.

Learning to observe objectively can be challenging. It is impossible to be entirely objective all of the time. Complete the exercise in Student Activity 1.3 to sharpen your objective eye.

Student Activity 1.3 _____

Objective Descriptions

Examine the photo. Then list four statements describing what you see.

Example: The teacher is pushing the tire swing.

1.

2.

3.

4.

You may want to find a classmate and compare your findings. Can each of you detect examples of objective and subjective recordings? Discuss your conclusions.

Learning to be objective (to the best of one's ability) is the fundamental skill necessary to travel on the road to sound observation. In Action Project 1.1, you have the opportunity to observe on your own. Many students have been surprised to find how subjective their initial practice observations were. You may find value in saving your initial observation and then comparing it with an observation made at the end of the class. This comparison can be valuable feedback and a true measure of the distance you have traveled.

Action Project 1.1
Recording Objective Statements

Following the general guidelines for observation, visit a school of your choice (preschool or primary) and record six objective statements about what you observe. Be sure to call ahead, go prepared, and stay 15 to 20 minutes.

1.

2.

3.

4.

5.

6.

Think About . . .

Suppose you read the following observation of a child coloring in the art area of a classroom:

Lupe (2;5) tightly grasps a purple jumbo crayon in her right fist, arm bent parallel to the table about one inch above the table. She makes circular strokes of medium intensity. After completing four imperfect circles, she looks up at her teacher with delight and exclaims, "I make doughnuts!"

You are pleased to note that the author of the observation was both objective and descriptive. What else do you need to know in order to make full use of this observation?

CHAPTER 2

Highlights of Development During the Preschool Years

The Chapter 1 Think About section describes a child's coloring activity; the carefully worded narrative clearly details what Lupe (2;5) did. Is the observer's job now complete? No. Once the observational information is collected, it needs to be thoughtfully analyzed and used. The results of this analysis, if applied by the teacher in the classroom, will enrich the curriculum and the activities planned for each child.

To facilitate Lupe's educational experience, the observer must understand Lupe's coloring within the context of child development. If the observer understands the development underlying Lupe's coloring and the development yet to come, then she or he has the necessary framework to guide activity planning. Asking the following questions is appropriate. What does Lupe's grasp indicate about her fine motor development? What does her assertion that the purple circles represent doughnuts demonstrate about her cognitive development? Notice her ease in sharing her achievements with her teacher. Understanding child development goes beyond appreciating children's current interests and skills or rejoicing in witnessing their achievements. Teachers need to know enough about child development to make good judgments about what is educationally appropriate for the children in their classrooms (High/Scope Educational Research Foundation, 1976).

Chapters 2 and 3 make no attempt to supplant the wealth of information in child-development textbooks. The purpose of these chapters is to highlight selected aspects of early childhood development so that the observer understands what growth looks like and what to watch for in the classroom; to serve this purpose further, many *growth indicators* are identified. Although both chapters feature sections on physical, cognitive, psychosocial, and creative development, the emphasis of this chapter will be on the preschool child; Chapter 3's emphasis will be on the primary grade child.

Selected Highlights of Physical Development

"Oh, I wish I had his energy!" remarked Clodine, as she watched her 4-year-old jetting around the play yard late in the day. Preschoolers often appear to be like little firecrackers, sparkling and bursting with fuel. These young children have mastered walking and have improved their balance and coordination through practice and maturation; they are now engaged in the adventures of running, jumping, hopping, galloping, skipping, kicking, catching, and throwing. Watch young children in the supermarket, in your neighborhood, or at the park. They seem to want and seek out opportunities to exercise a variety of motor skills.

Motor Development.   Motor development is defined as "learning to move with control and efficiency through space" (Gallahue, 1982, p. 3). Early childhood educators observe movement by noting growth and keeping records on chil-

Axiom	**Motor Development Example**
Development occurs at individual maturational rates. Each child possesses his or her own genetic time clock.	In a group of 3-year-olds some jump by mustering all the energy they can harness for the task; other children jump with quick, easy movements.
Developmental areas (physical, cognitive, psychosocial, and creative) overlap and are interdependent.	A child who is uncomfortable or shy around others may not participate in gross motor activities, thus limiting opportunities for physical development.
Motor development is predictable.	Children develop jumping abilities before hopping and hopping before skipping (see Box 2.1, Preschool Growth Indicators of Gross Motor Development).
Physical growth proceeds along a *cephalocaudal* (head-to-tail) pattern.	Babies can lift their heads before sitting. A young preschooler can more easily catch a ball than kick a ball.
Physical development advances in a *proximodistal* pattern, "from the central axis of the body outward" (Black, Puckett, & Bell, 1992, p. 125). Thus, children acquire gross motor control before fine motor control.	Two-year-old Morag scurries over to the riding truck on the outside yard, smiling broadly as she plops herself down and powers the truck forward using her strong thighs.
	Four-year-old Tristin spends many happy preschool hours manipulating tiny houses and small wooden people on the "village floor map" made of fabric.
Perfecting motor skills is subject to individual interest and practice.	Some children cannot tie shoelaces because no one taught them or they have always worn Velcro-fastened shoes.

Figure 2.1.   Developmental axioms.

dren's gross motor development (maturity and capabilities of large muscles, such as those of the arms and legs) and fine motor development (maturity and capabilities of small muscles, such as those of the fingers). Motor development rests on basic developmental axioms (see Figure 2.1). Review these axioms, and take time to reflect on the implication of each axiom for motor development.

Gross Motor.   Identifying motor skills and determining needed motor opportunities prepare the teacher for active observation. Begin the identification process by studying the growth indicators in Box 2.1; they offer general guidelines for age expectations in gross motor development. While reading the growth indicators, keep in mind that children within the same age range normally display various levels of skill development (first axiom). The growth indicators are meant to be guidelines—not commandments!

Another aspect of the identification process is recording how the child performed the motor skill. Adults may easily confirm that a child can run, but the trained observer uses developmental knowledge to ask questions of detail. For example, does the child run with speed, control, smoothness, and endurance? Is the child's hopping balanced and performed with confidence using a spring-like action, or is it stiff and accompanied by large arm movements? Observing speed, coordination, agility, power, and balance offers a more complete picture of the child's gross motor abilities.

In programs for preschoolers, children usually have daily outdoor opportunities to exercise their budding motor skills freely. Providing a sufficient number and variety of outdoor motor experiences supports children's development. Early childhood educators can augment the fixed equipment by frequently adding assorted items (e.g., obstacle courses, wooden crawl-through shapes, parachute activities, ring-toss games, or balls of various sizes). Movement activities assist in motor development and can be carried out even during inclement weather; children often enjoy moving to recorded music with directions. Planned activities for motor development are necessary for optimum growth.

Fine Motor.   Preschoolers display a wide variety of abilities in fine motor skills. Some children put puzzles together with the greatest of ease, whereas others appear to be "all thumbs," especially when the pieces are small. In addition, fine motor tasks often require auxiliary capabilities. Picture the young child pouring juice from a small plastic pitcher during snack time. This child must have not only control over her or his fingers but also good concentration and accurate judgment. The growth indicators listed in Box 2.2 provide the observational focus for these gradual developments.

Well-trained teachers are careful not to base evaluations of a child's development of fine motor skills on one task; observing the child in a natural setting and identifying the many fine motor tasks exhibited by the child provide a more accurate picture. To facilitate this expansive approach to assessment, Figure 2.2 identifies many examples of fine motor tools available in various classroom areas.

Box 2.1
Preschool Growth Indicators of Gross Motor Development

Locomotor Skill	Three-year-old	Four-year-old	Five-year-old
Running	Run with lack of control in stops and starts	Run with control over starts, stops, and turns	Run well established and used in play activities
	Overall pattern more fluid than 2-year-old	Speed is increasing	Control of run in distance, speed, and direction improving
	Run with flat foot action	Longer stride than 3-year-old	Speed is increasing
	Inability to turn quickly	Non-support period lengthening	Stride width increasing
		Can run 35 yards in 20–29 seconds	Non-support period lengthening
Galloping	Most children cannot gallop	43 percent of children are attempting to learn to gallop	78 percent can gallop
	Early attempts are some variation of the run pattern	During this year most children learn to gallop	Can gallop with a right lead foot
		Early gallop pattern somewhat of a run and leap step	Can gallop with a left lead foot
			Can start and stop at will
Hopping	Can hop 10 times consecutively on both feet	33 percent are proficient at hopping	79 percent become proficient during this year
	Can hop 1 to 3 times on one foot	Can hop 7 to 9 hops on one foot	Can hop 10 or more hops on one foot
	Great difficulty experienced with hop pattern	Hop pattern somewhat stiff and not fluid	Hop characterized by more springlike action in ankles, knees, and hips
	Attempts characterized by gross overall movements and a lot of arm movement		Can hop equally well on either leg

Box 2.1 continued
Preschool Growth Indicators of Gross Motor Development

Locomotor Skill	Three-year-old	Four-year-old	Five-year-old
Climbing	Ascends stairs using mark time foot pattern	Ascends stairs using alternate foot pattern	Climbing skill increasing
	During this year, ascending stairs is achieved with alternate foot pattern	Descends stairs with alternate foot pattern	70 percent can climb a rope ladder with bottom free
	Descending stairs mostly with mark time foot pattern	Can climb a large ladder with alternate foot pattern	37 percent can climb a pole
	Climbing onto and off of low items continues to improve with higher heights being conquered	Can descend large ladder slowly with alternate foot pattern	32 percent can climb a rope with bottom free
			14 percent can climb an overhead ladder with 15 degree incline
			Climbing included more challenging objects such as trees, jungle gyms, large beams, etc.
Balance	Balance beam walking pattern characterized by mark time sequences	Balance beam walking pattern characterized by alternate shuffle step	Balance beam walking characterized by alternate step pattern
	Can traverse 25 foot walking path that is one inch wide in 31.5 seconds with 18 step-offs	Can traverse 25 foot walking path that is one inch wide in 27.7 seconds with 6 stepoffs	Can traverse 25 foot walking path that is one inch wide in 24.1 seconds with three stepoffs
	Can walk 3 inch wide beam forward 7.4 feet, backward: 3.9 feet	Can walk 3 inch wide beam forward 8.8 feet, backward 5.8 feet	Can walk 3 inch wide beam forward 11 feet, backward 8.1 feet
	44 percent can touch knee down and regain standing position on 3 inch wide beam	68 percent can touch knee down and regain standing position on 3 foot wide beam	84 percent can touch knee down and regain standing position on 3 foot wide beam

Box 2.1 continued
Preschool Growth Indicators of Gross Motor Development

Locomotor Skill	Three-year-old	Four-year-old	Five-year-old
Skipping	Skip is characterized by a shuffle step	14 percent can skip	72 percent are proficient
	Can skip on one foot and walk on the other	One footed skip still prevalent	Can skip with alternate foot pattern
	Actual true skip pattern seldom performed	Overall movement stiff and undifferentiated	Overall movements more smooth and fluid
		Excessive arm action frequently occurring	More efficient use of arms
		Skip mostly flatfooted	Skip mostly on the balls of feet
Jumping	42 percent are proficient	72 percent are proficient	81 percent are skillful
	Jumping pattern lacks differentiation	Jumping pattern characterized by more preliminary crouch	Overall jumping pattern more smooth and rhythmical
	Lands without knee bend to absorb force	Can do standing broad jump 8–10 inches	Use of arm thrust at take-off evident
	Minimal crouch for take-off	Can do running broad jump 23–33 inches	More proficient landing
	Arms used ineffectively		Can do standing broad jump 15–18 inches
	Can jump down from 28 inch height	90 percent can hurdle jump 5 inches	Can do running broad jump 28–35 inches, vertical
	Can hurdle jump 3 1/2 inches (68 percent)	51 percent can hurdle jump 9 1/2 inches	Can jump and reach 2 1/2 inches
			90 percent can hurdle jump 8 inches
			68 percent can hurdle jump 21 1/2 inches

Note. From Karen DeOreo and Harriet G. Williams, "Characteristics of Kinesthetic Perception," in Charles B. Corbin, *A Textbook of Motor Development*, 2d ed. Copyright© 1980 Wm. C. Brown Communications, Inc., Dubuque, Iowa. All Rights Reserved. Reprinted by permission.

Box 2.2
Preschool Growth Indicators of Fine Motor Development

Growth Indicator	*Example*
Increasing ability to grasp and/or manipulate small objects	Outside, blowing bubbles, Lorna uses one hand to hold the skinny straw that is inserted into a hole on the side of the Styrofoam cup. With her other hand she holds the cup, turns it upside down, and dips the rim into a soap mixture. Turning the cup right side up, she blows through the straw; multiple bubbles flow out the top of the cup.
Increasing ability to fasten and unfasten	While playing Daddy in the house-keeping area, the child unbuttons and, for the first time, buttons the small fasteners on the coat of the 13-inch doll.
Increasing ability to cut with scissors	Moving from cutting play dough to cutting newspaper strips, the teacher reminds the child, "Cut from your belly button forward."
Increasing ability to insert and remove small pieces	Before December the puzzles in Maja's classroom contained a maximum of 10 pieces. Today the teacher introduces a 20-piece puzzle entitled "The City." Maja smiles triumphantly as she completes this puzzle on her first attempt.
Increasing ability to string or lace items	At the art table several children are creating collages with pieces of beautiful junk. T. J. brings over a long piece of yarn, methodically wraps the ends with tape, and slowly and carefully (sometimes dropping pieces) strings 12 items to make a necklace. He asks the teacher to tie it around his neck.

Area	Tools
Art Area	Paintbrushes, pencils, crayons, markers, scissors, paper punch, play dough utensils, large needles for stitchery, pipe cleaners.
Science Area	Magnifying glasses, magnets, toothbrushes for washing rocks, eyedroppers, small items for balancing and classifying.
Housekeeping Area	Silverware, small-handled cups and pouring utensils, dress-up clothes or doll clothes with fasteners (buttons, zippers), clip earrings, writing tools for making grocery lists.
Block Area	Small wooden people, small plastic animals, small cars, small blocks, interlocking train tracks.
Manipulative Area	Pegs and pegboards of different sizes, Legos, puzzles, lacing boards, interlocking cubes, Tinkertoys, bead stringing.
Music Area	Hand castanets, xylophone, triangle, hand bells, mallets used with tom-toms, cymbals with small knobs.
Language Arts Area	Felt-tip pens; crayons; pencils of various sizes; flannel board pieces; typewriters; hand puppets; plastic magnetic shapes, letters, and numbers.

Figure 2.2.   Preschool examples of fine motor tools.

A frequent observation made by teachers in the area of fine motor development is the child's grasp of tools. The Think About section at the end of Chapter 1 reported that "Lupe (2;5) tightly grasps a purple jumbo crayon in her right fist, arm bent parallel to the table about one inch above the table." To understand Lupe's development, consider the following questions presented by Cratty (1986) for observing advances in techniques using writing instruments. Does the child hold the crayon in her fist with only the point touching the paper? Or does she use a pincer grip (index finger and thumb), using her hand and wrist as one unit? Is the arm in the air or has it progressed to a comfortable position, resting

Opportunities to exercise fine motor skills help build concentration, judgment, and motor coordination.

on the paper? Perhaps the hand anchors and the fingers move together, using the pincer grip; children start to use this technique between the ages of 5 and 7. Based on Cratty's sequences, the Think About observation shows that Lupe's "tool-grasping" development is in the beginning stage.

Some teachers of 4-year-olds worry about kindergarten readiness when children in their classrooms cannot competently perform writing and cutting tasks. A specific concern centers around appropriate pencil size in the preschool classroom. Carlson and Cunningham's (1990) research on pencil size concluded "there was some evidence to support the existence of a positive relationship between management and performance. Therefore, the recommendation to preschool caregivers and teachers is that both large and small diameter pencils be provided for school graphomotor activities" (p. 279).

Even though much of motor skill development is driven by an individual's genes, the child must practice to use writing instruments efficiently (Kaplan, 1991). The teacher observes and notes whether (1) children have shown an interest and (2) children have had sufficient time to practice—beginning with easy tasks, such as using scissors to cut pieces of play dough or copying letters in their names using fluid marking pens. The following advice offers food for thought:

As growth continues, development moves from the wrist to the fingertips when children are 5 or $5\frac{1}{2}$ years of age. Only then can they have full control over the entire hand and perform the complex movements that misguided adults often ask them to perform at an earlier age. (Cherry, 1990, pp. 9-10)

In summary, understanding the developmental axioms, observing growth indicators, describing performance qualities, and making adjustments for individual needs is the power switch that turns on teacher effectiveness. To assimilate the information on motor development more fully, become an avid informal observer of children. Key into children's displays of motor skills. Discuss your expectations for children's gross and fine motor development with your peers. Check that your expectations are based on sound developmental information, and use your observations to build an experiential understanding.

The abbreviated treatment of the subject in this chapter does not allow us to discuss all aspects of preschool physical development; our focus has been limited to motor development. Refer to a child-development book to review the following areas not examined in this chapter: preschool growth curves for height and weight, bone growth, brain maturation (especially the cerebral cortex), motor perception, and hand preference.

Selected Highlights of Cognitive Development

The boundaries of the concept of cognition are far from clear-cut. Cognition is obviously involved when a child puts a puzzle together for the first time; the mind is similarly at work when a child watches a friend spin around a playground bar and attempts to do the same. At the very least, both activities involve the coordinated efforts of noticing details, remembering, and making judgments. In this text cognition is viewed as a fertile and complex concept—even though it is not easily defined. It is enough to say, at this point, that cognitive development refers to the changing and expanding intellectual processes of human beings.

Currently, four dominant views of cognition help to describe children's thinking and explain its development: the stage theory of Jean Piaget, and the information-processing, neo-Piagetian, and contextual approaches (Flavell, Miller, & Miller, 1993). These views need not be treated as competitors; rather, each contributes to a more complete understanding of cognition. "Piaget, more than anyone before him, changed our conception and understanding of the cognitive resources of children" (Beilin, 1992, p. 202) and "was among the first modern psychologists to insist on the active role the child plays as a learner" (Gelman & Baillargeon, 1983, p. 220). Rather than simply receiving information and registering it exactly as it is given, children make sense of it at their own levels of development. The mental structure of children changes qualitatively because of individual rates of maturation and active experience in the world.

Information-processing theorists view mental activities as analogous to the working procedures of a computer; they are interested in describing "what happens between (1) the moment a child receives impressions from the environment through the senses . . . and (2) the moment the child visibly responds" (Thomas,

1992, p. 367). The information-processing approach to cognitive development focuses on the processes of cognition, not only on the outcomes. For example, researchers study the procedures or "rules" children of different ages follow when trying to equalize weights on a balance scale or solve a two-digit multiplication problem. Various frameworks for studying cognitive processes have been proposed by several information-processing theorists.

Additional contributions to the understanding of cognitive development come from the neo-Piagetians and the contextualists. The former, while generally agreeing with Piaget's view, add new emphases and ideas to the specifics of cognitive change. The contextual approach views the child within a social environment and focuses on the inextricable connection between the social and cognitive realms (Flavell et al., 1993). Given the scope of the following summary and drawing primarily from the theories and research of developmental psychologists and information-processing theorists, the following highlights link children's growth to observable indicators. They offer the following sampling of topics rather than an exhaustive accounting: representational thought, language, limitations on reasoning, egocentrism, classification, seriation, number development, and memory.

Representational Thought.   Stop and recall your last trip in a car. Who drove, where did you go, and what route did you take? What did you pass along the way? Now analyze your memory of this trip. Did your thoughts contain mental images and/or words? Most readers will answer *yes*. Now let's consider infants. What is their thinking like? We know young infants do not rely on language; although the study of mental images is complicated, research does indicate that infants do not have the same abilities as young children to think about objects or experiences remote from the present. This is not to say infants do not think; their thinking is, however, somehow different. If a few 8-month-olds are asked to get their teddy bears, they can manage this trip even if it involves crawling through a room, up a flight of stairs, down a hall, and into their bedrooms. These babies had something going on in their minds, but once they reach early childhood, their thought processes will be qualitatively altered.

The remarkable advancement in cognition from the infant to the young child hinges on the expanding ability to think representationally—that is, "to make something—a mental symbol, a word, or an object—stand for or represent something else which is not present" (Ginsburg & Opper, 1988, p. 70). Infants begin to symbolize when they wave bye-bye and know someone will leave. Toddlers' dolls can represent people; toy cars can be models of the real vehicles children ride in daily. A scribbled circle can represent a doughnut and an upright block a high-rise apartment building. Words are symbols that stand for people, things, actions, and ideas. Dramatic play often includes complex representations of how children interpret other people's actions (often with a little imagination thrown in).

As preschool children mature, they also learn how to interpret others' representations and are delighted when they recognize pictures of familiar scenes, a city skyline, or a famous landmark. With maturation, experience, interest, and guidance, most preschoolers eventually learn to decode at least some numbers and letters before they begin kindergarten. (Numbers and letters are abstract symbols—bearing no physical resemblance to the concepts represented.)

Representational thought allows children to solve problems mentally. Infants need to try things out; given simple puzzles, 12-month-olds may turn large pieces all around to find a fit. Preschoolers, although still very concrete in their thought, are able to think of solutions; they may study the shape, color, and details of some puzzle pieces before accurately fitting them in place. Once children develop representational thought, they are forever changed. Try to fathom thinking without being allowed to use words or mental images. Difficult? Impossible? The ability to think in symbols is, indeed, an integral part of human cognitive processes.

Preschool children are internally motivated to practice and explore their expanding representational abilities—to pretend, play roles, draw pictures, and construct models. One job of early childhood teachers is to provide children with the materials, time, encouragement, and stimulation to do so in depth. Box 2.3 summarizes the growth indicators of young children's representational abilities to observe and support in the preschool classroom.

Although preschool children engage in representational thought, their thought remains concrete and they require an abundance of hands-on experiences to learn more about their world. Preschool, therefore, is not the place for worksheets and lectures. The concrete quality pervades young children's thinking in all areas. For example, Zachary (4;0) asked how big the earth is. His teacher tried to describe the immensity of our planet but obviously failed to convey an accurate image, for then he asked, "Is there a traffic cone at the end?" Here was concrete thought at work, trying to make sense of the child's world with his current mental capabilities. The understanding of such wondrous abstractions as the vastness of the earth would require years of gradual maturation and diverse experience.

Language.   The development of representational thought provides the means for children to understand that words can stand for people, objects, actions, places, desires, and ideas. Children learn to understand and speak their language remarkably well on their own. This competence is even more impressive when we bear in mind that the bulk of what they hear, comprehend, and speak is newly invented: speakers continually create new sentences. During the preschool years, most children become commendable participants in their native language as they unconsciously learn a limited set of rules of their grammar (Cazden, 1972). This achievement goes beyond the obvious communication benefits because language is a vital connector to more advanced forms of cognition. The growth indicators of language development in Box 2.4 may provide a starting point for classroom observations.

Language development during early childhood has practical implications for the early childhood educator. To promote growth, adults talk with children about meaningful topics, take them to interesting places, engage them with other

Box 2.3
Preschool Growth Indicators of Representational Thought

Growth Indicator	*Example*
Gestures	Preschooler uses fingers to try to represent a spider climbing up a water spout.
Uses language	Child asks her caregiver if she can look in a drawer, and the caregiver says, "Sure." Child repeats "Sure" to herself, then proudly exclaims to another child, "Tom said yes!"
Engages in pretend play	Child pushes toy car on the floor, saying "Vroom, vroom."
Engages in dramatic play	In the house area child takes the role of a dad to three stuffed animals and cooks them breakfast.
Draws and paints	
Makes models	Using sand in a large sandbox, a child constructs the local shopping mall, decorating favorite shops with feathers.
Decodes others' representations	Child carefully studies a pumpkin patch photo to find details observed on a field trip.
Begins to decode letters and numbers	Child recognizes own name on painting displayed on the classroom wall.

Note. From *Young Children in Action* by M. Hohmann, B. Banet, and D. P. Weikart, 1979, Ypsilanti, MI: High/Scope Press. Copyright 1979 by High/Scope Educational Research Foundation. Adapted by permission.

children, read to them, and model a rich and correct use of language—all activities that are part of a productive preschool. According to Vygotsky (1978), adults further children's thinking through their "guidance and collaboration" and help them progress from what they already know to what they could know with someone's help. Vygotsky termed this distance between the level of children's independent functioning and the level of their functioning with adult help the *zone of proximal development*. Language learning occurs within this zone, where adults play key roles in enhancing development. Evaluation of children's language may

Preschool Growth Indicators of Language Development

Growth Indicator	Example
Overgeneralizes some grammatical rules	Child says *foots* to indicate plural and *bited* to form past tense.
Learns many irregular constructions	Child uses *feet, sang, bit, taught.*
Advances, but does not complete, understanding of grammar	A grandmother coaches her young grandchild to record a message for her telephone answering machine.
	Child: Me and Grandma can't come to the phone right now....
	Grandma: Say, "Grandma and I."
	Child: OK. Me and Grandma can't come to the phone right now....
	The grandmother corrects twice more.
	The light seems to go on in the child's head, the grandmother pushes the record button, and the child proudly speaks.
	Child: Me and Grandma and I can't come to the phone right now!
Expands vocabulary	Child studies sand stuck at the entrance to a clogged funnel and mutters, "Now this is a perdicament."
Progresses in articulation, but limitations remain	Child: The wight's too bright for the wabbit.
Converses with increasing competence with adults and peers	Child sits chest-deep in wading pool.
	Child: I don't need to go under. I'm too little to go under. I'll go under later. I'll go under on Tuesday.
	Child cautiously puts face in water and gets out of pool to "think it over."
	Adult: Oh my! How brave you are! Are you going to think about how proud of yourself you are?
	Child: No, I'm going to think about how it scared me.
Constructs increasingly complex sentences (structure and length)	"This thumb is all right, but this thumb is not," declares a child clutching a thumb.

distinguish between typical development as children speak independently and growth observed with the benefit of adult exchanges (e.g., Pflaum, 1986).

Limitations on Reasoning.   Preschool children do not use adult logic to solve problems, and arguing about such matters of logic is usually fruitless as young children are simply prelogical. Piaget's classic conservation problems (Piaget & Inhelder, 1969) demonstrate this cognitive limitation of preschool children. (Conservation is the concept that something remains the same if nothing is added or taken away.) Beginning with two identical glasses of juice, a 4-year-old will agree they contain the same amount of juice. Next, the contents of one glass of juice are poured into a taller, narrower glass. While the child is comparing the two juice-containing glasses side by side, he or she is then asked if one glass has more or if they have the same amount of juice.

Most 4-year-olds assert that one of the glasses contains more juice because they base their judgments on final appearances rather than logical reasoning. Since the levels of juice are no longer the same, most 4-year-olds conclude that the glass with the higher level contains more juice. They center their attention on one aspect of the problem, the levels of the liquids, without also reflecting on the compensating feature, the diameters of the glasses. Preschool children seem to ignore the crucial transformation part of the conservation experiment and are unable to reverse the pouring process mentally.

Building on Piaget's intriguing work, developmental psychologists have studied how such a concept as conservation develops and how variations in tasks affect children's performance. This research tapped some of young children's abilities that were previously unrecognized. For example, when some conservation tasks were simplified, young children tended to answer correctly rather than being misled by their perceptions (e.g., Gelman, 1972). Typically, young children answer some conservation tasks correctly and some incorrectly, depending on their cognitive abilities, their experiences, and the difficulty of the tasks.

When children are given simple, direct conservation problems to solve, they can often respond correctly even at a young age; however, complex conservation tasks take longer to unravel. If teachers keep this in mind while trying to decide if a preschooler understands a specific concept (e.g., counting), they appreciate the complicated but fascinating business of assessment (see Box 2.5) and are

---

Box 2.5
Preschool Growth Indicator of Flexible Thought

Growth Indicator	*Example*
Usually cannot reason flexibly and logically to reach accurate conclusions	Child compares her broken cracker to her neighbor's whole one at snack time and complains, "Hey, Tillie got a bigger one."

careful to rely on more than one observation and consider the task difficulty before drawing a conclusion.

While preschool children have limitations in their abilities to reason, they do not need to be changed. They do, however, need nourishment to develop their reasoning abilities. The nourishment teachers need to provide consists of diverse materials and experiences, time to explore and represent, and an interesting environment in which their support of and participation in children's activities communicate their unwavering commitment. This nourishment does not spontaneously appear; it is the result of planning based on observation and is part of the early childhood educator's job.

Egocentrism.   The issue of task complexity reemerges in the study of egocentrism, which is the inability to distinguish one's own from others' points of view. Difficult experiments led researchers to conclude that children are egocentric until about the age of 7 (e.g., Piaget & Inhelder, 1967). Simple experiments, however, helped to modify this view and document young children's capacity for nonegocentric thinking (e.g., Flavell, Shipstead, & Croft, 1978).

Preschool educators are not as interested in the complete mastery of perspective-taking tasks as knowing whether or not preschool children are at all capable of taking another's point of view. For example, suppose a 4-year-old grabs a younger child's shovel in the sandbox. Should a teacher expect that the 4-year-old can consider the younger child's perspective, at least well enough to imagine the other's hurt or angry or intimidated feelings? The issue of preschooler's egocentrism is central to many common interactions in and out of the classroom. The growth indicators in Box 2.6 summarize the preschooler's preliminary, but not complete, abilities in perspective taking.

The preschool classroom offers a multitude of opportunities to stimulate and challenge children's blossoming understanding of others' points of view. A teacher, Ellie, calls up to Phung at the top of the jungle gym and asks what he sees from way up there.

"I see the pizza place across the street and the big tree and lots of cars driving past," he hollers down.

"What do you think I see from down here?" Ellie asks, interested to discover if the child recognizes that the wooden fence denies her the opportunity to see the pizza store, the cars, and the trunk of the big tree. If Phung's response indicates he understands that her perspective is different from his, she congratulates him for noticing that the fence blocked her view of the street. If, however, he assumes she sees what he sees, Ellie can cherish her next few moments as a teacher.

"I'll be right up," Ellie calls. "I want to admire your view." The teacher and child stand together on the jungle gym and talk about the tops of children's heads, the entire play yard, and the school roof as well as the pizza store, big tree, and passing cars. Ellie notices Maria jumping next to the fence. "Look where Maria is. I wonder what she can see. Let's go take a look." She promotes Phung's active learning about others' perspectives through this teachable moment.

Box 2.6
Preschool Growth Indicators of Perspective-Taking Ability

Growth Indicator	*Example*
Demonstrates perspective-taking ability in uncomplicated situations	Child builds a block tunnel and calls to a friend to look at her through the opposite end.
Demonstrates lack of perspective-taking ability in many situations	Using a computer face-making program, a child makes a face and exclaims that her teacher, 15 feet across the room, should see it. The child leans to one side so she no longer blocks the teacher's view but does not understand that her teacher is too far away to discern the details of the face.

Let's return to the 4-year-old who grabbed the shovel; is there reason to believe this child can take the other's feelings into consideration? Most likely, in the heat of the moment (the height of shovel desire), the 4-year-old never thought once, much less twice, about how the other child would feel when the shovel was grabbed away. If a teacher talked with the child after the act, however, some perspective taking would probably emerge. Over time, as young children's natural impulsiveness declines with maturation and expanded communication skills and as people help them take notice of others' perspectives (emotional and otherwise), children become less egocentric in social situations.

Classification.   Children and adults rely on classification to deal logically with objects and ideas in their everyday lives. Objects in homes are classified in appropriate rooms; for example, dishes are expected to be found in a kitchen. Classification also serves more detailed purposes. A third-grader might sort a list of spelling words into a group of those mastered and those requiring study. A junior high student may have several complicated ways of sorting baseball cards. For ease of access, a gourmet cook organizes jars of spices and an expert quilter sorts dozens of fabrics by color. When did this ability blossom? What classification behaviors can we expect to see in the early childhood classroom?

Young children are aware of similarities and differences of objects, and they find good reasons to sort them into groups. Irene, who just turned 3, sorts soft drink cans from food cans in her pantry just as her mother does and separates her crayons from markers in her art drawer. When her mother washed a silverware tray and asked Irene to put the silverware back where it belonged, Irene put all the silverware into three sections: one for knives, one for forks, and one for spoons. This is commendable classification for a young 3-year-old; in another year or so, her mother's further sorting of soup spoons and teaspoons, dinner forks and dessert forks, and large serving spoons and forks will make sense to Irene.

Early childhood classrooms offer abundant opportunities for children to classify objects. Using blocks, children might build enclosures to separate the wild from tame plastic animals, or they might construct a special road just for the trucks hauling supplies. The classroom environment may be organized so that children sort toys and supplies as they clean up, thereby encouraging children to notice similarities and differences and how things go together. For example, shaking instruments and percussion instruments might be sorted when stored on the pegboard in the music area. Look for the growth indicators listed in Box 2.7 to evaluate classification skills in the preschool classroom.

Chapter 10 provides a detailed classification example and outlines the steps young children take toward increasingly sophisticated sorting. Even without this information, however, think about what Irene needed to know in order to sort

A variety of materials offer preschool children interesting cognitive experiences.

> *Box 2.7*
> ## Preschool Growth Indicators of Classification
>
> | *Growth Indicator* | *Example* |
> | --- | --- |
> | Explores diverse attributes of objects | Child scrutinizes the parts of a coffee pot while working to reassemble it. |
> | Recognizes similarities and differences | Child remarks that the two guinea pigs have the same kinds of wiggly noses and whiskers but different kinds of fur. |
> | Sorts objects with increasing sophistication | After a nature walk, a child groups leaves of similar shape on a collage. |
>
> *Note.* From *Young Children in Action* by M. Hohmann, B. Banet, and D. P. Weikart, 1979, Ypsilanti, MI: High/Scope Press. Copyright 1979 by High/Scope Educational Research Foundation. Adapted by permission.

cans. She needed to know about the attributes of cans and how they are similar and different—in this case that some contain soft drinks and some food. Awareness of objects' attributes or characteristics is the underlying basis for all sorting. Providing teachers and environments that stimulate preschoolers to explore materials in detail lays the foundation for classification skills.

Seriation.   Seriation is arranging things or putting them in order according to one characteristic and is another cognitive ability that progresses as children mature and gain experience in their world. So often do teachers emphasize seriation by size (e.g., blocks or sticks) that they forget about the many other interesting attributes. Numerous objects available in the preschool classroom enable children to compare along various dimensions:

light to heavy	sweet to sour
short to long	light to dark
narrow to wide	clean to dirty
slow to fast	smooth to rough
high pitch to low pitch	young to old
loud to quiet	

In the preschool classroom, seriation begins with comparisons (Hohmann, Banet, & Weikart, 1979). For example, before children can line up several sticks from short to long, they first need to compare a short and a long stick. Comparisons begin with two objects: for example, wet and dry hands, sweet and sour lemonade, high- and low-pitched singing, fast and slow dancing, light- and

---

Box 2.8
Preschool Growth Indicators of Seriation

Growth Indicator	*Example*
Makes comparisons	At the sand table a child says, "Let's make this really soapy water be the ocean and this kinda soapy water be the lake."
Seriates a limited number of objects	Child arranges three triangles by size and glues them on a flat piece of wood.

Note. From *Young Children in Action* by M. Hohmann, B. Banet, and D. P. Weikart, 1979, Ypsilanti, MI: High/Scope Press. Copyright 1979 by High/Scope Educational Research Foundation. Adapted by permission.

---

dark-green paper, and fine and coarse tree bark. Comparisons support the seriation skills to follow (see Box 2.8 for growth indicators of seriation skills).

Number Development.   Young children spontaneously and informally learn about numbers before formal schooling (Flavell et al., 1993). Children seem to understand that *three* is more than *two* at a very early age; however, understanding that all numbers represent specific quantities and learning to count many objects accurately are not part of preschool children's cognitive repertoires. Young children's struggles to understand the one-to-one correspondence between objects and numbers may be appreciated by watching several 3-year-olds try to count seven objects. Some might touch all seven objects in sequence but count "1-2-3-4-5" aloud; they end up touching the seventh object and saying "5." The clear awareness that the end number (5, in this example) has to correspond to a specific quantity of objects requires some years of practice and maturation. The average 4-year-old has advanced to be able to count nine objects, the average 5-year-old about 20 objects (Ginsburg, 1989).

The preschool classroom can provide opportunities for children to compare amounts, practice one-to-one correspondence, count in order (to memorize the fixed sequence of numbers), and count objects. Over time, such activities, which allow children to use numbers in useful contexts, will strengthen their understanding of number (see Box 2.9 for growth indicators of number development).

Memory.   In the area of memory, "the basic neurological architecture that supports memory development is established in the first five years" (Schneider & Pressley, 1989, p. 199). Preschoolers and adults thus share the same "basic hardware" because both recognition and recall memory are evident during early childhood. A 4-year-old child might hear a song at preschool and instantly recognize it from a visit to his cousin's 4 months earlier. Recall memory, on the

---

Box 2.9
Preschool Growth Indicators of Number Development

Growth Indicator	*Example*
Compares amounts	Children slice bananas with plastic knives and then compare piles.
Develops one-to-one correspondence with objects	Child places one road sign on each cylinder at the top of a block "castle."
Counts in order	Children sing counting song during circle time.
Counts objects	Child counts four children at the sand table and goes to the art area and selects four containers for making molds.

Note. From *Young Children in Action* by M. Hohmann, B. Banet, and D. P. Weikart, 1979, Ypsilanti, MI: High/Scope Press. Copyright 1979 by High/Scope Educational Research Foundation. Adapted by permission.

---

other hand, requires mental imagery or language; preschoolers are capable of these representational skills. So when a 3-year-old "reads" her favorite story to her dad with very few errors, she demonstrates her recall memory. Although memories certainly advance from early childhood capacities and abilities, the processes of recognition and recall memory are already in place.

"What the head knows has an enormous effect on what the head learns and remembers" (Flavell et al., 1993, p. 255). In other words, what a person knows has a powerful influence on what information that person can store from the environment and remember. For example, chess experts remembered gamelike chess arrangements better than nonexpert players, even when the experts were 10 years old and the nonexperts were adults (Chi, 1978)! The experts' "heads" had more experience and skills with gamelike arrangements and thus were better prepared to remember them.

So it is with young children. Imagine a teacher reading a book about dinosaurs to a small group of children. Manuel listens attentively, having been read to at home about dinosaurs, having visited museums of natural history to see dinosaur skeletons, and having played with plastic models of dinosaurs for hours on end. Tanya plays with dinosaurs at school and is also interested in the book, but Jeremy is content to sit in his teacher's lap as he casually glances from the illustrations to the ongoing classroom activities. After reading about the stegosaurus, the teacher turns the page and asks if anyone knows the name of the next dinosaur.

"Oh, I know, I know," exclaims Manuel, struggling to retrieve a name from his memory.

"This is an armored dinosaur," the teacher remarks as they admire the illustration. "Do you remember the name yet, Manuel?"

Box 2.10
Preschool Growth Indicators of Memory

Growth Indicator	*Example*
Remembers by recognizing	"Oh wook!" exclaims a child to another while looking at a photo in the block area, "'member that 'ky 'craper?"
Remembers by recalling	Child incorporates a bridge, identical to the one observed the day before, into a block structure.
Demonstrates individual knowledge	On a walk to the corner grocery, child asks, "Can I pick these pansies and daffodils?"

"No, but I know it," groans Manuel.

"Ankylosaurus," says the teacher. "This dinosaur is an ankylosaurus."

"Yes, that's right. I know that. Ankylosaurus," pronounces Manuel easily.

The "heads" Manuel, Tanya, and Jeremy brought to the story time were unique. Manuel's head already knew a lot about dinosaurs, and he was confidently able to recognize the ankylosaurus's name even though he could not recall it on his own (perhaps next time). Tanya knew less but probably learned something—perhaps that ankylosaurus was an armored dinosaur. Time will tell. Jeremy might not have learned anything from the conversation, but that's all right; he enjoyed the pleasant company and atmosphere at story time. Thus, even in preschool, children have different heads stemming from their developmental levels and past experiences (see Box 2.10 for growth indicators of memory); teachers cannot expect that everything they say goes into those heads in the same way.

A Word of Caution.   Many interesting and important topics were not discussed in this section on cognitive development during the preschool years (e.g., young children's understanding of space and time and their expanding problem-solving abilities); readers may wish to study these topics independently. Also, although this section presented general trends in cognitive development, individual differences between children abound. These differences are normal and reflect human diversity.

Selected Highlights of Psychosocial Development

Human beings are social creatures, and who they become depends in large measure on the impact of their social worlds. Psychosocial development is the third developmental domain to be introduced. Although the domains of child development are categorized for practical study purposes, children are whole beings; their physical, cognitive, psychosocial, and creative developments are interrelated. For example, a preschool child's pumping skills on a swing set depend, in part, on large-muscle strength and coordination (physical development), understanding of when the legs go out and in (cognitive development), and encouragement from others (psychosocial development); once pumping is mastered, the child's creativity might stimulate the invention of new swinging skills. As in the other developmental domains, space and time permit only the consideration of selected topics for the early childhood educator: this section discusses the child's expanding attachments, self-concept, gender identity, play, fears, aggression, and impulse control.

Expanding Attachments.   Young children depend on their parent(s) or guardians for comfort and as communicating liaisons between their personal needs and desires and the larger world (Maccoby, 1980). Teachers of young children become sensitive to their own roles as new caregivers when they understand the resources inherent in and intensity behind the parent–child bond. For example, these teachers may formally inquire about each child's routines, needs, interests, and skills so that they can make the environment welcoming and familiar. Dump trucks with pegs for filling and emptying, which reproduce a favorite activity from home, are ready in the block area for one child's first day, and a special blanket is handy for rest time. Further, alert teachers consciously look for opportunities to build up their own relationships and styles of communication with each child. A teacher drives trucks in the sandbox next to a new child during free-choice time and, with a farewell hug, enthusiastically describes these activities to the parent at the end of the day.

To young children teachers are more than ships passing in the night. They are adults to whom young children reach out for security and companionship. To be effective, teachers establish their own positive relationships with each child in their care and arrange opportunities for child and adult to nurture the relationship. Then the separation from parents will be less traumatic, as children experience the emotional commitment from their teachers and thrive from their new variety of communication partners (see Box 2.11 for growth indicators of emotional attachment).

Box 2.11
Preschool Growth Indicators of Expanding Attachments

Growth Indicator	*Example*
Demonstrates strong attachment to parents	Child asks for the fifth time in one hour, "When's my dad coming?"
Establishes emotional bonds to nonfamilial people	Child runs to his teacher to kiss her good-bye at the end of the day.

Teachers and parents may profit from a discussion of strategies to ease children's separations from their parents. A videotape about *The Working Parent, Daycare, Separation and Your Child's Development* (Family Home Entertainment, 1986) stimulates discussion of nitty-gritty strategies, such as the insistence on *good-byes* from parents (instead of their sneaking out when the child isn't looking), acknowledging and affirming children's feelings about separation, matching the individual child to the style of care, and helping the child make a special friend at school. Being cognizant of the process of attachment and young children's potential difficulty in separating from their parents is the foundation of teachers' appropriate and nurturing responses.

Self-Concept.   Humans are unique as a species in their capacity for self-consciousness. The sense of self is a psychological construct nourished by expanding cognitive and social maturity, and "very young children already conceive of persons as having characteristics that are frequent and that endure across time" (Eden, 1990, p. 850).

During early childhood, children come to understand that they have a physical self that takes up space and has unique physical attributes and a psychological self that is not visible from the outside (see Box 2.12). By $3^{1}/_{2}$ or 4 years of age, children have some ability to distinguish between the outer and inner self and perceive that the latter involves a private, thinking self that is not accessible to others through simple observation (Flavell, Shipstead, & Croft, 1980). This burgeoning theory of the mind means that "children come to understand that the overt actions of self and others are the products of internal mental states such as beliefs and desires" (Wellman, 1990, p. 1).

Gender Identity.   A critical part of children's conceptions of themselves is their gender identity—that is, knowing whether they are a girl or boy. Most 3-year-olds correctly answer whether they are a boy or girl; if they understand that the genitalia determine one's gender, most also understand that gender is a permanent attribute (Bem, 1989).

Box 2.12
Preschool Growth Indicators of Self-Concept

Growth Indicator	*Example*
Aware of psychological selves	Child points to a picture in a book and describes the character, "She's mad 'cause this guy took her lunch."
Aware of private, thinking self	"Hi, Sireena. What are you doing?" a teacher says to a child nestled in a beanbag chair. "Just dinkin'," the child replies.

> ## Box 2.13
> ## Preschool Growth Indicators of Gender Identity
>
> | *Growth Indicator* | *Example* |
> |---|---|
> | Correctly identifies own gender | Child points to self and a playmate and declares, "I'm a boy, and you're a girl." |
> | Often rigidly applies gender roles | A young girl says she wants to be a nurse when she grows up even though her mother is a doctor. |

In general, young children conform to socially prescribed gender roles more than do children in middle childhood, so that there is "a consistent pattern of decreasing stereotyping and increasing flexibility during childhood" (Stoddart & Turiel, 1985, p. 1242). Because preschool children are only beginning to learn about the complex web of social conventions dealing with gender, Maccoby (1980) suggests they may exaggerate their gender roles so as to get them cognitively clear. A young 3-year-old girl with baby-thin hair publicly reaffirmed her gender every day by adamantly refusing to wear anything except dresses.

How an individual child construes gender roles (see Box 2.13) results from a unique blend of social pressure, imitation and identification, biological influences, and children's own self-regulation (Maccoby, 1980). For example, sometimes the strength of social pressure is evident as young children, having noticed the predominant gender of construction workers in their social environment, often use plastic men models to represent these workers in the block area. Personal experiences may, however, help children form nonstereotypic models. For example, a girl whose mother is a construction worker might well include a woman model in her block play or imitate the role herself.

Play.　Children are playful by nature (Rogers & Sawyers, 1988). More than being a diversion to keep children busy, play serves important functions during early childhood (Hendrick, 1992). Although children do not set out to learn about concepts in their physical world when they play, that indeed often happens. In preschool, an observer may be lucky enough to see children playing with materials and, incidentally, learning how to build a sturdy tower or combine the right amounts of sand and water to make a moldable mixture.

Often, young children's play facilitates social development (e.g., see Parten's classic 1932 study). Children may play independently next to other children, share common activities, or play cooperatively. Through endless hours of play graced with a multitude of playmates and adult support, young children learn a great deal about how to get along with others. Most children do so very well.

Through play, children "translate experience into something internally meaningful to them" (Hendrick, 1992, p. 48). A consequence of young children's

---

Box 2.14
Preschool Growth Indicators of Play

Growth Indicator	*Example*
Explores materials on own	Child explores toy trash truck and discovers one lever to raise the truck bed and one lever to open the back hatch.
Expands social interactions	In the sandbox several children industriously dig with scoopers next to one another, speaking occasionally, while others plan together to dig a moat around their "castle."
Engages in dramatic play	"Hurry up," one child prods another in the house area. "Hurry up an' get dressed, or we'll be late for work."

---

exposure to people is an interest in trying out various roles; as a result, children further their understanding of themselves and others. No one will scold children for being bossy if they are only pretending to be the neighborhood grouch. Or in the cloak of pretend roles, shy children can experiment with more assertive behaviors; they might find that the behaviors fit better than expected. Children also learn about their society through play, and they do so without personal risk. They might apply what they have learned about rules and punishments in a game of good guys/bad guys in which no one actually dies or goes to jail.

Play also serves the function of furthering physical development. Strength of large and small muscles, coordination, and flexibility are all advanced as young children play. The gross motor control of a 3-year-old is challenged by maneuvering a tricycle around traffic cones, and the fine motor skills of a 4-year-old are practiced by manipulating water table tools.

Observers of play may focus on play with objects and social play (e.g., Heidemann & Hewitt, 1992), but they always recognize the satisfaction play gives to children. Although the amount and type of play vary across cultures, keep the growth indicators listed in Box 2.14 in mind for most American children.

Fears.   Fears are a normal part of development. "They express the child's need for dependency and occur especially at certain times in a child's development" (Brazelton, 1984, p. 33). What are young and inexperienced children afraid of? First of all, they might be fearful of real objects, experiences, or people. Fears of this sort might come in the form of bathtub drains that make things disappear, loud noises, high places, people wearing masks, and strangers. Preschool children can think ahead and anticipate potential dangers. Depending on their culture, children might have a healthy fear of fast cars, rushing rivers, hot stoves, or galloping animals. These examples represent common fears for the young child.

The origin of some fears might also lie within. Brazelton (1984) argues that learning about the self carries a price during early childhood. The young child worries about controlling new feelings, such as aggression. As a result,

> children fall into a kind of imbalance in which they may become temporarily oversensitive to things and events around them. This increased sensitivity is likely to show up in the form of fearfulness or of expressed fears. These are an expression of the normal anxiety that goes with the reshuffling of one's ideas and awareness of aggressive feelings. A child with fears can be seen as asking for help from those around him— help to see the limits of the new feelings as well as the limits of his own capacity to deal with the situation. (pp. 38-39)

Preschoolers' representational thought provides entrance to a world of imagination that may feature frightening creatures or experiences (see Box 2.15). If young children talk about their dreams, it is often apparent that the line between a fantasy created by the mind and reality is not clearly drawn in early childhood. Monsters may seem real to children, and their fears are to be taken seriously.

Adults may help children face their fears by maintaining consistent controls on behavior, facilitating learning about the frightening objects, pointing out acceptable outlets for negative feelings, and assisting children in understanding and expressing feelings. Above all, adults working with young children should view most fears as normal and indicative of developmental spurts or adjustments to stress (Brazelton, 1984).

Box 2.15
Preschool Growth Indicators of Fears

Growth Indicator	*Example*
Fears of real objects, people, and experiences	Child backs away from viewing a sea anenome, thinking it is a sea "enemy."
	Child refuses to flush the toilet and wants to be out of the bathroom when the teacher does so.
Fears of situations involving imaginary creatures	After a nightmare child sticks close by teacher for the morning and begins to cry when teacher goes into a dim closet for supplies.

> *Box 2.16*
> **Preschool Growth Indicators of Changing Aggression**
>
> | *Growth Indicator* | *Example* |
> | --- | --- |
> | Instrumental aggression | Without making eye contact, one child grabs another's play dough. |
> | Hostile aggression | "You big fat baby!" one child yells at another who won't relinquish the lemon-scented play dough. |
> | Increasing reliance on verbal communication to settle disputes | "Can I have the play dough now?" Enrique asks Mary Alice. "No," Mary Alice answers firmly. "Well, gimme *some* then," he counters. |

Aggression.   "Aggression clearly has an instinctive component; however, the frequency and intensity of an individual's aggression and the targets selected are influenced by the social environment and the individual's place in the social structure" (Maccoby, 1980, pp. 156-157). Toddlers and young preschoolers usually do not mean to hurt others when they act aggressively; they are simply intent upon getting what they want. Their focus may be on a toy, a territory, or a privilege, such as being first to ride a tricycle. This aggression is descriptively called *instrumental* because the intent is not to hurt. True *hostile* aggression, however, is not far behind and is evident when children focus their anger on another and their intent is to hurt or dominate the other. A gender difference is noted: "throughout early childhood, most studies find more male than female physical aggression" (Konner, 1991, p. 376).

Although teachers (and parents) may be assured that aggression declines from early childhood onward, they can foster alternatives to aggressive behavior (see Box 2.16 for growth indicators of changes in aggression). Young children are rapidly developing their communicative abilities and, therefore, can be encouraged to substitute words for blows. The welfare of the victim, not the aggressor, is the focus of the adult's first concern. Adults can also sensitize children to the feelings of others; this strategy relates to an earlier discussion of egocentrism and perspective taking.

Impulse Control.   Often, parents and teachers put on narrow blinders and deal with children's misdeeds as isolated events instead of reminding themselves of where young children are in their development of impulse control and what can be done to foster it. A brief study of impulse control or "how children learn to organize and control their own behavior" (Maccoby, 1980, p. 198) enables one to see the forest of the development of impulse control rather than the trees of misdeeds.

The fact that young children are naturally impulsive is fundamental to an understanding of the development of impulse control. This fact should carry no harsh judgment. Young children typically act before they think about consequences and respond immediately to interesting or exciting objects, people, and events. Imagine a teacher lining up ten 3- and 4-year-olds on the edge of a grassy area for a race. The teacher describes the start—leaving a suspenseful pause between each cue: "On your mark, get set, go!" When the actual "go!" cue is delivered, however, most of the children are already scampering toward the finish! What happened? Nothing unusual—the starter of the race just witnessed a demonstration of the fact that young children do not wait easily. Adults who work with preschoolers should know that waiting is an acquired skill.

The development of impulse control hinges on children's ability to inhibit their actions and control their emotions. Inhibition applies to movement (e.g., waiting for the starter to say "Go!"), emotional outbursts (e.g., controlling excitement and frustration), premature judgments (e.g., searching for the best, but not necessarily the first, solution to a problem), and premature choices (e.g., learning that delay of gratification often brings satisfying rewards). What difference does impulse control make in children's lives? Self-control mechanisms allow children to develop a high quality of solitary play, attend to complex problems, anticipate dangers and guard their own safety, and sustain cooperative play with other children (Maccoby, 1980). Adults interested in fostering the development of impulse control in children (see Box 2.17 for growth indicators of impulse control) can profit from Maccoby's review of implications for child rearing:

- Provide children with a regular, predictable schedule in which novelty is regulated.
- Minimize the waiting time required of young children.
- Make the environment safe and childproof.
- Make appropriate decisions when children are too young to anticipate the consequences. Provide opportunities for age-appropriate decisions.
- Model self-control.
- Set clear limits and firm controls of children's behavior.
- Engage in joint activities with children.

The last strategy deserves a bit more attention. The hours teachers and parents spend working and playing with children will bear the fruit of self-control for the children in the long run. Joint activities allow children to participate in a complex sequence of events they are not yet able to manage on their own and to enjoy the rewards of delayed gratification. Consider a teacher making play dough with a small group of preschoolers. The children gain the experience of following several steps of an activity and produce a lovely product for their efforts. The teacher working alongside the children has the opportunity to model new ideas for children who are easily bored because they work superficially with materials.

Box 2.17
Preschool Growth Indicators of Impulse Control

Growth Indicator	*Example*
Usually acts before considering consequences	Upon awaking in the nap room where other children are still sleeping, child calls loudly to teacher.
Has difficulty waiting	Noticing problem behaviors every time preschoolers are lined up and asked to wait, the teacher abandons this procedure in favor of brief, direct transitions.
Benefits from joint activities with adults	Child, who does not often exhibit sustained attention on own, works intently on a sand-city when a teacher is involved.

Preschool children's progress in learning about themselves and their social worlds is remarkable. "Schools are the first large institution to which children come from their families and home neighborhoods and in which they are expected to participate individually and publicly" (Cazden, 1988, p. 3). At the end of the preschool years, most children are ready to venture further out into the world and meet the expanded social demands of elementary school.

Selected Highlights of Creative Development

Creativity is studied from various perspectives and in many different ways (Fabun, 1968; Taylor, 1991; Torrance, 1976). For this chapter, the definition of creativity is linked to the early growing years; creativity is "the process by which original patterns are formed and expressed. . . . The pattern need not be 'new' in the sense that no one ever thought of it before, but only that it be original with the person himself" (Fabun, 1968, p. 5).

Feldman's work (1980) explores two approaches to creativity taken by psychologists. He labels one approach the *trait approach* and the other the *process approach*. Feldman explains that the trait approach, fathered by J. P. Guilford, is characterized by the idea that creativity is innate and unfolds naturally. Creativity is motivated from within to express itself and will do so, except under extreme conditions. This approach holds that each person is born with a certain measure of creativity.

On the other hand, the process approach "focuses on the interaction between the organism and the environment—the ongoing, ever changing construction of behavior" (Feldman, 1980, p. 90). Creativity (see Box 2.18 for preschool growth indicators) is the result of possessing abilities and having conditions that allow for practice and improvement. For example, gifted children need interested parents and teachers to provide the necessary encouragement and opportunities to develop their abilities (Bloom, 1985a).

These two approaches, much akin to the nature-versus-nurture controversy, produce implications for the classroom. If we subscribed to the first approach— traits—teachers would need to do little. Today in the academic arena, however, the process approach is favored over the trait approach. Read on to learn how creativity is identified, facilitated, and cultivated in the early childhood classroom through the process approach.

"Young children express their originality and creativity primarily through the use of self expressive materials, imaginative pretend play, and creative thought" (Hendrick, 1990, p. 275). In developmental programs, children are involved with exploration, discovery, and new experiences. For the preschool child creativity is nearly synonymous with play. In quality schools preschoolers may be seen engaged in the creative process by constructing block structures and using accessory items; dressing up in high heels and a waltz-length silky nightie and carrying around precious baby dolls; laboriously struggling to solve puzzle patterns; waving scarves and moving to the music of a favorite record; making mud pies with wet sand; building with nails and wood; drawing with crayons, markers, and chalk; and dictating original stories as an adult's hand races to capture every spoken word. The examples continue to expand in these "electric" classrooms.

Simply observing the emerging signs of growth listed in Box 2.18 is not enough to support creativity. By using the information obtained from observations of individual children, the teacher makes strategy decisions. The teacher may provide enticing experiences based on a child's interests, offer encouragement related to the child's effort, ask open-ended questions, and/or arrange the environment to reflect a creative climate. Figure 2.3 offers suggestions for the teacher-in-training.

Let's take a closer look at two specific components of creativity: art and block play. When you are observing children engaged in these two activities, knowledge of the scope of growth is advantageous.

As children grow and develop at their own pace, they progress through defined stages of representational drawing. The individual growth rate is influenced by the child's cognitive development (e.g., representational thought), physical development (e.g., motor control), perceptual development (e.g., sensory awareness and space perception), and art experiences (e.g., opportunities to explore). Therefore, if the teacher understands and can identify the stage of growth represented by a child's artwork, an observational window opens.

Box 2.18

Preschool Growth Indicators of Creativity

Growth Indicator	*Definition*	*Example*
Expanding flexibility	Seeing alternatives, especially when one idea fails	While playing fire fighter, one child uses the only hose. Another child (who usually seeks the teacher's assistance) rummages through the dramatic play materials and uses a vacuum cleaner attachment as a hose.
Expanding sensitivity	Tuning into senses and seeing details in the world around us	On a walk the child carefully observes an ant diligently dragging a bread crumb toward the anthill and says, "Boy, he's working hard!"
Expanding imagination	Composing and utilizing mental images of things not present	Chester, using a block as a microphone and standing on top of an outdoor play structure, sways back and forth as he sings, imitating a popular country and western singer.
Expanding risk taking	Experimenting with possibilities, being open to divergent thinking and acting on it	Child adds one more block to a precarious structure.
Expanding resourcefulness	Trusting one's own perceptions	Child uses the wheelbarrow to transport selected toys to other side of play yard
Expanding skills in using creative materials	Developing use proficiency through practice and maturation (interrelated with fine motor and cognitive development)	A child's functional explorations and manipulations (e.g., stirring and mixing sand) become representational (as cakes are created).

Note. From *Beginnings and Beyond*, 3rd ed. (pp. 490–491) by A. Gordon and K. W. Browne, 1993, Albany, NY: Delmar Publishers, Inc. Copyright© 1993 by Delmar Publishers. Adapted by permission.

Condition	Examples of the Teacher's Role
Concrete experiences	Provide experiences that develop the senses. Plan abundant field trips. Tune into children's questions and interests on walks and field trips. Point out changes in nature.
Uninterrupted time blocks	Allow children large time blocks to use materials of choice in ways that are congruent with their development. Permit important projects to be left as is (e.g., block structure) and worked on later.
Sufficient space	Provide space that is appropriate to selected activity: sometimes off to the side and protected, free from invitations for passersby to intrude (blocks, easel painting); sometimes large enough for many (group mural painting, movement activities, and dramatic play).
Open-ended materials	Use a "help-yourself shelf" in the child-directed art area. Place a choice of items to draw, paint, paste on, or fold and tear; alternatives for fastening things together; tools to mark with; and an assortment of ever-changing materials. Provide multiuse materials and equipment for the sensory table and the defined areas of manipulatives, dramatic play area, and sand.

Figure 2.3.   Preschool classroom conditions affecting creative climate *(continued on next page)*.

While studying the stages of representational drawing presented in Box 2.19, compare the sequence of development for the scribbling and preschematic stages. Collect a few samples of each child's drawings over time, dating each sample. Then use Box 2.19 for interpretation of children's developmental growth in this area.

Teachers can also observe and keep notes when children work with three-dimensional art materials, such as play dough or clay. A sequential progression is also followed.

When the children are working with clay, the teacher can expect to see the following (Wolfgang, Mackender, & Wolfgang, 1981):

1. Random pounding
2. Controlled pounding
3. Rolling clay into snake-like rolls and later circles

Condition	Examples of the Teacher's Role
Accessible and organized materials	Minimize the child's need to hunt for materials and become distracted from selected activity.
	Define distinct areas of the room using low movable shelves or large area rugs of various colors.
	Label and classify materials within the areas; place crayons in color-coded cans or blocks on shelves labeled with corresponding paper cutouts.
Varied and abundant materials	Supply a set of unit blocks and baskets of small wooden people or plastic animals.
	Offer easel painting and another set-up activity (e.g., collages) as well as a help-yourself shelf in the art area.
	Count the children. Are there enough items, or will children need to wait a long time to have a turn to express themselves?
Teacher's supportive attitude	Respect each child as unique and important, accept child's level of expression, and use words that enhance rather than stifle the creative process. Help children to feel psychologically safe, and empower them to explore and take risks.
Teacher modeling	Exhibit curiosity, recognize curiosity in children, and encourage curiosity in daily experiences. Use your senses to explore with the children.
	Promote flexibility and sensitivity by asking open-ended questions rather than giving answers.

Figure 2.3.   Preschool classroom conditions affecting creative climate *(continued)*.

    4. Adding of pieces to the rolls and circles (facial features and body parts)
    5. Combining products, such as people in cars or a boy on a horse (p. 11)

When evaluating art experiences, consider the following warning: fostering creativity requires an art program that is process oriented (exploratory) rather than product oriented (crafts). In November many classroom walls are filled with paper-plate turkeys that have strips of colored paper stapled on to represent feathers. The head and feet are cut by the teacher. All the turkeys look alike. Did the children express themselves creatively? No, they simply followed the teacher's directions. The objectives of product art are not consistent with the development of creativity.

In addition, consider how children respond to the two different orientations. Watch children create by gluing all sizes and shapes of small, smooth wood pieces together. Then watch children pasting precut construction-paper face

Box 2.19
Preschool Growth Indicators of Representational Drawing

The Scribbling Stage, Two–Four Years: Beginnings of Self-Expression

Drawing Characteristics	Space Representation	Human Figure Representation
Disordered Scribbling:		
Motor activity utilizing large muscles with movement from shoulder	Utilizes drawing surface	No attempts made
Kinesthetic pleasure	Sometimes scribbles beyond paper	
Grasps tool with whole hand	Ignores previous marks placed on a page	
Swing of arm makes line		
Looks away while scribbling		
Controlled Scribbling:		
Smaller marks	Stays within drawing area	Circles, lines, loops and swirls made, which are prefigural
Repeated motions	Draws around previous marks on the page	
Watches scribbles while drawing	May concentrate on certain parts of drawings	
Uses wrist motion		
Can copy a circle		
Named Scribbling:		
Relates marks to things known	Scribbles placed purposely	A scribble may be pointed out by the child as being a person
Greater variety of line	Previous marks on the page are utilized	Action may be named, such as running, jumping, swinging
Holds tool between fingers	Empty space may take on meaning	
Identification of subject may change in the process of drawing	Lines become edges of shapes	
Longer attention span		

Box 2.19 continued
Preschool Growth Indicators of Representational Drawing

The Preschematic Stage, Four–Seven Years: First Representational Attempts

Drawing Characteristics	Space Representation	Human Figure Representation
Shapes for things are geometric and lose their meaning when removed from the whole	Objects seem to float around page	Head-feet symbol grows out of scribble
	Paper sometimes turned or rotated while drawing	Flexible symbol, constantly changing
Placement and size of objects are determined subjectively	Size of objects not in proportion to one another	People are looking at viewer, usually smiling
Objects drawn are not related to one another	Objects are distorted to fit space available	Gradual inclusion of arms (often from head), body, fingers, toes
Art becomes communication with the self	Space seems to surround child	Distortion and omission of parts is to be expected
Known objects seem to be catalogued or listed pictorially		Clothes, hair and other details expected by end of this stage
Can copy a square at four, a triangle at five		

Note. Reprinted with the permission of Macmillan Publishing Company from *Creative and Mental Growth: Eighth Edition* by Viktor Lowenfeld and W. Lambert Brittain. Copyright© 1987 by Macmillan Publishing Company.

Children's three-dimensional art
develops in predictable stages.

pieces onto precut construction-paper snowmen following a model. There is a
marked difference in the degree to which children engage themselves. Product
art offers only one right way, thus smothering creative flexibility and imagination. Schirrmacher (1988) advises

> There are too many activities that masquerade as creative art. Some of these include
> - Ditto, photocopied, or mimeographed sheets
> - Cut-and-paste activities
> - Tracing patterns
> - Coloring-book pages

- Dot-to-dot pages
- Crafts
- Holiday gifts
- Seatwork (p. 7)

Practitioners must be diligent not to cheat children of the most obvious and basic creative experience by substituting product art for process art.

Blocks are one of the most universal toys at home and school, and block play has been a part of early childhood education for over 75 years. The developmental values of block building are bountiful. Blocks help children develop imagination; awareness of balance, form, and spatial relations; representation and classification abilities; patterning skills; size, shape, area, volume, and equivalency understandings; eye–hand coordination; and fine motor skills. Eventually, blocks are used by children to set the scene for dramatic play, a rich source of language and cooperative play.

When first exposed to unit blocks, children need plenty of time to explore with them. Progressing at their own pace through sequential stages (see Box 2.20), children make new discoveries, including bridges, enclosures, or patterns; repetitions are also commonly observed. Children who enter block play at older ages (4 through 6) pass quickly through all beginning stages except that they skip the first, elementary one (Hirsch, 1990). Making sketches or taking photos of children's expanding block development is an excellent observational aid.

Blocks seem to hold a magnetic attraction for young children. There can, however, be times when children ignore the block area. In these situations the teacher may change the location of the block area, add accessories reflecting the

---

Box 2.20
Preschool Growth Indicators of Block Play

Stage 1   Child carries blocks around and piles or stacks in disarray.

Stage 2   Child repetitiously makes horizontal (on floor) and vertical (stacking) rows.

Stage 3   Child makes bridges.   ⊓⊓

Stage 4   Child makes enclosures.

Stage 5   Child makes decorative patterns; symmetry is present.

Stage 6   Child names structures related to their functions (houses, boats, stairs).

Stage 7   Child denotes familiar structures with buildings.

Note. From *The Block Book* (pp. 101–104) edited by Elisabeth H. Hirsch, 1990, Washington D.C.: National Association for the Education of Young Children. Copyright 1974 by the National Association for the Education of Young Children. Adapted by permission.

children's current interests (e.g., small plastic dinosaurs), or actively participate in block building. Strategies for teacher observation and interventions in block play are addressed in Chapter 11.

The growth and development of the preschool child is multifaceted. Certainly no two children develop along the exact same course; individual children show different progression rates in physical, cognitive, psychosocial, and creative development. Yet development follows a predictable path. Understanding development and the growth indicators along that path allows the teacher to identify each child's advances, missing neither the baby steps nor the giant leaps.

Think About . . . _____

A thought-provoking opportunity awaits the student of child development. From *Life* magazine comes an article about a child from Tibet making a perilous journey from her remote and isolated village in the Himalayas to a school 100 miles away. In a small entourage, Diskit and her brother traveled single file on a frozen river following the leader who, with a long stick, tapped the ice to test for strength. Stop and think for a moment how Diskit's secluded mountain life and unusual travel protocol might have shaped her perceptions of the physical world. Then read on.

> On the twelfth and final day, the landscape changes. The white of eternal ice gives way to the brown hills surrounding the valley of Ladakh. The exhausted travelers trade the frozen skin of the mighty river for a dirt road, and Lobsang and his children hitch a ride on a transport truck. Diskit cowers: The driver is a Sikh with a turban and a long moustache. She has never before seen an Indian who was not a Tibetan Buddhist. The vehicle overtakes a man on horseback. She tugs on her father's coat. "*Abale,*" she asks, using the native word for father, "have you seen? Here the donkeys walk backward."
>
> "No," her father replies. "It's just that we're moving faster than it is."*

Extraordinary, isn't it, from a Western, industrialized perspective that a primary grade child could perceive an object being overtaken as traveling backward? Think about an explanation.

*From "Journey to Knowledge," by O. Follmi, *Life*, December, 1989, pp. 109–116. Copyright © 1989 by O. Follmi.

CHAPTER 3

Highlights of Development During the Primary Grade Years

Diskit, whom you met in Chapter 2's Think About section, was a child with all of her mental faculties intact. Her perceptual error of thinking that a man on a donkey was traveling backward as she overtook him on a truck was understandable in the context of her cultural experiences. Growing up in a small mountain village dedicated to growing barley in the summer and surviving frigid winters had not yet taught her about the traffic patterns she first observed, without understanding, in town. As she learned from new experiences, Diskit would doubtlessly become incredulous that she was ever capable of such a misinterpretation.

As you reflect on the development of preschool children as described in Chapter 2 and read about the development of primary grade children (K–3) in this chapter, think about how the various cultures with which you are familiar influence and moderate development. Selected highlights of physical, cognitive, psychosocial, and creative development are presented to document general growth trends; as in Chapter 2, however, remember that individual and cultural diversity is always evident.

Selected Highlights of Physical Development

Body Growth.   As the active primary grade child's internal developmental timetable continues, the child proceeds to grow in a general stepwise pattern. On average, primary grade children's height increases by approximately 2 to $2^{1}/_{2}$ inches per year; their weight increases about 5 pounds per year.

An important growth consideration for the early childhood teacher is individual genetic rates of maturation. Attention to this factor is necessary when you are observing and assessing a child, even in the primary grades. In a room full of first or second graders, a general trend in physical growth and development is evident but individual differences in this area can easily be spotted. Think back for a moment to your primary grade years. Were you an "average" child? If not, did you get dubbed with a nickname reflecting your physical development—half-pint, shrimp, lefty, string bean, four-eyes, or boney maroney? Maybe you knew someone who did. Do you think these individual deviations from the norm in growth affect the primary grade child? Consider how physical development may influence a child's self-esteem as you read the psychosocial development section of this chapter.

And they are all the same age!

Motor Development.   The primary grade child's muscle strength and eye-hand coordination show continuous maturation, thus facilitating the development of motor skills. By the age of 6 or 7, the child can perform the fundamental motor skills of walking, running, hopping, climbing, galloping, skipping, jumping, pushing, pulling, bending, grasping, throwing, catching, and kicking. Children of primary grade age are refining and perfecting the fundamental motor skills. Studies record improved performance with age (Clark & Phillips, 1985; Du Randt, 1985; Kerr, 1985). To appreciate these advancements, consider one example: the progression of skills in learning to catch a ball (see Figure 3.1).

Children 5 to 8 years old begin to combine their motor skills in a complex fashion that requires more eye-hand coordination, shorter reaction time, and better balance than preschool children exhibit (Shaffer, 1993). Think about the change in the type of physical games usually played on the K–3 playground as compared with the physical activities in a preschool yard. How old are the children who are skillful at playing jacks, dodge ball, baseball, or jump rope? As motor-skill performance becomes more complex and specified, strength and judgment are also required to carry out the task. When were you able to ride a bike, skip rope, dribble a ball, hit a tether ball, or play soccer? What about your sister or brother? Even though most children can participate in these activities by age 8 or 9, Black et al. (1992) warn:

Initial Stage	There is often a definite avoidance reaction of turning the face away or protecting the face with arms
	Arms are extended and held in front of the body
	There is limited movement until contact
	The catch resembles a scooping action
	Uses the body to trap ball
	Palms are held upward
	Fingers are extended and held tense
	Hands are not utilized in the catching action
Elementary Stage	Avoidance reaction is limited to the child's eyes closing at contact with ball
	Elbows are held at sides with an approximately ninety degree bend
	Since initial contact made with the child's hands is often unsuccessful, the arms trap the ball
	Hands are held in opposition to each other: thumbs are held upward
	At contact, the hands attempt to squeeze the ball in a poorly timed and uneven motion
Mature Stage	Arms are held relaxed at sides and forearms are held in front of body
	Arms give upon contact to absorb the force of the ball
	Arms adjust to the flight of the ball
	Thumbs are held in opposition to each other
	Hands grasp the ball in a well-timed simultaneous motion
	Fingers make a more effective grasping motion

Figure 3.1. Stages of ball catching.

Source: From *Developmental Movement Experiences for Children* (pp. 175–176) by D. L. Gallahue, 1982, New York: Macmillan. Copyright © 1982 by Macmillan Publishing Company. Reprinted with permission.

Organized sports training and competition may not be desirable for children 6 and 7 or younger, whose fundamental coordinations are not sufficiently refined. For the 8-year-old, such organized activities must be pursued with understanding of the specific motor capabilities and interests of the individual child. (p. 369)

The growth indicators of gross motor development listed in Box 3.1 help guide ongoing observations and record keeping.

Corbin (1980) offers the following norms for fine motor development in the primary school years:

Five-year-olds begin to color within the lines, cut and paste simple things. They can draw triangles and begin to draw combinations of two or more forms. At six years, the child demonstrates fair control for block printing; however, some letters may be reversed. It is not uncommon for some children to reverse letters occasionally until around 8 years old. (p. 168)

The complex process of motor development is enhanced by appropriate experiences.

Box 3.1

Primary Grade Growth Indicators of Gross Motor Development

Growth Indicator	*Example*
Increasing strength of legs and arms	Mandy's knuckles whiten as she gives an extra kick with her legs while reaching for the last rung on the overhead parallel bars. Today she finally makes it all the way across!
Increasing speed	In the fourth game of neighborhood "hide and seek," whining complaints of the preschoolers echo in the streets, "Why do we always have to be *it?*" "Because we always catch you," laugh the older brothers and sisters, scampering off.
Increasing agility	Effren begins to feel confident as he successfully dodges the ball again and again and again in the second-grade game.
Increasing ball skills (throwing, catching, kicking, hitting)	"We want Misha, we want Misha," chants the first team to pick for a game of kick ball. "She's the best kicker in the whole room!"

In the primary grades fine motor skills are largely reflected in handwriting. The printing of letters and numbers is part of the K–3 curriculum, whereas cursive handwriting traditionally is not introduced until the second grade. Cratty (1986) reports that children's gradual reduction of letter size begins by printing their own first name using letters 5 inches to 2 inches tall (age 5) and advances to making letters and numbers, horizontally aligned, 0.25 inches tall (age 7). Even though growth norms provide standards, each child's handwriting must be evaluated individually. While studying the growth indicators of fine motor skills listed in Box 3.2, keep these wise words in mind:

> One of the most well-established premises of human development is that there is a wide range of individual variation that is well within the range of "normal" and, of course, the inclusion of children with disabilities and special abilities further expands the range of individual differences in any one classroom. (Bredekamp, 1992, p. 31)

ELEMENTS AFFECTING MOTOR DEVELOPMENT   Rates of maturational growth (affecting height and weight measures) also affect the development of motor

---

Box 3.2

Primary Grade Growth Indicators of Fine Motor Development

Growth Indicator	*Example*
Skillful use of writing tools, scissors, and small objects	Emanuel cuts an intricate snowflake out of folded paper, while his younger sister, Carmen, struggles to cut on a line.
Increasing ability to arrange numbers and letters uniformly	Kirsten (5;6) wrote:

Blake (7;10) wrote:

Increasing eye–hand coordination	While playing Stak Attack, the 8-year-old child carefully and slowly removes the bottom block from the stack, adding it to the top without toppling the 15-inch stack.

---

skills, advancing or delaying the process. A broad range of motor skills can be witnessed in the primary grade classroom. "A relatively tall 7-year-old might have the muscle maturity and coordination more typical of a 5-year-old" (Berger, 1991, p. 334). During the primary grade years, however, maturation is not the only influence on motor development. "A wide variety of meaningful movement experiences are necessary to help each child refine her or his movements to a point where they are fluid and adaptable to a wide variety of movement situations" (Gallahue, 1982, p. 22). Engaging in daily movement activities, structured and unstructured, helps children sharpen their basic motor skills.

Achievement is helped through practice when a child is competent in basic motor skills and maturationally ready to take on complex motor activities requiring strength, speed, agility, eye-hand coordination, and prehension. Practice opportunities are often linked to interests, motivation, cultural expectations, and geographical location. For example, children who live in California may easily combine the fundamental motor skills into more complex skills through riding a skateboard, playing baseball, or perhaps swimming in the ocean. Children who live in Vermont may perfect their skills through skiing, ice skating, or playing basketball. Urban children may play stickball, whereas suburban children may ride bikes.

Curriculum planning based on observation keeps in mind the primary grade child's need for ample opportunities to practice, exercise, and engage in physical play at school. Pay special attention to the following:

- Children who have long bus rides and then go directly into the classroom.
- Children who haven't developed social skills and appear to be "loners" on the playground, never entering into physical sports.
- Children who have poor diets and are overweight.
- Children in city schools when Stage 3 smog alerts prohibit them from playing outdoors.
- Classroom schedules that do not allow for enough movement and rigorous activity during the day. Is one recess at 11:00 A.M. the best way to aid attention span?

If a developmentally appropriate curriculum is used, one must provide adequate practice opportunities for the physical needs of primary grade children.

Another crucial factor that may affect motor development is limited social interaction. In a study of children's feelings of loneliness and their relationship to physical fitness (Page, Frey, Talbert, & Falk, 1992), it was reported that "lonely children were less physically fit and physically active than were those who were not lonely" (p. 211). This phenomenon presents another reason why motor development should not solely be left to recess time.

Early childhood educators question the effects of television watching on children's motor development. Certainly program quality is a vital issue, but the activities television replaces cannot be overlooked. Are children missing opportunities to develop gross and fine motor skills when they watch television? Did children have better motor development before television? Research is currently being done in this area.

In conclusion, K–3 children are moving into a social environment where motor skill performance is necessary for success in sports participation. Corbin (1980) points out, "Great emphasis is placed on the fundamental motor tasks during the elementary school years because of their importance to the more complex movements of sports and recreational skills" (p. 76). Fully developed fine motor skills are necessary for classroom success in writing, computer operation, and manipulation of art tools for creative expression. Providing practice opportunities, encouragement based on observations of individual interests, and realistic expectations are the responsibilities of primary grade teachers.

Selected Highlights of Cognitive Development

Representational Abilities.   Having gained experience with a great variety of concrete representations during the preschool years, primary grade children are prepared to construct and decode more abstract symbols. Older children can listen to a book with few picture aids and rely on their own mental imagery to aug-

> *Box 3.3*
> ## Primary Grade Growth Indicators of Representational Thought
>
> | **Growth Indicator** | **Example** |
> |---|---|
> | Expands complexity of preschool growth indicators | Kindergartners engage in "school" dramatic play and sound remarkably like the people they represent! |
> | Gestures | |
> | Uses language | A first grader constructs a personally designed car out of Legos. |
> | Engages in pretend play | |
> | Engages in dramatic play | A third grader draws a person in profile. |
> | Draws and paints | |
> | Makes models | |
> | Decodes others' representations | |
> | Able to decode and use abstract symbols (letters and numbers) | A second grader competently reads *The Cat in the Hat* to a kindergartner during after-school care. |
>
> (See Figure 7.4 in Chapter 7 for additional information on reading.)

ment the text. Further, their understanding of the meaning behind letters and numbers becomes more secure and skilled. See Box 3.3 for growth indicators of representational thought.

Consider this example of growing familiarity with the representational meaning of numbers. An advanced prekindergartner (4;9) arranged magnets on the refrigerator in spite of a missing 3 and 0.

1 2 ♀♀♀ 4 5 6 7 8 9 1◉

The child explained that she used three sucker magnets because she didn't have a 3 and that a small round magnet was "almost like" a zero; clearly, she understood the representations involved.

Because nothing about the symbol 3 suggests what it stands for, understanding numerals (and letters) as abstract representations is a critical cognitive step for primary grade children. This step results from maturing perceptual skills and from instruction. On one hand, maturing perceptual skills allow children to make increasingly fine distinctions between symbols (e.g., between *b* and *d*). On the other hand, no amount of contemplation of an "M" or "Σ" will result in children's correct deciphering of the letter unless they have been taught its meaning. Elementary schools are responsible for teaching children the abstract representational systems of letters and numbers.

Language. The most far-reaching change in language during the primary grade years stems from children's growing understanding of language as a means

Primary grade children can construct complex representational models.

of communication. Primary grade children become able to think about how they and others use language; language can be a powerful tool. Most young children enjoy conversing with others and become aware of themselves and others as givers and receivers of messages. Hopefully, teachers and parents of primary grade children provide encouragement as language skills (see the growth indicators in Box 3.4) develop in speaking and writing.

Children need encouragement and a safe environment in which to talk, write, and try out new words. Although more attention is paid to primary grade children's technical use of language (e.g., spelling and grammar) than to younger children's, continued emphasis on content before form reduces risks of failure. Teachers want to encourage children to speak and write fluently, and that requires lots of practice, experience, and confidence. If children are continually under the critical eye of adults waiting to pounce on a misspoken or miswritten word, they are apt to pull back from language.

A first-grade teacher delighted in the content of a child's story and ignored the many errors and lack of a title on the first draft. Try to figure out the words and enjoy a chuckle.

The day the teacher vanisted we panted the room fluorescent. Spied on the other classis. We acted up for 2 hoers and theen went home, for louch. Back at school we rearranged the class room. We never saw or teacher agin. intell we fowd out she had moived to massachousits.

Box 3.4
Primary Grade Growth Indicators of Language Development

Growth Indicator	*Example*
Expands vocabulary	A child describes a new friend as being "very considerate."
Understand there can be literal and figurative meanings of words	To describe what old people look like, a 6-year-old summed up, "They're very old, and they can't talk very good; their voices *ruffle*."
	During a first-grade story time, children laugh heartily as Amelia Bedelia literally follows directions to dust furniture, draw drapes, and dress chickens.
Discerns subtle differences among words	Child says, "Today the rain sounds sharp, not plunking like usual."
Uses and understands many grammatical rules and exceptions	Second grader is not confused by passive sentence construction (e.g., "Trent was teased by Riley").
Becomes a proficient communicator with adults and peers	Second grader states own point of view in class discussion. "The color of wind is whatever's behind it."
	To emphasize her anxiety before her first class play, a 6-year-old declares she has "monarchs" in her tummy.
Constructs increasingly complex sentences (structure and length)	A child informs a friend, "My favorite dinner is barbecued ribs with extra sauce on the side, cole slaw, and creamy potatoes, and for dessert I like baked apples with cinnamon."

(See Figure 6.1 in Chapter 6 for information on writing development.)

At the beginning of third grade, this child was a prolific and able writer. Consider this short piece about a grandparent.

Gaga and the Raccoons

My grandma's name is Gaga. She died when she was 70 that was 3 years ago. Gaga's real name is Marge Gaede. She taught first, second, and third grade before she retired. After she retired gaga worked at the hands on museum in ann arbor. Gaga loved raccoons very much and to her great joy discovered that many raccoons lived in the forest behind her house. Every night Gaga would make peanut butter samwitchs and then she would throw them all over her yard. My family, Gaga and her husband Gampa and I all sit on the porch and wait and watch. Soon the raccoons began to come they ate and ate and ate. When the raccoons were full they slowly began to leave and I went to bed. When Gaga was still teaching her stutents gave her a shirt that said Fuzzies and Raccoons go togather. Fuzzies are little balls of thered with eyes that Gaga loved to make. When I was at Gaga's feunroll all I could think was Raccoons and Gagas go togather.

This child's language development flourished in an environment that encouraged talking about a wide range of meaningful topics, reading books regularly, and writing as a method of communication about interesting subjects.

Logical Thought.   A major cognitive advancement during the primary grades is children's increasing ability to reason logically about concrete problems (Piaget & Inhelder, 1969). Primary grade children's expanded mental flexibility and concrete experiences allow them to understand logical operations, such as addition and subtraction. First graders who are beginning to learn math facts often treat $2 + 3 = 5$ and $5 - 2 = 3$ as two independent problems. Before the year is out, most will understand the logical connection between the two.

Primary grade children's logical thought may be demonstrated by asking them questions about conservation. In a conservation-of-length problem, two rulers are aligned and then one is simply moved over in full view of the child. If a young primary grade child asserts that the two rulers remain the same after the rearrangement and is asked why, the child is likely to justify this conclusion with a statement that focuses on the maintained identity of the objects: "It's the same stick" or "You just moved it over."

Given a variety of conservation problems, a primary grade child (particularly a 5- or 6-year-old) typically answers some correctly and some incorrectly. For example, the child who was right about the conservation-of-length question above might answer incorrectly on questions about conservation of mass and liquid 2 minutes later. This inconsistency is a bit perplexing. One would think that once a child understands that something remains the same if nothing is added or taken away, this reasoning could be applied across the board on a variety of tasks. If the child said that two rulers are the same if one is moved over, why wouldn't the

Box 3.5
Primary Grade Growth Indicators of Logical Thought

Growth Indicator	*Example*
Often reasons flexibly and logically about concrete problems	Child studies six cup hooks, four of which are empty, and says "I know what 6 take away 4 is."
Thinking remains concrete	Child looks at a photo book of Amish families with a parent who describes their religion and simple life. To exemplify the connection between beliefs and daily life, the parent explains the Amish reliance on hooks and eyes rather than modern zippers to fasten clothing. After attentive listening, child asks thoughtfully, "Do they believe in elastic?"

child also say that two masses of play dough remain equal if one is reshaped and two amounts of juice are the same if one is poured into a differently shaped container? Although the basic concept of conservation is the same across tasks, children do not become logical thinkers all at once. Some tasks are more difficult than others, even when they theoretically draw on the same cognitive concept; further, children have had varying experiences and have varying cognitive strengths. Adults should expect to see primary grade children draw on logical thought sometimes (but not always) and to observe individual differences among children.

The thinking of primary grade children (see Box 3.5 for growth indicators of logical thought) remains concrete, so they reason best about the here and now. For example, an 8-year-old listened to an older child tell a joke about two friends, Joe and Casey, who loved baseball. The friends agreed that whoever died first would try to return to Earth and let the other know if baseball is played in heaven. Joe died first, and one day Casey returned home to find him sitting in his living room. The 10-year-old delivered the punch line:

10-YEAR-OLD: So Joe said, "I've got some good news and some bad news. The good news is there is baseball in heaven. The bad news is you're scheduled to pitch tomorrow."
8-YEAR-OLD: I don't get it.
10-YEAR-OLD: Well, see, for Casey to pitch in heaven, he's gotta die first.
8-YEAR-OLD: (No laughter but a moment of thought.) So what did Casey die of?

The joke bombed! Concrete thought simply did not allow the 8-year-old to discern the hidden agenda.

Declining Egocentrism.   In general, primary grade children become increasingly adept at understanding the perspectives of others and responding accordingly (see Box 3.6 for growth indicators of perspective-taking ability), and there is practical evidence of declining egocentrism in primary grade children's everyday lives. Primary grade children's improved ability to take the needs of their listeners into account is an example.

If a 3-year-old talks to Grandma on the phone and tries to relate an incident, the child will probably jump into the middle of the story—not thinking that Grandma knows nothing about the circumstances. Hearing "That dog scared me," the grandmother wouldn't know which dog scared her grandchild, where, and how. A primary grade child is more apt to give some background information to put the incident in some context and might say something like, "When I was walking home from school, a big dog ran into the street right at me and. . . ." Adapting to the needs of the listener allows children to become improved communicators and is evidence of declining egocentrism.

Classification.   Classification skills undergo substantial development during the primary grade years. Although preschool children are generally content to sort a limited number of objects once, primary grade children can be challenged to sort and re-sort a larger number of objects. Thus, their greater mental flexibility enables them to select classifying attributes that guide their sorting and then abandon these attributes and begin again. Re-sorting is a notable achievement.

A first grader sorts and re-sorts a collection of leaves into the following piles and then says no more groupings are possible.

1. Big leaves
   Little leaves

Box 3.6
Primary Grade Growth Indicators of Perspective-Taking Ability

Growth Indicator	*Example*
Demonstrates skillful and accurate perspective-taking in many situations	Aware that a friend dislikes scary stories, a third-grader advises against reading a particular book.
Demonstrates lack of perspective-taking ability in some situations	"Come on, just jump," a child urges impatiently to another on the swings. "There's nothing to be scared of."

2. Green leaves
   Brown leaves
   Yellow leaves

3. Pointy leaves
   Roundish leaves

This child sorted real leaves on the basis of some concrete similarities and differences. First, size differences guided the child's groupings, then color, and then shape. This was a fine demonstration of sorting and re-sorting for a first grader.

As children's thinking becomes increasingly flexible (see Box 3.7 for growth indicators of classification abilities), they can sort and re-sort objects according to various concrete attributes. Young primary grade children, like the first grader

---

Box 3.7
Primary Grade Growth Indicators of Classification

Growth Indicator	*Example*
Sorts and re-sorts objects flexibly and usually by concrete attributes	An 8-year-old sorts model horses:

1. Bays   Grays
   Chestnuts   Whites
   Paints   Blacks

2. Black mane
   Brown mane
   Gray or white mane

3. Albino hooves
   Brown hooves
   Black hooves
   Gray hooves

4. Face markings
   No face markings

5. Famous or related to famous horses
   Unknown horses

Note: Grouping 5 stems from child's own knowledge about horses rather than concrete features of the models.

Compares whole class with its parts with increasing accuracy	Child beginning multiplication understands sets of objects and can group three sets of four objects.

who sorted the leaves, tend to select attributes of the objects themselves as the basis of classification and produce a limited number of groupings. As they enter middle childhood and gain knowledge about the objects being sorted, children produce more abundant groupings but remain predominantly concrete in their approach to classification tasks. By the end of elementary school, however, older children might draw on their personal stores of knowledge and, for example, sort leaves into an evergreen pile and a deciduous pile; thus, they are no longer tied to the objects' concrete attributes.

Toward the end of the primary grade years, children answer many class-inclusion questions correctly. Perhaps a 7- or 8-year-old has sorted a pile of buttons into two groups: 6 two-holed buttons and 11 four-holed buttons. With the piles in full view, the child is asked if there are more four-holed buttons or more buttons. Although this primary school child answers, "more buttons," a younger child would probably have answered, "more four-holed buttons." To answer correctly, a child must compare the group of four-holed buttons with the complete group of buttons and thus simultaneously think about a part and the whole. The gradual understanding of class inclusion demonstrates the increasing mental skills of 7- and 8-year-old primary grade children.

Seriation.   If 4- and 5-year-old children are given 10 sticks to seriate by length, typically they order a few but not all. By age 6, most children can seriate all the sticks, but they do so with some trial and error. For example, they may select a stick and try it in a few positions before being satisfied with the pattern they are making. Older primary school children work on seriation tasks systematically; they usually select the longest or shortest stick visually and continue adding sticks in order. Once the pattern is complete, these children can insert an additional stick in the series without difficulty.

Primary grade children's advances in seriation (see the growth indicators in Box 3.8) parallel their advances in classification and conservation; all rely on their ability to think flexibly and logically about concrete problems. Not only can primary grade children seriate objects by length, they can also effectively seriate objects by other criteria, such as texture, hue, and musical pitch.

Box 3.8
Primary Grade Growth Indicators of Seriation

Growth Indicator	*Example*
Increasing ability to seriate many objects systematically	A child arranges 15 stuffed animals from old to new.
Ability to insert new item into the series	Finding another stuffed animal under the bed, a child confidently places it into the arrangement.

Memory. Although preschool and primary grade children share the same basic memory processes (recognition and recall), memory skills become honed during the elementary years. Processing speed increases, and "a number of memory strategies emerge and develop" (Schneider & Pressley, 1989, p. 199). Most notable during the primary grades are the strategies of rehearsal and organization. Rehearsal is a common strategy; to remember a telephone number on your way from the phone book to the phone, for example, you might repeat the number over and over. Effective rememberers playing a game of memorizing a tray full of baby items at a baby shower try the strategy of organization. They think about which objects can be clustered together to avoid trying to remember a long string of unrelated items. Categories might include bath-time, feeding, and health-care items.

During the primary grade years, children begin to use rehearsal and organization spontaneously. First graders faced with the task of learning their very first set of spelling words simply don't realize that rehearsal would be an appropriate study strategy. By the third grade, however, most children can use rehearsal on their own and, if encouraged, can use this strategy effectively. The same is true of organization.

What makes the deliberate selection of memory strategies possible is the development of metamemory—knowledge about memory. Even during the primary grade years, children know something about memory. For example, when

---

Box 3.9
Primary Grade Growth Indicators of Memory

Growth Indicator	*Example*
Increasingly deliberate and spontaneous use of memory strategies	"I'm going to write that word five more times without peeking; it's still kinda blurry," reports a second grader preparing for a spelling test.
Early development of metamemory includes knowledge about people as rememberers, varying task difficulty, and appropriate memory strategies	Child writes homework assignments in notebook to avoid having to remember them.
	Children discuss pros and cons of stage plays versus radio plays and remark that the latter require less memorization.
	A third grader practices flash cards to study for a math test and reviews chapter self-quiz to prepare for a social studies test.

kindergarten and first-, third-, and fifth-grade children were asked if it would be easier to learn the names of the birds in town for the first or second time, many of the children (even the kindergartners) knew intuitively that the relearner would have the advantage (Kreutzer, Leonard, & Flavell, 1975). Ideas about memory (and the mind) gain clarity as 8- and 9-year-olds begin to distinguish between what they understand and what they have merely memorized (Lovett & Flavell, 1990). Further, not only do primary grade children have some knowledge about memory as a cognitive process, they also become more aware of when they must put out some effort to store or retrieve information; think about the growth indicators of memory presented in Box 3.9 in this light.

A Word of Caution.   The cognitive development highlights presented in this section are not comprehensive. You may be interested in reading about problem solving, reading comprehension, spatial relations, math concepts, etc. Although this section describes general trends in cognitive development, individual differences are always apparent. These differences are normal and reflect the beauty and complexity of human diversity.

Selected Highlights of Psychosocial Development

The psychosocial lives of primary grade children continue to broaden and mature. By the end of third grade, children have definite notions of who they are, and their lives outside of the family have become increasingly important.

Self-Concept and Self-Esteem.   In Chapter 2, we left the preschool child with a beginning understanding of the self as both a physical object and a psychological being. Children's ideas about the self grow more complex during the primary grade years. Gradually, through the primary grade years and beyond, children's self-concepts include more psychological assessments (e.g., "animal lover"), characteristics uncommon to others (e.g., "the shortest kid in class"), and descriptions of active abilities (e.g., "a really good gymnast") as well as many of the concrete characteristics cited by younger children (e.g., "curly hair"). Elementary school children also understand their own specific academic strengths and weaknesses. They can judge their often varying competencies in math and on verbal tasks, and their judgments are differential—not global (Marsh, Byrne, & Shavelson, 1988).

Although primary grade children feel more like unique individuals, they also feel more closely bound to a social network (Maccoby, 1980). As a result, primary grade children are likely to include membership in a group (e.g., an ethnic group, a sports team, or a scouting troop) when asked to describe themselves. Sustained experience in groups offers tremendous growth opportunities. Ethnic groups may guide children's development in many ways (e.g., expectations of how children treat their elders) and help them forge their identities. Within groups, children are also stimulated to see how their behavior appears to others (e.g., bossiness is not valued), to monitor their behavior, and gradually to make appropriate adjustments.

Most primary grade children have ideas about what they would like to be, and having an ideal self and setting high standards are part of the development of the self-concept (Katz & Zigler, 1967). The development of the ideal self is increasingly specified during elementary school, but even primary grade children have notions about what they want to be like in the future. The dreams of future glories are healthy and, further, are associated with impulse control; studies demonstrate that homeless children lack the long-term optimism to sustain such dreams (Stanford Center for the Study of Families, Children, and Youth, 1991).

Self-esteem is the evaluative component of the sense of self, and good self-esteem is possible when children's physiological needs and needs for safety, belonging, and love have been met (Maslow, 1970). Two essential ingredients that contribute to self-esteem are the warmth, acceptance, and respectful treatment given a child and the child's success as "measured against personal goals and standards" (Coopersmith, 1967, p. 242). So the origins of self-esteem lie not only with how children are treated by the important people in their lives but also with how well they do in the world. Children need not excel in everything they do in order to feel good about themselves, but reasonable competence in selected arenas is important to self-esteem.

A person's self-esteem is linked to his or her aspirations in specific fields of interest. Suppose, for a moment, that you found yourself in a chili cook off or perhaps a 10-K run during the past weekend—activities in which you are not particularly skilled nor do you care to be. If you did not do well, you might be mildly embarrassed but your self-esteem should not suffer. After all, you were a fish out of water. On the other hand, you care very much about your performance in areas in which you have chosen to compete—perhaps this class. This is your pond, and your performance is connected to how you feel about yourself.

The same process is true of children, but children are just beginning to find their ponds, and adults need to assist them in their searches by exposing them to a wide range of experiences without pressure. Trying out new activities includes the possibility of failure, so adults working with primary grade children can encourage this risk taking by being low-key. Adrienne, age 7, made a list of all the things she wanted to try; included were soccer, softball, ballet, violin, Brownies, jazz, horseback riding, and gymnastics. Her parents supported her interests with the stipulation that she had to commit for a season or school year. At the end of first grade, she crossed off three of the four activities she had tried that year: soccer (too hot and too much running), softball (too boring), and ballet (too embarrassing) and anticipated sticking with Brownies and trying out jazz in second grade. Through this process, Adrienne learned more about the kinds of activities she enjoys and can do well. Her self-esteem will be enhanced as she discovers the ponds she wants to swim in, develops competence, and is encouraged by those who love and teach her. Box 3.10 lists indicators of the growth of self-concept and self-esteem in primary grade children.

Box 3.10

Primary Grade Growth Indicators of Self-Concept and Self-Esteem

Growth Indicator	*Example*
Includes psychological assessments, uncommon characteristics, active abilities as well as concrete characteristics in descriptions of self and others	Child reports to parent after school, "I really like the new kid in my class; he's kinda shy like me, and I think he likes the monkey bars too!"
Considers group ties as part of self-definition	Child proudly wears a scouting uniform to school.
	Child shares photos of the Acoma Pueblo, "I'm this kind of Native American, just like my mom, who lived here when she was 10."
Develops sense of ideal self	Child says he wants to pitch for the Pirates when he grows up.
Searches out areas of interest that contribute to self-esteem	Much to the children's delight, a second-grade class plans a hobby/collection/interest day so that each child may share her or his personal "passion."

Gender Identity.   Young children (and adolescents) regard "the crossing of stereotyped gender boundaries as more wrong and expressed a greater personal commitment to sex-role regularity, than [do] children in middle childhood" (Stoddart & Turiel, 1985, p. 1241). Primary grade children's increased freedom from rigid adherence to gender stereotypes stems partly from their secure understanding that their gender is constant and that gender roles are societal conventions rather than absolute requirements (see Box 3.11 for growth indicators of gender identity). As Western society continues formally and informally to reduce its gender-stereotyped expectations and restrictions, children may recognize and embrace their life options wholeheartedly.

Advances in Play.   During the elementary school years, children increasingly participate in cooperative play with other children and enjoy games with rules (Scarr, Weinberg, & Levine, 1986). Cooperative play is sustained as maturation and experience stimulate children to give and take actively in their encounters. Board games are popular as primary grade children readily learn rules and

Box 3.11
Primary Grade Growth Indicators of Gender Identity

Growth Identity	*Example*
Does not rigidly adhere to all stereotyped gender roles	"I'm really good in math," a child proudly tells her mother after school.
Becomes aware that gender roles are societal customs	A third grader reads *Little House in the Big Woods* and compares the diversity of his sister's activities to those of Laura Ingalls Wilder.

understand that they apply equally to all players. Whereas younger children might use a modified set of rules while playing Monopoly, older children are more able to follow the instructions. Even in children's unstructured play (e.g., school, fort, house), rules command an increasingly prominent role (see Box 3.12 for growth indicators of play).

Relationships with Peers.   Children's relationships serve as important models of future relationships (Hartup & Moore, 1990).

Box 3.12
Primary Grade Growth Indicators of Play

Growth Indicator	*Example*
Participates in cooperative play	"Ya wanna play fort? one child calls to two friends. "I'll build the walls, and you can build the roof, and we can all decorate it. OK?"
Participates in and makes up games with rules	"You're out!" several children call to a child hit by the ball in dodge ball.
	"Let's say you don't really have to go to jail when you land here," says one child to another while playing Monopoly.

Cooperative play and games with rules characterize play during the primary grade years.

Primary grade children's friendships become less centered on conveniently shared activities (e.g., neighbor children riding bikes together) and more focused on mutual loyalty, intimacy, as well as interests (Bigelow, 1977). Children count on their friends to come to their aid and stick up for them, share their secrets, and engage in leisure-time experiences together. Generally, "children find same-sex play partners more compatible, and they segregate themselves into same-sex groups, in which distinctive interaction styles emerge" (Maccoby, 1990, p. 513). Children learn how to disengage from conflict to "increase the likelihood that [their] relationships will continue once the disagreement ends" (Hartup, Laursen, Stewart, & Eastenson, 1988, p. 1600).

Increasingly throughout middle childhood (and adolescence), peer groups offer the individual security and a sense of belonging, but they also exert pressure to conform. Much of this conformity centers around participation in activities (e.g., playing four-square at recess), clothing (e.g., wearing the "right" brand of t-shirts), and allegiance to peer-group members. Some peer groups expect conformity in antisocial activities. In general, children are inclined to go along with their peer groups until midadolescence (Shaffer, 1993); therefore, the types

> *Box 3.13*
> ## Primary Grade Growth Indicators of Relationships with Peers
>
> | *Growth Indicator* | *Example* |
> | --- | --- |
> | Increasingly focuses friendships on loyalty and intimacy as well as mutual interests | "I like Melody more now 'cause she really stuck up for me at recess," a child reports. |
> | Usually prefers same-gender play-mates | On the playground, most girls and boys play in gender-segregated groups. |
> | Increasingly aware of and vulnerable to peer-group influences | "I can't wear this shirt to school, Mom," a child whines. "All the kids will laugh." |

of peer groups children are involved in warrants scrutiny. Box 3.13 lists growth indicators of primary grade children's relationships with their peers.

Moral Reasoning.   Preschool children tend to base moral judgments on the material outcome of an action rather than the intent of the person involved. In contrast, primary grade children begin to understand that many moral questions pivot around a person's intent. Their earlier preoccupation with surface details (e.g., how much paint was spilled) is gradually abandoned for a deeper evaluation of the situation's complexities and relevant issues (e.g., Was the spill accidental? Was the person being careless?). See Box 3.14 for growth indicators of moral reasoning.

There are strategies to promote children's moral behavior (Maccoby, 1980). Seizing opportunities to help children think about others builds and challenges their perspective-taking skills. For example, parents may talk about others' experiences or discuss inferences from stories or television programs. Second, a reasonable amount of control over their own lives provides children with experience in responsibility. Third, arbitrary discipline that undermines children's sense of control and responsibility is rejected. Clear connections between a child's actions and their consequences will help the child consider consequences when faced with moral choices.

Managing Stress.   Everyone has stress in daily life, and children are no exception. How children cope depends on two factors: their competence (social, academic, and creative) and their social support (Werner & Smith, 1982). Critical problems arise when these factors are in short supply and/or when the stresses multiply (e.g., divorce plus a move plus the mother returning to work plus lower family income).

The modern tendency to pressure children to hurry through their childhoods has resulted in unnecessary stress (Elkind, 1988). Parents hold high expectations

---

Box 3.14
Primary Grade Growth Indicators of Moral Reasoning

Growth Indicator	*Example*
Increasingly evaluates the intent of the actor	"We know you told us to stand still," a brave child tells the substitute, "but Robby would have gotten hit by the ball if Shuichi hadn't knocked it away. He really wasn't being bad."
Increasingly takes into account the relevant issues of a moral situation	"No way!" a child vehemently argues. "Marcin shouldn't get any 'cause he didn't help."

---

for their children's successes, but their demands may be inappropriate to the children's developmental levels. Children are enrolled in an abundance (often, an overabundance) of extracurricular activities and allowed access to information formerly reserved for the more mature (e.g., adult problems, violence, and sex in the media). What can adults do? Here are some of Elkind's suggestions:

1. Cut back on the demands placed on children and increase your supports. Look for a reasonable balance of developmentally appropriate responsibilities and adult support and commitment. For example, a teacher encourages the parents of a 7-year-old who goes home each day to an empty house for three hours to enroll their child in an after-school program. After the child becomes noticeably happier, the parents decide to devote half of a weekend day to a leisure-time activity with their child.

2. Provide opportunities for unstructured play, such as opportunities for creative expression—a natural antidote for hurrying. Competitive and instructional activities, although they may be an important part of children's lives, do not reduce stress.

3. Model living in the present and smelling the roses in your own life. Remember that children carefully observe and imitate the important adults in their lives; through example, you can model ways to enjoy life and moderate stress .[1]

These suggestions are further supported by research on the relations between stress and school activities. Children in developmentally inappropriate classrooms exhibited more stress than did children in appropriate classrooms; partic-

---

[1] From *The Hurried Child,* © 1988 by David Elkind. Adapted with permission of Addison-Wesley Publishing Company, Inc.

ularly stressful times were transitions, waiting, and workbook/worksheet activities (Burts, Hart, Charlesworth, Fleege, Mosley, & Thomasson, 1992).

Psychosocial development is affected by children's individual natures, developmental strengths and limitations, unique social surroundings (their family, friends, school, and extended social networks), and cultures. Against the backdrop of the developmental trends discussed above, cherish the inevitable differences among children.

Selected Highlights of Creative Development

Primary grade children's expressions of creativity ("The process by which original patterns are formed and expressed" [Fabun, 1968, p. 5]) are more clarified and intricate than are preschoolers' expressions. Two examples follow: a 4-year-old may draw a person, a house, or an animal of disproportionate size in space, whereas a 6-year-old may recall and illustrate a favorite scene from a field trip using detailed figures in an organized drawing that includes a baseline and a skyline with air in between (Lowenfeld & Brittain, 1987). Preschoolers may shake musical instruments to the rhythm of a favorite song; K–3 children may construct their own music-making devices. During the early elementary school years, nonverbal, verbal, and written expressions become more complex and representational than they were during the preceding years.

Another difference between primary grade and preschool children's creative development is emerging individuality. Children's creative interests and strengths begin to bud during the preschool years, but they bloom during the primary grade years. When the dictated stories of two preschoolers, Ona and Whitney, are compared, they would probably have some observable differences. If, however, Ona continues to nurture her interest and ability in writing and Whitney finds writing less appealing than science experiments, the differences in these two girls' third-grade stories become increasingly pronounced. Ona and Whitney, along with other primary grade children, begin to recognize and develop their individual creative talents through abundant and varied opportunities.

During these important years, maturing individual strengths can be appreciated and supported when creative interests and abilities are identified. The growth indicators of creativity listed in Box 3.15 are the basis for teacher observation and lead to recognition of development.

There are diverse pathways for creative expression in the primary grades. Individual strengths emerge and develop in writing, music, dance, drama, problem solving, and art. Early in elementary school, many children delight in organizing and participating in backyard circuses and plays, building tree houses, and inventing new games or revising old ones. In the classroom, evidence of creativity is proudly displayed at open house: artwork, science and social studies projects, and original stories.

One specific pathway, creative art, has been singled out and spotlighted over the years. The stages of art growth have been studied and defined through ado-

Box 3.15
Primary Grade Growth Indicators of Creativity

Growth Indicator	*Example*
Expanding representations, moving from single idea to interrelated ideas	Chase's preschool drawing of his family displays each member as distinct and separate, without background. Chase's second-grade drawing of his family shows each member involved in roles: Mom is at the computer, Dad's cooking dinner, and his two brothers are working on homework—all in one room!
Expression of individual strengths	Jaime enthusiastically volunteers for the lead in the first-grade play, *Are You My Mother?* Toma shares a poem he wrote after his kitten was run over.
Expanding flexibility	"Two five-year-olds, Missy and Eric, want to build a school, but they have no blocks or pieces of wood. They consider using shoe boxes, which are fairly durable and stackable, for a base" (Schirrmacher, 1988, p. 48).
Expanding sensitivity	The child (6;2) leafs through the *Great Book of French Impressionism*, looks up, and says, "Why do they paint pictures of people without their clothes on?"
Expanding imagination	Tori is whirling around and clapping her hands in patty-cake fashion. She tries frantically to keep the beat of the rock music that's playing. She flaps and flops her hands over her head. Then she opens and closes her hands quickly like little signal lights. She calls out, "I'm dancing like a peacock." The rest of the children begin to clap with her. As she raises her floor-length skirt a few inches above her ankles, she calls out, "Someday I'm gonna be a dancer on stage."

Box 3.15 continued
Primary Grade Growth Indicators of Creativity

Growth Indicator	*Example*
Expanding risk taking	Having had a lot of practice riding her two-wheeler with training wheels, Najeeba seeks out her big brother. She says, "I want you to take off these training wheels. I'm going to teach myself how to ride without them."
Expanding resourcefulness	While the children are playing the game Simon, the pattern becomes too difficult for the children to duplicate with the four different-colored buttons. One child suggests that each child concentrate on only one color. Therefore, as a team, the group could successfully reproduce long patterns.
Expanding skills in using creative materials	"This is the best story I've ever written about dinosaurs," says Peter. "I think I'll illustrate it. Let's see, should I use watercolors, tempera paints, construction paper cutouts, markers, or block prints?"

Note. Flexibility, sensitivity, imagination, risk-taking, resourcefulness, and creative-skills indicators adapted from *Beginnings and Beyond*, 3rd ed. (pp. 490–491) by A. Gordon and K. W. Browne, 1993, Albany, NY: Delmar Publishers, Inc. Copyright© 1993 by Delmar Publishers. Adapted by permission.

Drawing is one avenue of self-expression.

lescence (Herberholz & Hanson, 1990; Kellogg, 1970; Linderman, 1990; Lowenfeld & Brittain, 1987). These stages follow a predictable pattern. Does that mean that a child leaves one stage one day and suddenly zips into another stage the next? No. A child in transition may teeter from one stage to the next before fully exhibiting the characteristics of the succeeding stage. Bountiful opportunities for unrestricted practice and experimentation are needed. A word of caution—art activities duplicating a model are not creative; they stifle growth.

The growth indicators in Box 3.16 are a guide for observing the stages of representational drawing during the primary grade years. The characteristics of the preschematic stage (found in Chapter 2) are repeated, together with the characteristics of the schematic stage.

"Is creative expression really important?" ask educators who are pressured to demonstrate classroom proficiency in academic areas. Absolutely! Creativity assists independent thinking, fosters self-esteem, relieves emotional tension, and

Box 3.16
Primary Grade Growth Indicators of Representational Drawing

The Preschematic Stage, Four–Seven Years: First Representational Attempts

Drawing Characteristics	*Space Representation*	*Human Figure Representation*
Shapes for things are geometric and lose their meaning when removed from the whole	Objects seem to float around page	Head-feet symbol grows out of scribble
	Paper sometimes turned or rotated while drawing	Flexible symbol, constantly changing
Placement and size of objects are determined subjectively	Size of objects not in proportion to one another	People are looking at viewer, usually smiling
Objects drawn are not related to one another	Objects are distorted to fit space available	Gradual inclusion of arms (often from head), body, fingers, toes
Art becomes communication with the self	Space seems to surround child	Distortion and omission of parts is to be expected
Known objects seem to be cata- logued or listed pictorially		Clothes, hair and other details expected by end of this stage
Can copy a square at four, a triangle at five		

Primary Grade Growth Indicators of Representational Drawing

The Schematic Stage: Seven–Nine Years: The Achievement of a Form Concept

Drawing Characteristics	*Space Representation*	*Human Representation*
Development of a form concept which is repeated again and again	Establishment of a base line on which objects are placed and often a sky line, with the space between representing the air	Repeated schema for person
Schema is altered only when special meaning is conveyed	Two-dimensional organization of objects	Body usually made up of geometric shapes
Drawing shows concept, not percept	No or little overlapping	Arms and legs show volume and are usually correctly placed
Bold, direct, flat representation	Subjective space representation common	Exaggeration, omission, or change of schema shows effect of experience
Drawings reflect a child's active knowledge of the environment	a. simultaneous representation of plan and elevation	Proportions depend on emotional values
	b. X-ray drawings	
	c. fusion of time and space	
	Multi-base lines	
	Environment symbolized	

Note. Reprinted with the permission of Macmillan Publishing Company from *Creative and Mental Growth: Eighth Edition* by Victor Lowenfeld and W. Lambert Brittain. Copyright© 1987 by Macmillan Publishing Company.

The guide contains information for reading, vocabulary, structural analysis, and guided and independent reading. The following activities are samples of using the story across the curriculum.

Theme: Animals. Daytime/Nighttime.
Story: *Good-Night Owl!* by Pat Hutchins

Sample Activities:
- Put up a bird feeder and have the children identify the visiting birds and record their findings in a bird-watching journal.
- Have the children create paper-plate masks representing the various story animals. Use the masks for retelling or dramatizing the story.
- After discussing various birds, have the children write a story about being a bird from the bird's point of view.
- Using familiar tunes (e.g., "Skip to My Lou"), assist the children in writing a song about an owl.

Figure 3.2. Integrated curriculum example.
Source: From *A Guide to a Shared Reading Experience* by Linda Crosswhite, 1991, Jacksonville, IL: Perma-Bound. Copyright © 1991 by Perma-Bound. Adapted by permission.

helps children discover that their own uniqueness is special, valued, and important in the world (Cherry, 1990; Torrance, 1977; Wright & Fesler, 1987).

How can creativity be promoted in the classroom? If "a primary goal of education is to enable children to develop their minds and intellectual capabilities, using all forms of creative intelligence as means for achieving this goal" (Getty Center for Education in the Arts, 1985, p. 11), then using a curriculum design that embodies creative development becomes a critical choice for the teacher. The integrated curriculum approach, which is based on thematic units (Schwartz & Pollishuke, 1991), is an excellent example of such a design. Children's language arts experiences are related to a theme (sometimes originating from the children's interests, sometimes offered by the reading program). All other curriculum areas are woven around the language arts experience but taught full strength (Gunderson, 1989). This approach promotes creativity by providing an atmosphere of directed exploration, accepting individual ideas, and linking disciplines together. In Figure 3.2, Crosswhite (1991) illustrates how the integrated curriculum approach facilitates development of creativity in the primary grades.

In summary, promoting creativity is one of the teacher's main challenges. The primary grade child's maturing creative expression and emerging strengths develop best when:

- Creativity is incorporated into the curriculum.
- Indicators of creative growth are fostered.

- Children's creative interests are encouraged.
- Ample opportunities for children to grow at their own rate are provided.

To avoid redundancy, the approaches of creativity (trait versus process art), the conditions influencing creativity, and the teacher's role are excluded from this chapter. Review the creativity section in Chapter 2 for more information.

The primary grade child is developmentally different from yet similar in many ways to the preschool child. Children within both age groups show individual rates of maturation, follow predictable patterns, and draw on their own experiences and genetic makeup. In this chapter, however, we have highlighted how the primary grade child continues to advance physically, cognitively, psychosocially, and creatively. Identified growth indicators help the teacher zero in on developmental strides through continued observation.

Think About . . .

> Often, when Fiona thinks of one of her students, Warren, her ponderings begin with "if only." If only Warren would wander less. If only Warren would pay more attention in class. If only Warren would complete his assignments. If only Warren found school interesting. If only. If only.
>
> Warren does, however, wander in class, and he does not pay attention or complete assignments or find school interesting. How can Fiona begin to uncover the roots of the behaviors that frustrate her best intentions as a second-grade teacher? Think about this question before you begin the next chapter.

PART II

Observing Individual Children in the Early Childhood Classroom

Observing the Development of Individual Children by Using Running Records

In the years following Fiona's difficult experience with Warren, she often wondered what became of this little boy. As described in the Chapter 3 Think About section, here was a child who resisted her every effort to control, guide, and teach him. With hindsight and training in observation, Fiona wishes she had known more about running records and had felt confident enough to observe Warren with this method. She suspects she would have understood patterns in Warren's behavior that were overlooked in the daily demands of teaching a difficult child. The aim of this chapter is to show how to write running records that describe characteristics of children's development in depth.

Overview of Observing Using Running Records

Description.   The *running record* is a detailed, objective, sequential recording written while the event is happening. Researchers in child development depend on running records (at times called specimen descriptions) to gain insights into development. Piaget relied on his detailed observations of children to help him conceptualize and describe cognitive growth. In many of Piaget's books, portions of running records are reproduced to demonstrate his theoretical points; many of Piaget's original accounts are thus available for you to study.

Here is an excerpt from *The Origins of Intelligence in Children* (1963) describing 16-month-old Lucienne's reactions to an old-fashioned match box and watch chain. Previously, Lucienne had discovered how to turn the match box over to dump the chain out and how to pull the chain out with her finger if the box was slightly closed. Piaget then added a new twist to the game; he closed the box almost shut and gave it to Lucienne. Piaget described her "curious reaction" when she could not reach the chain with her finger.

> She looks at the slit with great attention; then, several times in succession, she opens and shuts her mouth, at first slightly, then wider and wider! Apparently Lucienne understands the existence of a cavity subjacent to the slit and wishes to enlarge that cavity. . . .
>
>   Soon after this phase of plastic reflection, Lucienne unhesitatingly puts her finger in the slit and, instead of trying as before to reach the chain, she pulls so as to enlarge the opening. She succeeds and grasps the chain.[1]

[1] From *The Origins of Intelligence in Children* (p. 338) by J. Piaget, 1963, New York: W. W. Norton. Copyright © 1952 by International Universities Press, Inc. Reprinted with permission.

Piaget was the right person at the right time to capture this marvelous snapshot of a child edging out of infancy and into early childhood.

In a running record the observer writes down everything possible that the child says and does during a specified length of time or designated activity. Detailed, objective recordings are made in sequential form while the event is happening. "The observer in making a narrative record records a wide slice of life. No attempt is made to filter what occurred in any systematic way" (Evertson & Green, 1986, p. 177). The observer is not looking for or interpreting any specific behavior; the goal is simply to gather as much raw data as possible. Because of a high yield of information, the running record is a valuable observational method for teachers of young children.

Perhaps an analogy is in order. Compare the writing of running records to imagining an observer as a human videotape. The observer's eyes are focused on the subject, and the observer records what is seen and heard. The qualification of *human* is essential; although the observer would like to be able to capture absolutely everything, keeping up with an active child and being as objective as possible makes recording a challenging task. Practice allows the observer to become more proficient at collecting a large quantity of facts.

Teachers learn about the development of individual children through careful observation.

In practice, no hard-and-fast rule determines the amount of detail to record. The best guideline to follow is to keep the purpose and setting of the observation in mind. This focus will help determine which facts are essential to record and which may be safely omitted. In a running record in Chapter 1, for example, it was essential to record Cyd's language in the sand area as clear evidence of his ability to seriate three objects by size; noting his clothing, however, would not have added useful information. In contrast, if several unfamiliar children are being observed, recording what each child is wearing could be vital in distinguishing one child from another! The observer, always improving with experience and practice, makes on-the-spot decisions regarding the appropriate amount of detail to record.

A well-written running record is a rich account of naturally occurring behavior. The observer can return again and again to its deep well of unbiased details to study a child with a new purpose or perspective. As an objective chronicle, the running record is preserved not only for the recorder, but for all observers to come. Think of the countless number of students who have deepened their understanding of child development by studying Piaget's running records; in the same light, anticipate future teaching colleagues who will one day learn more about individual children by reading your running records.

To heighten the future value of a running record, a brief conclusion is added to its end. Imagine teachers preparing for parent conferences and sifting through the contents of a few running records on each child to refresh their memories. Think about the time involved in this chore. If, however, the teachers had written a conclusion at the end of each running record, the contents would be quickly and effectively accessible. A conclusion briefly summarizes the development demonstrated by the behavior or event observed and recorded in a running record. Pay attention to this valuable service provided by the conclusions in the running records in Figures 4.1 through 4.4.

Observational studies may be quantitative or qualitative. "Quantitative studies are dependent on numerical or statistical treatments of data; qualitative studies are not" (Genishi, 1982, p. 567). Clearly, the narrative data collected in running records are qualitative; observers scrutinizing the data focus on "holistic chunks of information" (Brause & Mayher, 1991, p. 137) rather than numbers.

Purpose.   The intent of the running record is to learn more about the many aspects of a child's total development from the objective and precise recording of this child's actions and language. Running records can be particularly helpful to teachers trying to understand individual children's problems or getting to know a new child in the classroom. In the following example, Paley's (1986) running record of a conversation documents 3-year-olds' difficulty in thinking about something not present.

> Over the weekend, an unsafe climbing structure has been removed. The doll corner window overlooks the area that housed the rickety old frame.
> "Can you tell what's missing from our playground?" I ask.

"The sandbox."

"The squirrely tree."

"The slide."

"But I can *see* all those things. They're still in the playground. Something else was here, something very big, and now it's gone."

"The boat."

"Mollie, look. There's the boat. I'm talking about a big, brown, wooden thing that was right there where my finger is pointing."

"Because there's too much dirt."

"But what was on top of the place where there's too much dirt?"

"It could be grass. You could plant grass."

Libby and Samantha see us crowded around the window and walk over to investigate. "Where's the climbing house?" Libby asks. "Someone stoled the climbing house."

"No one stole the house, Libby. We asked some men to take it down for us. Remember how shaky it was? We were afraid somebody would fall."

The threes continue staring, confused.[2]

Reading a running record at the end of the observation day or a week later or 2 months later provides a replay option that allows the observer to continue to draw conclusions and note each child's developmental strengths or limitations. Paley's running record provides her with a permanent account against which to gauge future development.

Running records support classroom planning. Teachers may use their observations and conclusions to plan supportive and stimulating daily activities; more specifically, "appropriate curriculum planning is based on teachers' observations and recordings of each child's special interests and developmental progress" (Bredekamp, 1987, p. 3). The brief running record shown in Figure 4.1 provides diagnostic information about a child's incorrect (but consistent) mathematical procedures. This information may guide the teacher's planning of follow-up math activities for this child.

Teachers may also use running records to augment information in other observational formats. For example, in the next chapter a running record provides the data for an anecdotal record. When completing a checklist or rating scale to assess a child's growth (topics of Chapters 6 and 7), a teacher may draw on a child's bank of running records for supportive data. The information gathered in running records also serves to enrich parent conferences as teachers share specific, wide-ranging accounts of children's behavior, language, interests, and interactions in the classroom.

Guidelines for Writing Running Records.　Typically, running record observation times are 10- to 30-minute periods, whereas short spans of 3 to 5 minutes are appropriate for students first practicing their skills. The raw data of a

---

[2] From *Mollie is Three* (pp. 69-70) by V. G. Paley, 1986, Chicago: University of Chicago Press. Copyright © 1986 by University of Chicago. Reprinted with permission.

Running Record of Felipe During Math

School/Grade: Delta Elementary/Third Grade

Date: 3/6   Time: 9:07–9:10 a.m.

Observer: Seth   Child/Age: Felipe/8;11

Comments

$$\times \underline{\begin{array}{r} 56 \\ 32 \end{array}}$$

Given the problem $\times \underline{32}$, Felipe hunches over his desk with his   *9:07*
eyes about 10 inches from the paper, taps his right foot rhythmically,
and whispers, "2 times 6 is 12; put down the 2 and carry the 1." He
methodically writes "2" in the ones' column and a "1" above the 5. In   *Seems*
a louder voice he says, "3 times 5 is 15 plus 1 is 16." He unhesitating-   *confident*
ly writes "16" in the hundreds' and tens' columns. His answer is 162.

Conclusion: Felipe displays an incorrect understanding of two-digit
multiplication problems. He vertically multiplies the ones' digits and
the tens' digits, skipping the intermediate step.

Figure 4.1.   Brief example of a running record.

student's 4-minute running record in Figure 4.2 provide information about a child's motor control and representational interest.

What guidelines smooth the transition from reading about running records to actually writing them? The following suggestions have been helpful to many observers viewing children's development through the observational lens of running records.

- Begin by reviewing the general guidelines to observation in Chapter 1.
- Prepare a heading to include the setting (center, date, and time) and people present (observer, child).
- Record only the facts. Be objective, and do not add any inferences. (In the example in Figure 4.2, the observer crossed out "decides to," realizing she had inadvertently interpreted Miette's behavior.)
- Write exactly what is happening in the present tense.
- Record events in sequence, as they are occurring.
- Stay focused on the child being observed. Conversations, noise, or activities going on simultaneously in the classroom may be distracting; resist!
- Jot down in a margin the time when the activity changes or at least every 5 minutes. Knowing how long a child was engaged in an activity can provide information about the child's interests and attention span.
- Use abbreviations or short phrases if helpful. The flow of activities can be so rapid that even an experienced observer can have trouble keeping pace with

Running Record of Miette Outside

Center: Learning Time Children's Center

Date: 9/17   Time: 10:25–10:29 a.m.

Observer: Paige   Child/Age: Miette/3;9

Comments

10:25

A blanket is spread out on the grass area adjacent to the swings. On the blanket are plastic toys that can be fit together to make animals. Included in the pieces are interlocking shapes that resemble legs, bodies, necks, and heads.

Miette approaches the blanket. She stops before stepping onto the blanket and looks down, surveying the toys. As she is looking, she slowly bends down into a squatting position. Once there, she picks up one of the plastic toys, a double-legged piece. She then ~~decides to~~ plops down on the blanket with one leg (right) straight out and the other leg (left) tucked crosswise under her bottom. Searching for a moment and finding an identical piece and a body, she pushes the three pieces together. She then takes her newly joined pieces and sets them upright on the blanket. Changing her position, Miette moves onto her knees and hands, now in a crawling position. Synchronizing the movement of arms and legs, she crawls across the blanket, moves several pieces around, and selects a new piece. With a neck piece in her hand, she crawls backward to her original place on the blanket. Pushing with her arms, she raises her upper body. Sitting on her legs, knees bent and with her feet under her bottom, Miette attaches her new piece to the body without effort. Finding a head piece within reach and using a steady hand, she fastens it onto her construction. Once this task is accomplished, she stands up, holding her completed animal for another child to see. "I made a dog!" Miette exclaims.

Coordinated

Conclusion: Miette's balanced action and synchronized movements show evidence of large motor control. The fitting together of the plastic toys displays small motor control. Her use of representational thought is demonstrated by her model of a dog.

Figure 4.2.   Student running record example.

the action; you should, however, write complete quotes to produce evidence of a child's language ability. The exact words a child said will be difficult to remember and fill in later.

• Provide space to jot down notes that are not a part of your running record (e.g., additional information about an activity).

- When you have completed the observation, go back and fill in the needed details as soon as possible while they are fresh in your mind. Running records are rich with description.

- At the end of the running record, write a brief conclusion summarizing the development (cognitive, psychosocial, physical, or creative) demonstrated by the child.

- Keep the records confidential; don't leave them lying around the classroom.

- Organize each child's running records in his or her portfolio. (More on this in Chapter 9.)

Pitfalls.   The pitfalls of running records include subjectivity and general and vague descriptions. Novice observers might initially find subjective statements sneaking into their running records. Candidates for revision might be sketches of a *well-adjusted* or *happy* child or one who colors *nicely*. One adjustment to make is to record actual behaviors rather than inferences. To stop making such subjective inferences, observers focus on the behaviors that led to their assumptions. Instead of writing that the child is happy, they write down what they actually saw and heard. Perhaps a child was observed smiling from ear to ear or singing a snappy little tune while putting a puzzle together. Accurate conclusions can be drawn only from objective recording that fully describes the behavior.

Some contrasting examples from Chapter 1 emphasize the importance of objective recording and the pitfalls of subjective recording. The following excerpts illustrate critical differences in the abilities of two observers.

Student A	*Student B*
[Cyd] tells [the teacher] that the biggest dinosaur is the boss, probably what he wants to be all the time.	He spins around to the teacher and announces as he points to them in lined order, "Tyrannosaurus is the boss 'cause he's the biggest. The stegosaurus is the next boss 'cause he's next biggest. The dimetrodon is the baby. He's not very big."

The first student's general summary and inference about Cyd's motives leave the reader with an incomplete and misleading picture. In the second example, however, a reader can clearly visualize what the child is doing. The objective portrayal of the event is enhanced by Student B's use of explicit words and exact quotations. When the observer uses specific words to characterize the actions and language of the child, the reader can form an accurate mental image of the event. Thus, the second pitfall of writing running records (general and vague descriptions) is avoided.

Capturing children's developmental moments in detail is a valuable observational skill to cultivate; using explicit words is the key. After writing a running record, the observer checks to see if some words are general or vague and need to be replaced with specific words to describe a behavior clearly. For example, a general statement might be, "The girl plays with the blocks in the carpeted area." What specific words would explain how she might have played with blocks? Did the observer consider stacks, forms enclosures, or balances? Descriptive words precisely characterize the child's behavior and provide the teacher with accurate developmental information. Student Activity 4.1 presents an opportunity for you to apply your new understanding of word choice.

Student Activity 4.1
Descriptive Word Practice

Write some descriptive words to further specify the following activities of children. You may use a thesaurus if you wish.

Example: Looks—squints, peeks, stares, scans

1. Builds

2. Colors

3. Tells

4. Runs

5. Writes

Selecting descriptive modifiers (e.g., adjectives, adverbs, and prepositional phrases) increases the clarity of each observation. Study the following examples, and find the modifiers. How are they helpful to the reader of the observations?

Example A	*Example B*
Antonio walks down the stairs one step at a time.	With head bent down, Antonio (2;3) takes slow, precise steps—right foot and then the left foot on each tread as he eases himself down the narrow staircase.

What words would accurately describe these four children's facial expressions?

Example C
Delia rolls balls
down different-sized
ramps made of
blocks.

Example D
Delia (4;2) stacks three
blocks and places a long, flat
board from the top of the
blocks to the ground. Then
she rolls a ball down the
incline, watching where it
stops. Next, she adds two
more blocks vertically so
that the incline is even
steeper and rolls another
ball down the higher ramp.
As the second ball races
down the incline and speeds
past the first ball, a jubilant
smile fills her face. Quickly,
she constructs a ramp seven
blocks high and again rolls a
ball down the ramp.

Modifiers and descriptive words can provide information about the child's facial expressions, movements, appearances, tones of voice, gestures, and problem-solving methods.

Striving to record an accurate picture is the job of the trained observer. Avoid the pitfalls of subjective inferences and vague descriptions; and remember that details, details, details pave the way to sound observations in running records.

Integration of Developmental Theory and Observation

Preschool Example.   A teacher committed to studying the development of her day care students observed a $3\frac{1}{2}$-year-old boy in the dramatic play area. Jeffrey, as usual, was the first child to arrive at the day care center, and his teacher, Gita, thought she would have 10 or 15 minutes to observe him working alone before the next child needed to be welcomed. After Gita hugged him good morning and he put his jacket in his cubby, he headed straight for the dramatic play area. This area seemed to be his favorite spot in the early morning. Gita sat on a small chair next to a low shelf with her notepad and filled in her heading; she was about 12 feet away from Jeffrey, where she could maintain full view of the dramatic play area and the entrance door. Read Gita's running record in Figure 4.3.

INTERPRETING THE DATA   Later in the day, when Gita reads over her running record (Figure 4.3), she is able to draw detailed conclusions about specific areas

---

Running Record of Jeffrey in the Dramatic Play Area

Center: Peaceable Kingdom Day Care

Date: 2/8   Time: 6:40–6:55 a.m.

Observer: Gita   Child/Age: Jeffrey/3;6

Comments

Jeffrey stands sleepily at the entrance to the dramatic play area and rubs his eyes. With his hands on his hips, he slowly turns his head from one end of the area to the other, looking at the materials. He stands, without moving, looking back and forth at the area for 50 seconds. He slowly walks to the far corner and looks down at the heap of dolls and stuffed animals. He bends over, picks up the brown bear, and holds it under his left arm while he pulls out the rabbit and pink bear. He takes this load and dumps the animals on the round table and goes back to the pile. This time he goes down on his knees to rummage through the heap of mostly dolls. He extracts a dog with a torn ear and missing eye and nose; after turning it all around, he discards it to the side. He pulls out a dirty, limp lamb and quickly puts it with the dog. He rummages again. Lifting his head, he calls to me, "Hey teacher, we got any more animals?"

6:40

"No," I reply, "I think you found them all."

Standing up, Jeffrey returns to the round table. He puts the animals in three of the four chairs around the table and scoots each one in. He picks up the pile of full-sized plates from the stove and goes to the brown bear. Holding the plates in his left hand, he pats the brown bear on the head with his right hand and announces, "Barney." He puts a plate in front of Barney. Moving clockwise around the table, he reaches the pink bear. "Mimi," he says and gives it a plate. He pauses with his hand on the rabbit's head for 15 seconds. "Casey," he says tentatively; then, "No, Wally." He gives Wally a plate.

6:45

Figure 4.3.   Preschool running record example *(continued on next page).*

of Jeffrey's development. First, there is wonderful evidence that Jeffrey enjoys using his cognitive ability to represent.

- Jeffrey allows one thing to stand for another. The animals were given names and referred to as *babies*. He pretended that the tomato was bacon and eggs and the apple was pancakes with bananas.

- Jeffrey is able to take on a role. He pretended that he was the dad and talked to the animals with raised intonation. He gave each animal a plate and started to pass out forks.

- Perhaps he is imitating action and language he has observed. Perhaps he has heard his father call someone "my little chickadee" and watched the table-setting process.

Jeffrey walks to the cupboard and gets the plastic fruit and a large, long-handled spoon from the bottom shelf. He puts the plastic tomato on the spoon and, balancing it carefully, walks over to Wally.

"Here you go, Wally," Jeffrey says with a smile, enthusiasm, and a slightly raised voice. "Your favorite, bacon an' eggs." He tips the tomato onto the plate.

"Now for you, my little chickdee," Jeffrey sing-songs on his way back to the fruit. "What my little darlin' want to eat?" (He pauses, looking at the fruit.) "Oh? We got some that too." He puts the plastic apple on the spoon, carries it over to Mimi's plate, and tips it on. He briefly glances at two children who are being greeted by Dolores (the aide).

After studying the animals at the table, Jeffrey rummages through the stove, sink, and cupboard without removing anything. Opening the refrigerator, he smiles and collects with both hands an oversize handful of real flatware from the top shelf. Walking slowly toward Barney, he transfers the flatware to his left hand; as he tries to pull out a fork with his right hand, several pieces drop to the floor. He picks them up and tries again. Again, he loses several pieces, but this time, he gives Barney a fork before collecting the pieces. The fork he tries to pull out for Mimi gets tangled, and the whole handful tumbles to the floor. Frowning, Jeffrey scoops the flatware up and dumps the pieces in the sink.   *Yipes! Clean up.*

Noah and Lene arrive at the entrance to the dramatic play area and are warmly greeted by Jeffrey. "Hi, wanna play with me? I'm feeding my babies. He got bacon an' eggs, and she got pancakes with 'nanas. I'm the dad, OK?"   *6:55*

Conclusion: Jeffrey's dramatic play with stuffed animals, dishes, and plastic fruit demonstrates his representational ability. His initiation and independence allow him to play on his own, although he also welcomes other children.

Figure 4.3.   Preschool running record example *(continued)*.

Gita also finds information about Jeffrey's developing number skills.

- Jeffrey is able to maintain one-to-one correspondence with small numbers. He successfully passed out plates to the three animals, although he took the whole stack with him to the table rather than counting out three at the stove. It appeared that he planned to give each animal a fork but abandoned the idea when the handful of flatware proved to be unwieldy.

This running record also provides information about Jeffrey's development in other areas that will not be pursued at this time. In the psychosocial realm, for example, Gita observed a child who worked beautifully by himself and yet was cordial to arriving children. Running records often provide a wealth of information in various developmental areas.

FOLLOW-THROUGH PLANS   As a student of early childhood, you will practice the observational methods presented in this book as part of your education. As a

Children's interests and abilities are continually on display in the classroom.

result, you will learn about the potentials of the various methods and how to utilize them competently. As a teacher (future or present), however, you want to conduct observations in order to enrich the lives of the children in your classroom. You will want to press your running records and interpretations into service. Remember, "teaching is not one activity and inquiring into it another. The ultimate aim of inquiry is understanding; and understanding is the basis of action for improvement" (McKernan, 1991, p. 3).

Therefore, in anticipation of teaching responsibilities, let's follow Gita's example of putting her running record to practical use. She notices how long it took (15 minutes) for Jeffrey to set up his role play. The dolls and stuffed animals were all jumbled together. The plates, flatware, and plastic fruit seemed to be located in random places; the flatware was in the refrigerator and the plastic fruit in the cupboard. Gita wonders how much more Jeffrey's role play might have developed if he could have easily located his props in predictable places. Consequently, Gita decides to do a general housecleaning and organization of the dramatic play area.

Gita continues to study the materials-and-equipment issue. She concludes that plastic fruit is a poor substitute for bacon and eggs or pancakes and bananas as it does not allow the child to mix things together or practice fine motor skills by ladling food onto dishes. Further, because plastic fruit clearly represents real fruit, some children might feel constrained to use it only as fruit. She plans to fill one canister with open-ended materials, such as various wooden shapes, which will add to the ease and enjoyment of the children's pretending.

Gita ponders what else might be changed in the dramatic play area to support children's representational thought. What else can Jeffrey do as a make-believe grownup? Are there materials to support pretending to write checks, make a shopping list, read a cookbook, take care of a baby, and chat on the telephone? If Jeffrey wanted to pretend to be someone other than a family member, could the dramatic play area provide the foundation? Are props and space available to be a shopkeeper, bank teller, flight attendant, chef, fire fighter, etc.? Gita's running record stimulates an evaluation of the materials available and the use of space throughout the classroom.

Noticing that Jeffrey exhibits one-to-one correspondence with three animals and three plates, Gita wants to find out if this skill extends to larger numbers. She decides to ask Jeffrey to pass out napkins to the eight children at the snack table tomorrow. She plans to provide Jeffrey with opportunities to count objects so as to evaluate his number development further.

Gita's running record also gives her pause to appreciate Jeffrey's thoughtfulness; he did not act impulsively in the dramatic play area. He studiously surveyed the area before commencing play. He was not distracted during his cumbersome search for the stuffed animals. Jeffrey appeared to plan his role play mentally and carry it out with great deliberation. Gita recognizes the importance of being responsive to this individual characteristic. If she rushes him, she will not bring out the best in Jeffrey.

Primary Grade Example. Going one step further than being a "human videotape," a primary grade teacher arranged (with parental permission) for a student teacher to videotape Thienkim, a child in his kindergarten class. To minimize classroom disruption, the camera was set up near a wall and the zoom feature used to follow the child. Pablo, the teacher, was concerned about Thienkim's behavior in the classroom and called a child-study team meeting of the principal, resource specialist, and himself to explore the necessity of special help for Thienkim. Pablo promised to supply a videotape so the team could share a common frame of reference, and he transcribed a portion of the tape in the form of a running record (Figure 4.4) for Thienkim's file.

INTERPRETING THE DATA After the child-study team views the videotape, Pablo presents Thienkim's problems as he sees them. Pablo describes an insecure, timid child whose behaviors limit her potential enjoyment of friends, school, and learning. Pablo is bewildered by some of Thienkim's behaviors: Thienkim said she did want to work with Luciano and then chose not to; further, she held up her index finger while recognizing two ducks on a Lotto card. Pablo admits feeling unsuccessful with Thienkim and wonders if she should be placed in a special class with more individualized attention.

Fortunately for Thienkim, the resource specialist is of Vietnamese ancestry and is able to explain some of Thienkim's behaviors to Pablo and the principal. In Thienkim's culture, shaking hands and hugging are not acceptable methods of greeting between teachers and children; a slight bow is appropriate. As an indication of courtesy and comprehension, Vietnamese often answer a question

---

Running Record of Thienkim During Greeting Time

School/Grade: Glade Elementary/Kindergarten

Date: 9/17   Time: 8:00–8:20 a.m.

Observer: Pablo   Child/Age: Thienkim/5;4

	Comments
Thienkim arrives at school, barely visible behind the coat of her mother. With a gentle nudge, the mother guides Thienkim through the doorway into the classroom and departs quietly. Thienkim stands motionless with her eyes cast downward.	*8:00*
"Good morning, Thienkim," Pablo says cheerily and reaches out to grasp Thienkim's hands, pull her close, and hug her warmly. Thienkim's body stiffens, and she recoils from Pablo's embrace as soon as she is released.	
Thienkim goes to the cubbies via the outskirts of the classroom, avoiding eye contact with the other arriving children. She puts her lunch away, sits on the rug circle, and patiently studies her hands until the class is gathered to begin the day.	*8:03*
During Pablo's calendar and counting activities, Thienkim remains motionless and silent. Thienkim does not volunteer when Pablo begins free-choice time and asks, "Who wants to work with blocks?" nor does she express interest in any other available activity. All children leave to start on self-selected activities. Only Thienkim remains on the circle.	*8:10*
"Would you like to work with Luciano and the puzzles?" Pablo asks.	
"Yes, I don't want to," replies Thienkim in a soft voice. She gets up, walks swiftly to the small-toys area, chooses a Lotto game, and spreads the cards on an empty table with her back to the center of the classroom.	
"How many ducks are there?" asks Pablo later, pointing to a card.	*8:20*
"Two," answers Thienkim without hesitation, holding up her hand with her middle, ring, and pinky fingers bent down.	*Holds up one finger —why?*

Conclusion: Thienkim withdraws from friendly interactions with the teacher and class participation. She chooses to work alone with a structured game and correctly enumerates two objects.

Figure 4.4.   Primary grade running record example.

A running record is often the key to an expanded understanding of a child.

with "yes" and then go on to reply to the message. Regarding Thienkim's ability to count, the resource specialist notes that Vietnamese begin counting with their thumbs—so the index finger is the usual sign for *two* (Buell, 1984).

FOLLOW-THROUGH PLANS   Grateful for the resource specialist's gentle and gracious cultural education, Pablo resolves to make his classroom more hospitable to Thienkim. Review Pablo's running record in Figure 4.4, and write down your suggestions in the exercise below.

Student Activity 4.2 _____

Putting Pablo's Running Record to Practical Use

List ways Pablo can make use of the information from his running record of Thienkim.

Example: Greet Thienkim with verbal warmth but physical restraint.

1.

2.

3.

Applications

Strengths and Limitations.   The fundamental benefit of using the running record method is the collection of raw objective data, usually on one child. The data can be gathered in short periods (5 minutes) or rather long observational sessions (20 to 30 minutes). This observation method records a child's behavior and language and allows developmental conclusions to be drawn. Running records may be saved and used throughout the year (or longer) for analyzing, assessing, and marking the changes in children over time. Running records may also serve to stimulate the planning of developmentally appropriate activities and the evaluation of the classroom.

Both the experienced and the inexperienced observer can easily recognize the major difficulty with the running record. The setting alone, an active early childhood environment, can be problematic. Young children may change their activities frequently as the observer frantically writes. Perhaps classroom noises or interferences distract the observer. Myriad factors might cause the observer to neglect to record some behaviors or verbalizations. Being a "human videotape" requires the constant use of imaginary blinders, a well-tuned ear, and a fast hand.

Another problem is scheduling. Even though the running record method is easy to use, requiring only a paper and pencil, the busy classroom teacher encounters many obstacles to finding time to observe a child. The day-to-day demands on an early childhood teacher can be overwhelming, so running records are best spaced out. It takes a diligent teacher who is willing to plan for (and an administration that is willing to support) the practical implementation of observational time.

A running record for Warren, the child discussed in Chapter 3's Think About section, might have yielded a wealth of new understanding; for example, it might have revealed his keen interests, how long and under what conditions he worked on task, how he responded to peer tutors, and his active concern with practically oriented problems. Given the demands of an elementary school classroom, however, Warren's teacher probably would have required help from the principal, a specialist, or a parent to accomplish this running record. Fiona could have asked this person to free up her time in order to give Warren her full attention for a short period. If the person were trained in observation, Fiona would have had the option of asking him or her to use the running record method to observe Warren.

As you gain expertise in the observational methods presented throughout this text, you will become able to put the running record in perspective: one plate in a smorgasbord of observational options. You will use the running record selectively when you need raw, objective data to learn more about a child or profit from an overall picture. Then, the time investment required by the running record will pay off; review the educational follow-through plans for Jeffrey and Thienkim if you have any doubts.

Student Activity 4.3 _____

Running Record Exercise

Now is your opportunity to practice running records. Pick a partner. One of you is A, and the other is B. Partner A is given a sheet of notebook paper and a pen or pencil. Partner B is given a piece of paper and a box of children's crayons. Partner B may color in any way she or he chooses when the activity begins. Partner A observes and records the exact coloring behavior of Partner B for 2 minutes in a running record. Copy the form below, adding space for your recording.

Running Record

School:

Date: Time:

Observer: "Child":

                                                                        Comments

Running record:

Conclusion:

When you are finished, change roles with your partner and repeat the activity. Follow the same procedures.

Then, to verify accurate recording, work with someone else in the class. Slowly read the running record you have written, and have that person act out the scenario. Circle any behaviors incorrectly acted out, and clarify them on your paper when you are finished.

You probably want to write a few more running records to practice and solidify your skills. The first step is to move from adult partners to observing young children. You may watch your own or friends' children or unfamiliar children at a neighborhood park. Or perhaps you are an assistant or volunteer in a classroom in which you can gain some experience. Students are most successful in the beginning by keeping the observation to 2 or 3 minutes and recording a single child involved in a solitary activity. Gradually work on building up to a longer observation. Some students use tape recorders, which they can later stop and start at their own convenience while they write their final copy. Action Project 4.1 provides an excellent opportunity to begin observing; try it after you review the critical elements of running records summarized in Points to Remember.

Action Project 4.1
Running Record Activity

Observe a child working alone for 3 to 5 minutes, and record his or her actions and language in a running record. As you make your selection, remember that you will want to draw some conclusions about the child's development in all pertinent areas. Also remember to include the following information on your recording form.

Running Record

Center or School/Grade:

Date: Time:

Observer: Child/Age:

Comments

Running record:

Conclusion:

Points to Remember

Running records offer observers the means to explore the development of individual children, especially those who are most puzzling. Teachers who make the time to use the running record are well rewarded for their efforts. They have an objective narrative, unhampered by subjective or premature interpretations, that describes the actions and verbalizations of a child in detail. The running record stands alone as raw, qualitative data and is available for later study—stimulating evaluation and profitable follow-through plans. To maximize the usefulness of each running record, check that it

- Has an informative heading
- Is written in the present tense
- Is as objective as possible
- Uses explicit words, modifiers, and details to describe behaviors

Think About . . .

Gita, the teacher, is sitting on her chair with note pad in hand when Noah and Lene arrive at the entrance to the dramatic play area. Jeffrey cordially invites them to play. Gita's running record of Jeffrey's role play has progressed smoothly, and she has the time and desire to continue. She anticipates that Jeffrey's interactions with the other children will be interesting to observe.

Gita continues with her running record, now focusing on the three children. What problems with using a running record in this situation do you foresee?

CHAPTER 5

Observing the Development of Individual Children by Using Anecdotal Records

While preparing a pretend breakfast for Barney, Mimi, and Wally, Jeffrey (3;6) actively engaged in solitary dramatic play in Chapter 4's example of a preschool running record. The Think About section asked you to picture the teacher using the running record method to observe Jeffrey's interactions with two newcomers to the dramatic play area. Jeffrey's teacher, Gita, wanting to extend her understanding of Jeffrey's social skills, seized the opportunity to record the behaviors of the trio. Imagine Gita's frantic attempt to write down every action, reaction, interaction, and verbalization of all three children in a running record!

A running record is an excellent method to employ when the observer wants to gather wide-ranging data on one child. Gita certainly collected an impressive display of developmental information about Jeffrey. There is, however, another method that can efficiently summarize incidents and is especially useful when detailed accounts are not feasible. It is the anecdotal record.

This chapter investigates the use of the anecdotal method as a powerful teacher's tool for building an understanding of the whole child; it is a way to collect and analyze significant happenings. Although the focus of this chapter is on the observation of individual children, anecdotal records can also be helpful for teachers observing small groups of children, students observing master teachers, or supervising teachers observing student teachers. So what are anecdotes? Read on, and find out about one of the most popular observational methods in the early childhood classroom.

Overview of Observing Using Anecdotal Records

Having returned from a memorable vacation, I frequently delight in sharing brief accounts of the trip with friends. Often, the happenings are humorous; often, they are unusual or unfortunate; always, they are anecdotal. One such recent anecdote is as follows:

> There I was staring down a very steep and difficult ski run. My legs seemed as stiff as boards; my hands were desperately gripping my poles. I vaguely noticed out of the corner of my eye a 3-year-old girl zipping down the slope, her dad standing adjacent to me. In the next instant she stopped, turned, and hollered, "Look at me, Daddy; I'm halfway down the mountain." I turned to her dad, paused, and asked, "Can you buy that kind of confidence?"

Have you had similar experiences of recounting personal happenings? Most likely we all have. An anecdote, then, is not a new idea to any of us. We all seem to have a sense of what it is all about.

Description. In the early childhood classroom an *anecdote* is more than something interesting or amusing to share. It is a short, concise narrative

> 10/5   Kristi (3;3).   During the fire fighters' classroom visit, Kristi cried and crawled into the teacher's lap when Ryan's mom (one of the fire fighters) put on her uniform. (Psychosocial—Fear)

Figure 5.1.   Example of a preschool anecdote.

summarizing one directly observed incident, usually chosen for its developmental significance and recorded after the occurrence. This transcribed memory account traps golden developmental moments and provides a permanent record of growth trends. Figure 5.1 displays an anecdote denoting a child's fear; notice that the data available for study are qualitative.

Anecdotal records are most reliable if jotted down as soon as possible after the event, thus capitalizing on a clear memory. In bustling classrooms, however, writing a detailed anecdotal entry immediately after the observed incident is not always possible. The teacher in Figure 5.1, having acquired the competence to spot significant behaviors, observed a noteworthy incident and only had time to make a quick memorandum using key words on a nearby scratch pad.

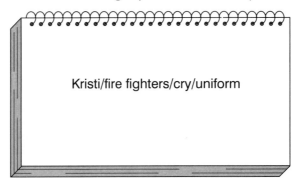

Kristi/fire fighters/cry/uniform

Later, the teacher transcribed the key words into a few meaningful sentences (Figure 5.1) and placed the anecdote in the child's portfolio.

When based on key words or short phrases, anecdotal records take little time and are easy to record on a daily basis. Anecdotes require no particular setting, no forms, and no time structures; the observer needs only to capture the essence of what occurred. The observer may draw on the *journalistic approach* and record the factual accounts of the *who, what, where, when,* and *how* of a single incident (reporting *when* and/or *where* is not always necessary; observers should use their own judgment).

Well-written anecdotes give brief information about location to build a visual image of the setting, summarize how the incident happened, and use descriptive words to tell what was said and done. Consider the language anecdotes shown in Figure 5.2 that were extracted from individual portfolios.

The journalistic approach assists the observer in remembering the essential components of anecdotes.

The teacher recording the language anecdotes in Figure 5.2 considered them developmentally meaningful; in so doing, the teacher appraised the child's age, the vocabulary choice and usage, the expression of relationships, and the concise communication of a complex idea. Language anecdotes may also be collected to evaluate sentence length, articulation/clarity, word order, and conversation skills. In addition, K–3 teachers may observe and record children's use of expanded sentences, past-tense words, pronouns, and accurate grammar, just to mention a few examples.

Purpose.   The fundamental aim of the anecdotal record is to note significant and ongoing evidence of children's development or growth through selected observations. "Emphasis should be on events that demonstrate a child's typical behavior or strikingly unusual behavior" (Goodwin & Driscoll, 1980, p. 82). Teachers observe and record behavioral patterns, changes, progress, milestones, or uncommon happenings. Typical topics for early childhood anecdotes are language and literacy development, social interaction patterns, problem-solving skills, aggressions, and achievements. The recordings may involve only a single child or child–child interactions or adult–child interactions.

Anecdotes chronicling a child's development can provide the basis for the teacher's planning of appropriate environmental support, activities, responses, and experiences. Posting one or two anecdotes a week for each child gives the teacher a collection of valuable information to offer a learning program that germinates from emerging individual needs.

Example 1: Tatiana (2;0). While sitting on the floor in the art area peeling the wrappers off crayons, she looked up as the caregiver drew near and said, "I making the crayons all naked."

Example 2: Maggie (4;8). I listened as Maggie chattered on and on as the two of us cleaned up the block area. Finally I winked and said, "It all sounds like baloney to me." Maggie quickly asked, "What's baloney?" I replied, "It's a word that means you made all that up." She thought for a few seconds and said, "No, it's salami!"

Example 3: Matthew (7;4). While discussing *In A Dark, Dark Room and Other Scary Stories* by Alvin Schwartz, Matthew thoughtfully shared, "Do you know what kind of scary things I like best? Things that are halfway between real and imaginary." The teacher started to ask, "I wonder what...?" Matthew quickly replied, "Examples would be aliens, shadows, and dreams coming true."

Figure 5.2.   Examples of language anecdotes.

"Taken regularly, anecdotal notes become not only a vehicle for planning instruction and documenting progress, but also a story about an individual" (Rhodes & Nathenson-Mejia, 1992, p. 503). Recordings gathered over a period and representing all requisite domains of development (physical, cognitive, psychosocial, and creative) supply enough information to create a story and, thus, a holistic understanding of the child. In addition, parents can fully appreciate this story when preserved anecdotes are shared at conference time.

Students who have had teaching experience may believe they know the strengths and weaknesses of the children in their classroom and conclude they don't need to write down individual observations. It is, however, impossible to remember the wonderful growth, in detail, of 8 to 15 (let alone 20 or 30) children over the course of the year. Regular and systematic anecdotal recording documents up-to-date information needed for individual planning and productive parent conferences.

Guidelines for Writing Anecdotes.   Over the years, researchers, teachers, and observers have developed helpful hints to ensure success using each of the various observational methods. The following are suggestions to assist in writing useful anecdotal records:

• Begin with a clear understanding of the developmental characteristics of the age group being observed. Be able to identify growth indicators for physical, cognitive, psychosocial, and creative development.

• Be aware of significant happenings in each child's daily activities.

• Jot down brief notes on paper or adhesive note paper or dictate into a small tape recorder as soon as possible after a directly observed incident. Record

Teachers observe and record anecdotes to note developmentally significant incidents.

significant language passages verbatim. Tuck them away in a folder or in a pocket designated for anecdotal records. (Remember that all records must be kept confidential.) At the end of the day, use the journalistic approach to transfer those cursory notes into readable sentences.

- At the beginning of each anecdote, enter the date of the observation and child's age (year;month).
- Be factual, objective, and concise; summarize.
- State the developmental significance (e.g., physical, cognitive, psychosocial, or creative) in the anecdote itself or in parentheses at the end. In the primary grades, cognitive development may be categorized into the relevant subject areas (e.g., language arts, math, social studies, and science).
- Guard against haphazardly tossing individual anecdotal records into a catchall file. Enter the finished anecdote in the child's portfolio of observational records.
- Check portfolios periodically to verify the recording of a variety of developmental incidents for each child.

To practice using the guidelines, slowly read the anecdotal record examples listed in the next activity and determine if each is an acceptable or unacceptable anecdote. For each anecdotal example, decide if changes must be made.

Student Activity 5.1 _____

Anecdotal Examples for Analysis

If the anecdote meets the guidelines, place an ✗ in the box marked *correct*. If, on the other hand, the anecdote does not meet the guidelines, place an ✗ in the box marked *incorrect*. In each case, describe your reasoning in the space marked *analysis*.

Example:
5/8 Willie (4;5). Willie is cognizant and watchful while playing with others. He can communicate well. Does like to create own play with other objects but keeps his playmates in mind. (Psychosocial—Play)

☐ Correct
☒ Incorrect

Analysis:
The observer has written an overall evaluation using inferences rather than an objective journalistic summary of one specific incident. Recording quotes would indicate Willie's communication skills. The last sentence is subjective.

Example:
11/24 Ernestina (3;3) and Meghan (3;9). When Meghan saw Ernestina in the doorway crying and clinging to her mother's leg, she walked over and gently placed her cheek touching Ernestina's cheek. The girls stood quietly cheek to cheek for a few moments, and Ernestina's mom departed. (Psychosocial—Separation)

☒ Correct
☐ Incorrect

Analysis:
The observer has identified a significant incident in the psychosocial development of Ernestina and Meghan. The narrative summary is written concisely yet contains information on the *who*, *what*, *where*, and *how* of a single incident.

2/15 Jeffrey (3;6), Noah (3;8), and Lene (3;3). At Jeffrey's invitation Noah and Lene joined in dramatic play. Jeffrey directed and Lene cooperated in the feeding and napping of Jeffrey's "babies." Noah dressed up in men's clothes and pretended to wash the dishes. (Psychosocial—Play)

☐ Correct
☐ Incorrect

Analysis:

12/7 Hien (4;2). Hien picks one marker out of the container with his left hand, smelling it (scrunching up his nose). "Um pink," he says. He draws carefully constructed parallel lines with it and puts it back. He sorts through the container and picks up a thinner marker, smells it, and looks it over. Hien asks if all the markers smell as he drops the thin one back into the container. He takes out a green marker, smells it, and draws on the paper using a circular motion. He uses his right hand to steady the paper. "I'm gonna make a target for us," he says. Putting back the green marker, he takes out the red marker and bangs it on the table and then lays it down. Next, he takes out the blue marker and uses a circular motion to draw inside the green circle.

The teacher asks, "So, that's a target?"

"Not yet," Hien says. He returns the blue to the container and takes out a purple marker. Quickly, he draws with purple in a circular motion inside the blue circle and says, "Now, that's a target." (Cognitive—Representation)

❑ Correct
❑ Incorrect

Analysis:

10/5 Isaiah (4;5). Drew a jack-o'-lantern: eyes, eyelashes, ears, mouth with teeth, nose, forehead, and curly hair. (Creative—Two-dimensional)

❑ Correct
❑ Incorrect

Analysis:

4/11 Thelma Lou (6;4). I am quite worried about Thelma Lou's fine motor development. While working with small puzzles, she seems to have a plan to begin with but asks for help over and over.

❑ Correct
❑ Incorrect

Analysis:

6/23 Cassandra (7;11). In a small, cooperative math learning group assigned to create a new pattern using plastic links, Cassandra stood up and gathered the links that had been placed in the center of the table. After unlinking each one, she announced, "We all have to have the same amount; I'm going to pass them out!" (Psychosocial—Relations with peers)

❑ Correct
❑ Incorrect

Analysis:

Integration of Developmental Theory and Observation

Knowledgeable teachers jot down anecdotal records that reflect all areas of development. Periodically they check each child's portfolio to see if they are collecting a variety of anecdotes in different settings. Individually or as a team, teachers read the newly added anecdotes and a sampling of the old ones to broaden their understanding of each child. They look for developmental growth patterns as they study individual recordings and plan activities based on assessed needs.

Two classroom anecdotes are reproduced in Figure 5.3 to represent preschool and primary grade topics. As you read through them, see if you can determine why the teacher chose to write each one down (the developmental significance) and begin to think of some plans the teacher could make to further each child's growth.

1/13 Song (3;3). While watching a puppet show in another classroom, Song responded with tear-filled eyes when he was mocked by the two 4-year-old boys sitting next to him. One boy poked the other and said, "Look at him; he's Chinese. He looks like this." With his hands he pulled down the corners of his eyes until they were partially closed.

9/18 Lissy (7;5). In the computer lab Lissy asked how to spell *through.* I responded, "Let's sound it out together." Lissy said, "I know how to write it that way, but I want to know the correct way to spell it."

Figure 5.3.   Examining anecdotal records.

Not all anecdotes necessitate follow-through plans. The examples in Figure 5.3, however, beg for teacher interpretation. "Interpretations are constructed through our active mental work; they are not part of the immediately given environment. They grow out of our theories, our past experiences and our present observations" (McCutcheon, 1981, p. 5). Listed are possible teacher plans based on the anecdotes in Figure 5.3. These plans model the process that teachers follow when interpreting anecdotal information to further individual growth.

Preschool Example

Preschool Example — Song

Developmental Significance: Psychosocial—Self-Concept

1/3 Song (3;3). While watching a puppet show in another classroom, Song responded with tear-filled eyes when he was mocked by the two 4-year-old boys sitting next to him. One boy poked the other and said, "Look at him; he's Chinese. He looks like this." With his hands he pulled down the corners of his eyes until they were partially closed.

INTERPRETING THE DATA   The teacher in this incident looked firmly at the two boys and only had time to say, "Song is not Chinese; he is Korean. You hurt his feelings when you make fun of his eyes. Eyes can be all different shapes." And then the teacher looked at Song and said, "It's OK to tell them that you don't like that."

After the children had gone home, the team teachers in Song's class evaluated the day. They began by looking at the anecdotes they'd written. Song's was first. The teacher who interacted with Song and the two boys shared her feelings related to this incident. She said she was a little surprised but very pleased with her response. In the past she hadn't responded this appropriately to delicate situations. The other teacher readily responded that he personally had been afraid to step in when sensitive matters occurred. Both teachers spent time talking about their own discomfort. Realizing that their biggest fear was uncertainty regarding the right words to say, they reviewed other responses teachers might make in similar situations.

"That's very hurtful when you say _____. I can't allow you to hurt someone's feelings."

"I'm sorry Logan and Ricardo hurt your feelings."

"I think you're wonderful just the way you are."

The teachers agreed that knowing the kind of words to say was important, but they must steer away from pat answers that become litany. Each situation would be different; their responses must come from an active involvement.

The teachers then shifted their attention to Song's discomfort and inability to stand up for himself with 4-year-olds. They discussed how they could affirm Song. In their 3-year-old classroom they continuously represented several cultures, including Korean, with dolls, pretend food, books, pictures on the classroom walls, and snacks. As the teachers read back through other anecdotes they had collected about Song, they saw a clear picture that Song showed confidence in dealing with and communicating his feelings with children his same age in his classroom; however, he is the first child of young parents and could benefit from more exchanges with older preschoolers in their school.

FOLLOW-THROUGH PLANS   After much discussion about Song's reticence and the other boys' insensitivity, the teachers decide to invite the same class of 4-year-olds back to share an art party with the help of parent volunteers. Their art party will have several different art activities set up throughout the room; the children will freely choose one art activity to participate in.

Song's teachers confer with the teachers of the 4-year-old class and choose the theme, "I'm Me and I'm Special" (York, 1991, p. 73). The teachers referred to the books *Anti-Bias Curriculum* (Derman-Sparks & A.B.C. Task Force, 1989) and *Roots and Wings* (York, 1991) for some of the following ideas.

At the first table the teachers decide to have hand mirrors; black, brown, beige, peach, and white paper; and several boxes of crayons, including various skin-tone crayons. The children who choose this activity will be able to look into the mirrors and draw what they see. The teacher at this table will talk with the children about differences and similarities as they come up, affirming that it's wonderful and important to be who we are—"you and me."

At the second table there will be long pieces of butcher paper, many shades of skin-tone tempera paint, primary-color tempera paints, craft sticks for mixing paints, paint cups, crayons, pencils, scissors, and a full-length mirror. The children will be offered the big paper to trace around each others' bodies on the floor. Then, with the aid of an adult, they will mix the skin-tone paints to reflect the color of their own skin and help each other paint their portraits on the butcher paper, adding hair, facial features, and clothes. The adults at this table will talk about our skins' many beautiful shades of color and how no two seem to be exactly alike.

At the third table will be magazine pictures of eyes of various shapes and colors along with scissors and glue for making collages. Again, mirrors will be handy to help the children identify their own eye shape and color.

At the fourth table, close to the sink, will be long strips of butcher paper, skin-tone tempera paints to be mixed to individual shades, buckets of soapy water, paper towels, and paintbrushes. Here, the children can take their shoes off, mix the paint the color of their feet, paint the bottom of their feet, and make footprints on the paper. Perhaps they will also want to make handprints. The teacher at this table can talk about the marvelous variety of sizes, colors, and shapes.

A resource table will be available with an array of other art materials that children from any table may need: yarn, crayons, marking pens, glue and tape, various colors of construction paper, large and small pieces of fabric, and wallpaper sample books.

After all the projects are complete, the adults plan to assist the children in displaying their creations in the classroom for everyone to admire. The teachers from both classrooms will help the children to talk about and celebrate their differences and similarities.

The art party took place 2 days later and was a success for all. The teachers of the two different ages planned more times when the two ages could be mixed: a trip to the park, snack time, and a musicfest. Subsequent anecdotal records noted that Song slowly and steadily gained confidence with older children. The two 4-year-old boys became more accepting of diversity, and the use of the anti-bias curriculum began to gain momentum in the school. Daily the teachers were more aware of their own reactions as well as the children's to cultural diversity. They were watchful not to ignore subtle comments. They used opportune moments to point out differences, likenesses, options; they modeled acceptance and joy in who each person is. Working toward a bias-free environment is a perpetual process necessary to help children develop a positive sense of self and others.

Primary Grade Example.   Consider the anecdote about Lissy in the computer center.

Primary Grade Example — Lissy

Developmental Significance: Cognitive—Language

9/18 Lissy (7;5). In the computer lab Lissy asked how to spell *through*. I responded, "Let's sound it out together." Lissy said, "I know how to write it that way, but I want to know the correct way to spell it."

INTERPRETING THE DATA   Lissy, now in second grade, has been going to the computer laboratory since kindergarten. In this laboratory, the children are encouraged to write words phonetically, using invented spelling, so as to avoid being bogged down by spelling refinements. She writes terrific stories, many about the exciting adventures of a princess; one of her stories was recently chosen for the school newspaper.

As the teacher enters this anecdote and checks previously logged anecdotes, she notes Lissy's continuous literacy development. Lissy enjoys writing and reading her stories and readily shares them with other class members. Her stories already have well-developed plots, thus showing her ability to comprehend sequence. The incident recounted in the anecdote was, however, the first evidence that Lissy is aware that printed materials need to be consistent for readers. Documenting Lissy's emerging personal interest in spelling illustrates the natural step children can make in a whole-language curriculum when they are ready and able to use correct spelling without it limiting their creative writing. Lissy's teacher is pleased to see that Lissy has made this connection.

As often happens, the teacher noted other children who seem to have the same need: in this case, an interest in spelling words of their choice. The teacher plans a small-group time to demonstrate ways to spell words using different sources. Lissy's teacher will show the children how to use one of their well-known

A child's enthusiasm soars with the opportunity to use a computer to compose stories.

reading stories to locate the spelling of a word that they know, and she will introduce the use of the picture dictionary. The teacher will also help the children create their own personal dictionaries—blank papers stapled together with one letter of the alphabet on each page. When the children need to look up a word in the picture dictionary or if they need teacher assistance for spelling, they can record the word in their personal dictionaries, thus having it for future reference.

FOLLOW-THROUGH PLANS   Enthusiastic about the small group information, Lissy showed avid interest in using the picture dictionary. She was also delighted to have her own personal dictionary. She immediately inscribed words on several pages. Her teacher later observed that Lissy sometimes illustrated the new word she added to her dictionary. (What a resourceful idea!) To capitalize on the children's spelling interest, the teacher gradually put up charts on the walls with lists of commonly used descriptive words, action words, and prepositions. Lissy's fervor for writing continued to increase because her developmental need was met at the right time.

If teachers view each child as an important and unique person, they will consciously select curriculum activities and experiences based on observed individual needs. Analyzing anecdotal records unlocks the doors to the appropriate curriculum cupboards.

Anecdotes and Other Forms of Recording

A cohesive portrait of each child's development is drawn through the use of many forms of classroom observations. The use of various methods allows the teacher to see through the looking glass with clarity and confidence.

Some teachers find it difficult to work with the large amount of raw data collected through running records. Although many running records document abundant and varied happenings, their conclusions cannot stand alone without the running record. Running record conclusions are seeds for several anecdotes (for clarification review the running record and conclusion in Figure 4.2). For this reason teachers pick out individual incidents in each of their running records, rewrite them as anecdotes, and file them in the child's portfolio. These shortened, one-incident recordings usually prove to be much more useful than the long descriptive passages of running records when the teacher is analyzing, planning, and conferencing.

Likewise, anecdotes are a possible source for some of the information requested by checklist or rating scale assessments discussed in the next two chapters. For example, a child's gross motor abilities recorded in several anecdotes could be transferred to a motor development checklist or rating scale. Language anecdotes are also a likely topic. Reflect on other potential topics as you study checklists and rating scales in Chapters 6 and 7.

Applications

Strengths and Limitations.   In the early childhood classroom, anecdotes are one of the most widely used observational methods; their strengths are numerous. To begin with, "teachers report that they see and hear with more clarity when using anecdotal records, by focusing more intensively on how children say things and how they interact with each other" (Rhodes & Nathenson-Mejia, 1992, p. 508). Weekly anecdotal recordings supply the teacher with specific examples of each child's growth patterns and developmental characteristics. These valuable records are then analyzed and, when appropriate, used in planning to facilitate individual learning.

Many teachers maintain that an important advantage of anecdotal records is their ease in use. Writing anecdotes takes no more than paper and a pencil (or a pocket-size tape recorder). Anecdotes are written at the teacher's convenience after the event has occurred. Because an anecdote is a concise statement, little time is needed to record the major elements. Many experienced teachers also enlist the help of assistants who can be trained effectively in anecdotal record collecting; some schools provide excellent in-service training for assistants.

Anecdotal records are a treasure chest of documented incidents that can be compared and contrasted with other recorded observations. These gems, used in conjunction with other kinds of observational records, can help the teacher form a precise understanding of each child's unique growth patterns, changes, inter-

Teamwork enhances the observational process.

ests, abilities, and needs. This wealth of information is the foundation for teacher planning and conferences.

Many would argue that teachers' biases may influence what they choose to record. Teachers may fail to see an important developmental step if they have formed preconceived ideas about a particular child or children in general. "This halo effect can work in either direction; an initial negative impression can affect our subsequent observations of the child, as can a positive one" (Phinney, 1982, p. 19). For example, a primary school teacher may think boys are better in math than girls are. Or a preschool teacher may judge a child's behavior on the basis of a sibling's competence displayed in a previous year. Practicing anecdote writing and receiving feedback from others is an excellent way to uncover hidden biases and avoid this potential limitation.

On the other hand, the teacher may unknowingly miss an important milestone for one or more children because of the many demands for a teacher's attention. Teachers avoid this pitfall by using aides or enlisting parent volunteers as classroom helpers and relying on well-organized systems of record keeping (more on this in Chapter 9). Devising creative classroom management techniques allows for needed "release time" to stand back, observe, and listen to individual children as they play and work.

Action Project 5.1
Anecdote Exercise

You are now ready to practice writing some anecdotes of your own. One of the best ways is to turn on a videotape of prerecorded incidents. (Beginning writers of anecdotes think that the replay button is mighty helpful!) Because we cannot play a videotape in this textbook, we will move to the next best option. This exercise gives you the opportunity to practice writing anecdotal records by extracting them from a running record.

Study the running record for Evan at the workbench, and then write one anecdote embedded in the scenario.

Running Record of Evan at the Workbench

School/Grade:	Cornerstone School/Kindergarten			
Date:	9/25	Time:	10:15–10:23 a.m.	
Observer:	Mariah	Child/age:	Evan/5;2	

Comments

As the door swings open to the outside yard, Evan makes a beeline to the workbench. He leans over and roots around in the large scrap-wood box, finally selecting two long (about 15 inch) rectangular pieces. As he places the wood pieces on top of the bench, he arranges one piece of wood perpendicular and on top of the other, forming a T shape, both lying flat. As he holds the top rectangle in place with his right hand, his left hand retracts the hammer from its hanging position on the pegboard that is attached to the back of the workbench. He lays the hammer down on the workbench and lets go of the wood with his right hand. The two wood pieces stay in the T position without support. Evan opens the drawer under the workbench top with both hands and picks out three nails with his left hand, placing each one on the workbench. He grasps the hammer in his left hand and a nail in his right hand. Holding the nail at the intersection of the two wood pieces, he raises his left arm almost shoulder height and whacks the nail; he misses and instantly pulls his right hand away. The top wooden rectangle falls off the bottom one, and Evan lets go of the nail. Still holding the hammer in his left hand, he once again repositions the wood into a T shape. He picks up another nail with his right hand and holds it in the same place. Again, he raises the hammer shoulder height and brings it down toward the nail with great speed. Again, he misses! With the hammer in his left hand and the nail in his right, he puts both hands on his hips and sighs deeply.

Shaina (5;4) approaches the workbench and says, "Wanna play chase?" "No," responds Evan, "I'm making 'un airplane, but this nail's falling." Shaina walks around the workbench, looking at Evan's structure as Evan re-joins the two pieces he has been working with. "Wait, wait!" hollers Shaina as she raises her hands into the air. "You gotta use the vise." "The what?" asks Evan. "This thing," Shaina replies as she reaches up and takes the vise from its position on the pegboard. "My daddy showed me how to use this; it works!"

10:18

Evan steps back one step with eyes glued on Shaina's actions as she clamps the   *very skilled*
two pieces of wood together and securely fastens them on the edge of the workbench with the vise. "Now it won't move. Try it and don't pound so hard," she says
as a broad smile fills her face.

With his right hand he chooses another nail and moves it into position. This time,   *10:21*
he holds the nail with his whole hand. Evan bends slightly at the knees, raises the
hammer about 1 foot above the nail and, with a slower speed, taps the nail. This time
he makes contact. With tongue now gripping the right side of his mouth, he lifts the
hammer and strikes the nail again. He repeats his successful motion six times, each
time making contact. When the nail is securely driven in, he looks up at Shaina, eyes
wide, lips together, gives one nod of his head. Before Evan has time to utter one
word, Shaina exclaims, "I'll bet that's a DC-10!"

Conclusion: (The conclusion has been omitted so that your selected anecdote will
not be influenced.)

Write your chosen anecdotal record for Evan (5;2) or Shaina (5;4).
Remember to summarize the incident and use the journalistic approach. Think
through any needed follow-up plans.

Points to Remember

Observing and recording a child's developmental progress through anecdotal
records requires little time. Anecdotes can easily be used to collect qualitative
data in all areas of growth. Contents state the *who, what,* and *how,* and sometimes
the *where* and *when* of an observed behavior. Using an in-the-nutshell recording
format, anecdotes are written after the incident occurs. They are placed in each
child's portfolio and used in planning. As preserved treasures, anecdotes enrich
parent conferences.

Anecdotal record keeping necessitates the use of objectivity to the best of
one's ability, a thorough understanding of child development, and the commitment to regular recording for each child. Anecdotes are often considered the
backbone of portfolios.

Think About . . .

Nicole is the teacher of an early childhood group. Today she has set up an obstacle course outside. She has carefully designed the course to challenge and assess the children in several areas of gross motor development, such as climbing, hopping, jumping, and balancing. To further complicate matters, there are other classes of children outside at the same time; these children may also choose to use the obstacle course. Nicole plans to target her observational attention on the developmental strides of her group.

If Nicole chooses the anecdotal method to collect the data in this situation, what do you surmise would be her dissatisfactions?

CHAPTER 6

Observing the Development of Individual Children by Using Checklists

As Nicole observes the children in her class going through the obstacle course discussed in the Chapter 5 Think About section, she wants to document their abilities. She rejects the running record method because her hand could never keep pace with quickly moving children. Anecdotal records would also be cumbersome. Imagine writing something like this for each child: "In my prepared obstacle course, Linnea (5;7) ran gracefully around the tree, hopped in two Hula-hoops on her right foot, jumped over the 12-inch foam cube from a standing position, and balanced halfway down the balance beam." Nicole wants to assess each child's gross motor abilities efficiently; this chapter introduces an observational method for her to consider.

Recall how you brush your teeth at night, and check off which of the following descriptions apply to you:

Name of brusher:

- ❏ Uses fluoridated toothpaste
- ❏ Brushes for at least $1\frac{1}{2}$ minutes
- ❏ Uses dental floss
- ❏ Uses gum massager of some kind

You have just completed a short checklist that required no special skills other than knowledge about your toothbrushing practices. You have used a checklist—the topic of this chapter.

Overview of Observing Using Checklists

Description.   A *checklist* is a register of items that the observer marks off if they are present; behaviors or details not on the checklist are ignored. Good checklists have clear items that leave little room for observers' subjective judgments. Checklists usually focus on skills or easily observed behaviors. For example, children's social or motor skills or teachers' story-reading skills might be studied on one or more occasions. In the introductory example, Nicole wants to assess the presence of specific abilities—that is, whether each child can run in a coordinated fashion, hop on one foot, jump over a low obstacle, and walk on a balance beam; a checklist is the appropriate observational method.

Checklists may be filled out during or after an observation. In either case, the observer brings the checklist and paper for note taking to the observational session. The quality of data recorded on checklists depends on the clarity of the items and the observer's ability to assess each item accurately. Therefore, the observer must be familiar with the content of each item and know what constitutes an earned check; instructions on checklists may serve to clarify potential ambiguities.

Information to complete a checklist may be gathered from a single or several observations, or the observer may want to include data from other observational records on the subject. The choice depends on the purpose and type of checklist used. A one-time observation may be sufficient to assess an environment, whereas a teacher completing a multiple-subjects checklist for a child would want to draw on the widest possible information base.

This chapter examines checklist items that focus on children's progress, the environment, and explicit teaching skills. First, let's look at portions of a checklist (Figure 6.1) assessing children's progress in emergent writing (Houghton Mifflin, 1989). Appreciate how the ordering of items illustrates developmental growth.

The High/Scope Educational Research Foundation developed a checklist to evaluate the implementation of its curriculum (Hohmann et al., 1979). The following item concerning the sand and water area is from the room arrangement checklist.

> 21. The sand and water area includes the following:
> ❑ an appropriate sand/water vessel.
> ❑ a cleanable floor surface.
> ❑ materials for pretending, scooping and digging, filling and emptying.
> ❑ additional sand-like materials for variety (beans, styrofoam bits, etc.).[1]

The items are clear and straightforward, allowing the observer to record their presence or note their absence.

Other portions of the High/Scope checklist assess the skills of teachers in supporting the program's goals. Because the development of representational thought during the preschool years was summarized in Chapter 2, consider an item pertaining to experiencing and representing.

> 5.   Adults encourage and support children's representational activities by:
> ❑ playing sensory-cue games.
> ❑ helping children notice and make imprints and shadows.
> ❑ encouraging children to imitate actions and sounds.
> ❑ comparing models to the objects they represent.
> ❑ encouraging children to represent in a variety of two- and three-dimensional media.
> ❑ taking dictation from children about what they have made, done, seen, or experienced.[2]

---

[1] From *Young Children in Action* (p. 297) by M. Hohmann, B. Banet, and D. P. Weikart, 1979, Ypsilanti, MI: High/Scope Press. Copyright 1979 by High/Scope Educational Research Foundation. Reprinted with permission.

[2] Ibid, p. 309.

Writing: Developmental Checklist

Center or School/Grade:

Date: Time:

Observer: Child/Age:

Date   *Skill*

[   ]   Mimics writing; scribbles

[   ]   Draws recognizable pictures of people, animals, and objects

[   ]   Dictates words and short phrases

[   ]   Dictates complete sentences

[   ]   Dictates stories

[   ]   Traces upper- and lower-case letters

[   ]   Traces words and sentences

[   ]   Identifies and forms upper-case letters

[   ]   Identifies and forms lower-case letters

[   ]   Uses letters and numerals to mimic writing; no sound–symbol asso-
               ciation

[   ]   Is aware of left-to-right sequence of letters and words

[   ]   Is aware of spaces between letters in words

[   ]   Is aware of spaces between words in sentences

[   ]   Copies words and short phrases

[   ]   Copies sentences

[   ]   Writes words and short phrases using invented spellings; demon-
               strates awareness of sound–symbol associations

[   ]   Writes complete sentences using invented spellings; demonstrates
               awareness of sound–symbol associations

[   ]   Writes stories using invented spellings; demonstrates awareness of
               sound–symbol associations

[   ]   Writes stories that include some words with standard spellings

[   ]   Writes stories with a distinct beginning, middle, and end

[   ]   Writes detailed, imaginative stories that reflect an awareness of stan-
               dard spelling, capitalizations, punctuation, grammar, and usage

Figure 6.1.   Checklist example.

Source: Adapted from *Houghton Mifflin Literary Readers. Selection Plans and Instructional Support,
Book 1.* Copyright © 1989 by Houghton Mifflin Company. Reprinted by permission of Houghton
Mifflin Company.

Checklists are used for assessment. In this photo, a university professor consults with a student about her story-reading techniques.

The High/Scope checklist focuses on precise teaching skills that help to implement a general goal and serves to keep teachers on track in meeting program goals.

Purpose.   Checklists are primarily used to assess the current characteristics of an observational subject (child, teacher, curriculum, or environment), to track changes in these characteristics over time, and to provide information for program planning. Consider the examination of current characteristics. A teacher might be interested in verifying which of the children in a classroom build stacks, rows, bridges, and enclosures with blocks and which are beginning to name, add details to, and pretend with block structures. Having casually observed children's developing building skills over the first few months of school, the teacher now wants to condense these observations onto an accessible form. A checklist is an appropriate observational method to meet this teacher's needs.

Below is an example of using checklists to examine current characteristics of teachers-in-training. A university professor of children's literature devises a checklist to observe students reading stories to children in the laboratory school. The first few items on this checklist are the following:

During story time, the practicing student:

❏ provides a brief introduction connecting the story to the children's experiences.

❏ maintains eye contact with the children.

❏ asks the children open-ended questions throughout the story.

❏ provides opportunities for the children to comment about the story.

Later, after pilot testing the entire checklist (trying it out and making appropriate revisions), the professor adds space for comments at the bottom of the form. Here, particular strengths, words of encouragement, areas of concern, or illustrative anecdotes may be jotted down.

The second purpose of checklists is to track changes over time. Nicole may reuse her checklist to monitor children's advances in gross motor skills. The teacher observing building skills can use the same checklist periodically over the course of the year to chart developmental growth. The university professor can use the story-time checklist as a pre- and post-test to document the students' progress.

The third purpose of checklist assessments is program planning. Teachers not only receive information about the skills and development of the children in their classrooms, they also develop ideas for their daily plans. For example, the block-building observer might need to plan exploratory experiences for the novice builders and add more diverse building materials for the experienced builders. Checklists (and observations in general) are not completed just to be entered in children's portfolios or cumulative records. Rather, the information they provide about individual children is for teachers to use in planning supportive activities, in evaluating program effectiveness, and in planning appropriate adjustments.

Guidelines for Constructing a Checklist.   Many useful checklists are available to the early childhood educator, and portions of two of these have served as examples (a writing checklist and a curriculum checklist). As a student of observation, however, you should gain the ability to construct your own checklist to study early childhood issues that are of specific interest and concern to you (see Box 6.1 for guidelines for designing a checklist).

Checklists are constructed to assess the skills or behaviors of children and teachers or specific characteristics of programs and environments. The topic under examination is thoroughly researched, and the checklist items are carefully worded. Pilot testing (trying out the observational instrument) is essential because items may not be added after data collection has begun (Evertson & Green, 1986). Chapter 12 addresses pilot testing in greater detail, but for now, participate in the following activity by selecting some appropriate subjects for checklists.

Box 6.1
Designing a Checklist

1. Select an appropriate topic.
2. Research the topic in libraries and classrooms.
3. Identify clear, distinct items.
4. Design a recording form.
   • Add check boxes.
5. Pilot test the instrument.

Student Activity 6.1
Checklist Topics

List five topics that may be appropriately assessed by checklists. You may include topics concerning children, teachers, curricula, and/or environments.

Examples:

• Children's understanding of numbers
• Presence of culturally diverse materials

1.

2.

3.

4.

5.

Return to the toothbrushing checklist, which I made up at my desk after reviewing what I know about toothbrushing. You and I have no confidence that my checklist identifies the essential components of good toothbrushing. I failed to research my topic in the library and in the field; consequently, the checklist suffers. If I want to design a checklist that accurately assesses a person's oral hygiene, I must do some research. I might visit a school of dentistry and interview professors about oral hygiene and ask them to critique my checklist. I could talk to my own dentist, observe people brushing, and then move to a literature search.

What are the possible flaws in my checklist? Perhaps to do a thorough cleaning job, the brusher needs to brush for 3 minutes rather than 1½ minutes. I simply don't know how long an effective toothbrusher brushes, but the experts may. If not, this item should be omitted. Further, I worry that my last two items overlap and, therefore, are not mutually exclusive—that is, one item might be included in another. Does flossing serve to massage the gums in addition to cleaning between the teeth? I think so, but I'm not positive. I don't know if you need to use a gum-massaging agent in addition to floss. I do not know if the advice my dentist has given me about my own teeth is universally applicable or if mouths, like children, vary considerably.

On the surface the topic of toothbrushing appears simple and straightforward; yet we quickly learned that the construction of a checklist, regardless of the topic, requires research and care. I hope you conclude that I had no business constructing a checklist without researching the topic, despite my years of brushing. Apply this lesson to early childhood education, and understand that even knowledgeable researchers review the relevant literature to ensure an accurate and current list of items.

Integration of Developmental Theory and Observation

Preschool Example.   To experience the process of constructing a checklist, we join Cecily and Dave, who are inexperienced preschool teachers of 4-year-olds and who want to know if the children in their classroom have age-appropriate gross and fine motor abilities. Because these teachers do not yet have a clear understanding of the range of normal physical development, they read several chapters on the physical abilities of preschoolers in reputable child-development texts. They are drawn to the convenient checklist format, which readily allows them to assess the skills of individual children.

Cecily and Dave read that gross and fine motor abilities show marked development over the preschool years, so they know that one list will not be appropriate for preschool children of all ages. Therefore, they decide to work on a list of items suitable for 4-year-olds and remind themselves that the items describe abilities most children develop between the ages of 4;0 and 4;11; these skills are not commonly in place at age 4;0.

1. Hops on one foot for seven to nine hops
2. Catches a large ball with two hands and extended arms
3. Dresses self
4. Draws designs
5. Alternates feet while climbing up and down a flight of stairs
6. Fastens buttons

7. Uses pincer grip on pencil

8. Jumps 8 to 10 inches from standing broad-jump position

9. Runs with control from start to finish and around turns

10. Cuts on or close to a predrawn line

11. Takes a step forward when throwing a small ball

Dave and Cecily certainly like the simplicity of this list and anticipate that the data will not be difficult or time-consuming to collect. They decide to rearrange the items to clarify the distinction between gross and fine motor skills. In order to monitor children's development over time, they insert space to record the date when the items are observed and plan to use the checklist three times over the

---

Physical Development of 4-Year-Olds

Center: Lomas Day Care

Date/Time: 10/24/NA   Date/Time: Date/Time:

Observers: Cecily and Dave   Child/Age: Gilberto/4;2

Date

10/24   ☑   1. Runs with control from start to finish and around turns

        ☐   2. Alternates feet while climbing up and down a flight of stairs

10/24   ☑   3. Jumps 8 to 10 inches from a standing broad-jump position

10/24   ☑   4. Hops on one foot for 7 to 9 hops

10/24   ☑   5. Catches a large ball with two hands and extended arms

10/24   ☑   6. Takes a step forward when throwing a small ball

        ☐   7. Manages typical fasteners (buttons, jean snaps, zippers, belts, or laces)

10/24   ☑   8. Draws designs

10/24   ☑   9. Uses pincer grip on pencil

        ☐   10. Cuts on or close to a predrawn line

Comments:

Figure 6.2. Preschool checklist example.

course of the year. After pilot testing the checklist and making some adjustments, they observe the children's physical skills over the course of a week and then fill out a checklist for each child. (They plan to expand their checklist in the future to include items for 3- and 5-year-olds so as to help in assessing 4-year-olds who are not "average.") Figure 6.2 presents the checklist as completed for Gilberto.

INTERPRETING THE DATA   Gilberto performed every gross motor item on the checklist except alternating feet while climbing up and down a flight of stairs. Cecily and Dave observed this item on a walk to the neighborhood park because Lomas Day Care does not have a full flight of stairs. Afterward, the teachers asked the children if they have stairs at home, and most, including Gilberto, reported that they do not. What an important revelation!

Gilberto is a young 4-year-old, and therefore his teachers are not concerned that he has trouble fastening his jean snaps and cutting close to a predrawn line. Cecily and Dave also note Gilberto's strengths in fine motor development.

FOLLOW-THROUGH PLANS   The checklist results stimulate Dave and Cecily to plan some walking trips to nearby places that have stairs in order to provide a variety of

The assessment of individual children's physical development leads to the planning of supportive follow-through activities.

opportunities for the children to climb up and down. Together, the teachers and children also build obstacle courses that include a few treads for practice. Gilberto's checklist is filed in his portfolio with a reminder tab to check his progress after several months—to allow time for the effects of maturation and practice.

Other 4-year-olds in Cecily and Dave's class demonstrate motor strengths and weaknesses different from those of Gilberto. The teachers' heightened awareness of individuals after assessments stimulates them to take advantage of opportunities for the practice of specific skills with specific children. For example, Sarvenez (who runs awkwardly) may enjoy trotting around the yard with the security of a teacher's hand to announce it is time to go inside. Charlotte may be just the child to help cut out a new magazine picture of a freeway system to hang in the block area. And Hubie may be the perfect candidate to stand next to the ball bin and catch the balls to put away at the end of outside time.

Data from checklists may be used, as above, to plan supportive activities for individual children; although specific children are targeted, others may benefit as well. The teacher trotting around the yard with Sarvenez may soon find they are accompanied by a whole herd of children becoming more proficient runners. The benefits to one often extend to many.

If the teachers study the results for all of the children in the class, the checklist might also yield information about the strengths and limitations of the program and environment. Suppose almost none of the 4-year-olds can catch a ball. Cecily and Dave scratch their heads for a second before realizing that they hardly ever take the balls out of the storage closet! They need to correct this oversight. Or perhaps the teachers do not know if the children can manage their own fasteners because these tasks are usually done for them; after all, Dave and Cecily are so much more efficient at buttoning and snapping than the children are. This, too, can change. Checklists, here, provide valuable information about how well curriculum goals are being met.

Primary Grade Example.   A kindergarten teacher wants to keep close track of his students' math development. The teacher, Aram, decides to use the detailed curriculum checklists supplied by the teacher's manual (Baratta-Lorton, 1976) to assess each child's progress; Aram is thoroughly familiar with the meaning of each item, assessment procedures, and appropriate math activities to support children's growth. The section on counting is adapted for Figure 6.3.

INTERPRETING THE DATA   Aram assesses his students' counting skills in mid September and determines from the results that several children, including Blanca, are ready for practice in counting on.

> The skill of counting on is a useful problem-solving tool in solving addition problems. It involves the child being able to perceive the number of objects in one group and count from there to obtain the total. Children who have this skill solve addition problems more quickly. When faced with a group of four objects and a second group of three objects, for example, these children *know* that there are four objects in the first

Counting Checklist Items

School/Grade: Hidden Ridge Elementary/Kindergarten

Date: 9/13

Observer: Aram   Child/Age: Blanca/5;3

1. Memorizing the sequence of number names
   - ☐ From 1–5
   - ☐ 6–10
   - ☑ 11–20
   - ☐ 20+

2. Counting objects (1:1 correspondence)
   - ☐ Groups of from 1–5
   - ☑ 6–10
   - ☐ 11–20
   - ☐ 20+

3. Invariance or conservation of number
   - ☑ With the numbers from 1–5
   - ☐ 6–10

4. Instant recognition of small groups
   - ☐ 2
   - ☐ 3
   - ☑ 4
   - ☐ 5

5. Counting on

   Verbally
   - ☐ Starting with any number between 1–10 and counting to 10
   - ☐ 11–20 and counting to 20

   To solve a problem using objects
   - ☐ Starting with any number between 1 and 10 and counting to 10
   - ☐ 11–20 and counting to 20

6. Counting backward (to 1)

   Verbally
   - ☐ Starting at any number from 1–10
   - ☐ 11–20

   To solve a problem using objects
   - ☐ Starting at any number from 1–10
   - ☐ 11–20

Figure 6.3. Primary grade checklist example from a teacher's math manual.

Source: From *Mathematics Their Way* (pp. A-4 and A-5) by M. Baratta-Lorton, 1976, Menlo Park, CA: Addison-Wesley. Copyright © 1976 by Addison-Wesley. Reproduced with permission.

group so they merely count from there: *four*; five, six, seven. Children without this skill must find the total by counting both groups: one, two, three, four, five, six, seven. A child who has this skill quickly discovers that the total can be found by counting on either group, which encourages flexibility and a concrete understanding of the associativity of addition. (Baratta-Lorton, 1976, p. 103)

FOLLOW-THROUGH PLANS   After the September 13 assessment, Aram plans two activities from the math text (Baratta-Lorton, 1976) to give Blanca and several of her classmates the opportunity to discover and practice counting on. The first, "Bite Your Tongue" provides a gross motor experience of counting on.

Ask the children to bend to one side two times, counting silently, then bend to the other side, counting aloud from three to six. This cycle is repeated over and over again with the children "biting their tongue" so the first two beats are silent. (p. 105)

The second activity, "Cover Up" provides practice counting on with objects after a teacher demonstration. Aram, pleased with the usefulness of the checklist, plans to reuse it again in 2 or 3 weeks after introducing counting on and counting backwards.

When teachers accurately assess children's current abilities, they can respond appropriately to individual needs.

Applications

Strengths and Limitations.   The checklist is valued for its simplicity. In the evaluation of a child or a classroom, observers sometimes simply want to assess whether a skill, behavior, or program characteristic is present. Checklists provide this kind of information. Think about preparing for parent conferences: teachers may want to be able to tell the parents if their children can run, hop, throw and catch a ball, etc. A checklist is a useful tool of evaluation. The examination of checklist results can promote teaching strategies and activities aimed at supporting specific areas of children's development and provide feedback about curriculum success.

Guard against the tendency to see skills or other characteristics as simply as they are portrayed on the checklist. The checklist only notes whether a characteristic is present; it does not indicate gradations of development within an item. Think about two children who cannot hop on one foot for seven to nine hops. An observer cannot use a checklist to document that one child has almost mastered the coordination whereas another hasn't the slightest notion of how to hop. The checklist only marks the success. Consider an added complication. Suppose a child who fails to hop 12 times does so easily the next day. Is one demonstration sufficient for a check? Checklists are often lax about specifying criteria for a check (e.g., "uses dental floss" versus "correctly uses dental floss at least three times a week"). This limitation can cause serious confusion among checklist users.

Further, reliance on checklists does not help educators figure out how to encourage the development of the characteristics not checked. A good teacher will evaluate data from checklists and other observational methods to maximize understanding of the characteristics of individual children or programs. Then, the remarkable teacher will design activities to promote the unique growth of each developing child and make adjustments to increase program effectiveness.

Each checklist is only as good as its items and cannot make accommodations for exceptional cases; an item is either present or absent. Suppose a teacher uses an age-appropriate physical development checklist to observe Sarah (5;9), the youngest of four close-knit sisters, and discovers that Sarah does not know how to gallop. The teacher knows, however, that Sarah is a superb rope jumper and is capable of some fancy footwork. The teacher suspects that Sarah has the physical capabilities to gallop but perhaps has never been taught or bothered to learn because of lack of interest. As an observer, the teacher may not check the galloping item but regrets that the checklist does not accurately reflect Sarah's gross motor skills.

Action Project 6.1
Checklist Exercise

Imagine you are a preschool or kindergarten teacher planning a field trip. You have parent volunteers who will accompany groups of four children, and you want to be sure that all children benefit from the varied learning experiences available. Decide on an interesting field trip, and construct a checklist that would allow the parent volunteers to assess whether the individual children in their groups experience all components of the field trip. In your orientation of the parent volunteers, you clarify that although you want each child to participate as fully as possible in the field trip activities, children's refusals (e.g., refusal to pet a pig) are to be respected.

Points to Remember

A checklist is an efficient, usually convenient observational method to assess the presence of specific behaviors, skills, or characteristics. The observer may focus on individuals, curricula, or environments and collect useful information, which is preferably augmented by data collected by various methods. Not only do checklists provide the observer with the opportunity to learn more about the subject, but the data should also help lay the foundation for responsive teaching strategies and activities as well as program fine tuning.

Think About . . .

September is a time of rededication and enthusiasm in America as most children and teachers return to school. The mood at South Gate School was energetic. Committed to increasing parental involvement, the staff included parent representatives on several committees and expanded means of communication between school and home.

In May a parent/teacher committee is formed to evaluate the home–school connection and propose changes. Members of the committee begin writing a checklist for parents' feedback but quickly become dissatisfied with the quality of the information they expect they would gather. Think about some of the committee's initial checklist items:

During the current school year, did you

❏ Receive school newsletters?
❏ Attend parent seminars?
❏ Volunteer at school?
❏ Participate in the home study program?

How would the committee's information be limited by the checklist method?

CHAPTER 7

Observing the Development of Individual Children by Using Rating Scales

The staff of South Gate School launched the academic year with an exciting new parent-involvement component. There was much enthusiasm for the development of parent partnerships. Joint projects were undertaken, parent/teacher committees were formed, and new ideas blazed. Now it is May, time to evaluate and formulate next year's goals. The end-of-year questionnaire referred to in the Chapter 6 Think About section would serve as an essential evaluation tool and guide to program planning. As the committee members explored various methods of gathering information, they soon realized they did not simply want to know if the parents received newsletters, attended parent seminars, volunteered at school, or participated in the home study program. The committee wanted the parents to appraise the effectiveness of each of these home–school communication projects. The committee chose to develop a rating scale, the method to be examined in this chapter.

Each of us has had opportunities to experience *rating scales*, which are predetermined measures of evaluation. Restaurants, hotels, movies, child care centers, and children's academic progress on report cards are rated. Consider, even, our own unconscious ways of rating ice cream, the neighborhoods in our communities, or the attitudes of people around us.

This chapter addresses the use of rating scales in observing young children. First a note of caution. Because of the familiarity of itemized assessment methods (e.g., checklists or rating scales) and their ease in use, early childhood teachers are tempted to rely heavily on these methods. Thus, the important factor in this chapter is knowing when the rating scale method is appropriate.

Understanding of children's growth can be bolstered by the appropriate use of rating scales.

Overview of Observing Using Rating Scales

Description.   Rating scales are observational "instruments used to assess the quality of a particular trait, characteristic, or attribute with assessment usually based on pre-determined criteria (scale)" (Kapel, Gifford, & Kapel, 1991, p. 467). In the early childhood classroom, rating scales are used to evaluate children, teachers, programs, or environments. Although this chapter concentrates on observation of individual children, a few examples of rating teachers and programs demonstrate the versatility of this method of observation.

When using a rating scale, the observer is asked to make an appraisal by assigning a value to each of the listed characteristics along a continuum; the observer estimates the frequency of occurrence or degree of intensity for each item. Judgments can be based on direct observations, past observations (preferably documented observations, such as anecdotes or running records), or overall impressions. Kerlinger (1986) refers to this latter type of observation as "remembered behavior or perceived behavior" (p. 494).

The use of rating scales is familiar to those preschools applying for accreditation through the National Academy of Early Childhood Programs. Reproduced below are three items from the *Guide to Accreditation* (1991), part of the self-study program for teachers and directors. In this rating scale, marking 1 indicates *not met*, marking 2 indicates *partially met*, and marking 3 indicates *fully met*.

A-8b Staff help children deal with anger, sadness, and frustrations by comforting, identifying, reflecting feelings, and helping children use words to solve their problems. (p. 25)	1	2	3
B-7c Encourage children to think, reason, question, and experiment. (p. 29)	1	2	3
J-3 Individual descriptions of children's development and learning are written and compiled as a basis for planning appropriate activities, as a means of facilitating optimal development of each child, and as records for use in communications with parents. (p. 62)[1]	1	2	3

Rating scale items all require the observer to make a judgment but may be presented through several different designs. Let's explore three: graphic, numerical, and category.

[1] From *Guide to Accreditation*, rev. ed., by the National Academy of Early Childhood Programs, 1991, Washington, D.C.: National Association for the Education of Young Children. Copyright © 1991 by the National Association for the Education of Young Children. Reprinted by permission.

Rating scale designs offer choices to meet varying purposes and preferences.

"The *graphic rating scale* provides a continuous straight line with cues or categories along the line to guide the rater" [italics added] (Remmers, 1963, p. 334). The visual representation of the continuum gives this scale its name. Figure 7.1 shows three arrangements of graphic rating scales. The third scale uses a *semantic differential arrangement* (Osgood, Suci, & Tannenbaum, 1957). In this format "the observer places a mark on a point between the two units to reflect which variable occurred most frequently or the intensity of the occurrence of the variable" (Evertson & Green, 1986, p. 175). In all three rating scale arrangements (see Figure 7.1), the observer makes an overall assessment by marking the quality of each characteristic.

When using the simple graphic rating scale form, the observer must know the child's abilities well and use caution to remain as objective as possible. Medinnus (1976) delivers the following warning:

> Since rating scales are attempts to quantify observation, the validity of such ratings depends largely on the adequacy of observations that the ratings are based on. The adequacy is determined by the amount of time spent observing the child as well as by the number of different settings and situations in which he is observed. (p. 25)

The *numerical rating scale* offers choices designated by assigned number values. Those whose jobs are related to preschool may be familiar with the *Early Childhood Environment Rating Scale* (Harms & Clifford, 1980). An example of one clear item under Gross Motor Activities demonstrates a well-constructed numerical rating scale (Figure 7.2).

The *category rating scale* "presents the observer or judge with several categories from which he picks the one that best characterizes the behavior or characteristic of the object being rated" (Kerlinger, 1986, p. 494). The example of a category rating scale (Figure 7.3) is one item from the Child Observation Record (COR) (High/Scope Educational Research Foundation, 1992a). Notice that this instrument uses a vertical continuum.

Example 1 – Fine Motor Skills

Shows control of hands and fingers	Always	Sometimes	Never
Shows coordination of hands and fingers	Always	Sometimes	Never
Shows flexibility in using hands, fingers, and wrist	Always	Sometimes	Never

Example 2 – Fine Motor Skills

Very controlled	Controlled	Somewhat controlled	Not at all controlled
Very coordinated	Coordinated	Somewhat coordinated	Not at all coordinated
Very flexible	Flexible	Somewhat flexible	Not at all flexible

Example 3 – Fine Motor Skills

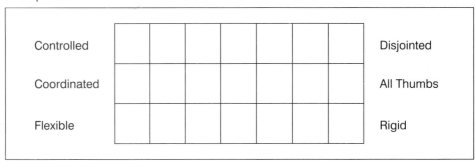

Controlled — Disjointed

Coordinated — All Thumbs

Flexible — Rigid

Figure 7.1.   Graphic rating scale examples.

	1	2	3	4	5	6	7

Space for gross motor activity

No outdoor or indoor space specifically set aside for gross motor physical play

Some space specifically set aside outdoors or indoors for gross motor/ physical play

Adequate space outdoors and some indoors with planned safety precautions

Planned, adequate, safe, varied, and pleasant space both outdoors *and* indoors

Note. For a rating of 5, space must be adequate for the size of the group using the space. Find out if small groups rotate or if the total group uses the space. Some facilities may have adequate space indoors and some space outdoors (reverse of item) and rate a 5.

Figure 7.2.   Numerical rating scale example.
Source: Reprinted by permission of the publisher from Harms, Thelma & Clifford, Richard, *Early Childhood Environment Rating Scale.* (New York: Teachers College Press, © 1980 by Thelma Harms and Richard M. Clifford. All rights reserved.), p. 23—Item 17.

Follow these general instructions when completing the COR ratings: Based on the notes of your observations, check off on each item the highest level of the child's typical behavior: 1, 2, 3, 4, or 5. (p. 1)

V.   Language and Literacy

    R.   Speaking

        Child does not yet speak or uses only a few one- or two-word phrases.   (1)

        Child uses simple sentences of more than two words.   (2)

        Child uses sentences that include two or more separate ideas.   (3)

        Child uses sentences that include two or more ideas with descriptive details   (4)
        ("I stacked up the red blocks too high and they fell down").

        Child makes up and tells well-developed, detailed stories, rhymes, or songs.   (5)

Notes: _____

_____

_____

Figure 7.3.   Category rating scale example.
Source: From *High Scope Child Observation Record for Ages 2 $1/_2$–6* (pp. 1 and 12) by High/Scope Educational Research Foundation, 1992, Ypsilanti, MI: High/Scope Press. Copyright © 1992 by High/Scope Educational Research Foundation. Reprinted with permission.

There are many different designs of rating scales; we have surveyed three. When constructing your own instrument or choosing an existing instrument, check that the format yields clear results. The next activity provides just such practice.

Student Activity 7.1

Examination of Rating Scale Design

Select two items from the following list of prosocial characteristics (Beaty, 1990, p. 129) and construct a graphic, numerical, and category rating scale item for each characteristic.

Prosocial Characteristics:

- Shows concern for someone in distress
- Shows delight for someone experiencing pleasure
- Shares something with another
- Gives something of his or her own to another
- Takes turns with toys or activities
- Waits for turn without a fuss
- Helps another do a task
- Helps another in need

The following is an example of a graphic, a numerical, and a category rating scale for the first item in the list (i.e., "shows concern for someone in distress").

Graphic:

| Shows concern for someone in distress | Often | Occasionally | Never |

Numerical:

1	2	3	4
No behaviors showing empathy for someone in distress	Actively consoles a distressed friend	Actively consoles a distressed person who is nearby	Actively consoles distressed people no matter where they are in the room

Category:
_____ Shows no empathy for other children in distress
_____ Shows empathy for a selected friend in distress
_____ Shows empathy for a distressed child who is close by
_____ Shows empathy for all children in distress

After you have constructed the rating scales for Student Activity 7.1, evaluate each type of rating scale design for clarity, ease in use, and personal preference.

Purpose.   Rating scales are used to evaluate children, teachers, environments, or programs in a specified area by positioning each assessed item (from minimum to maximum) on a continuum. This method can be used for assessing single or multiple subjects. For example, if teachers of 4-year-olds are interested in children taking the initiative, they could use a rating scale to measure initiative taking for one child or for the whole class.

"Assessment provides teachers with useful information to successfully fulfill their responsibilities: to support children's learning and development, to plan for individuals and groups, and to communicate with parents" (National Association for the Education of Young Children & National Association of Early Childhood Specialists in State Departments of Education, 1991, p. 32). Repeated use of rating scales for individual children can provide information about developmental change over time. For instance, rating scales can be used throughout the year to assess the advancement of fine and gross motor skills, a child's degree of social maturity, the growth of language, the recurrence of aggressive behaviors, or a grade school child's reading stages. The same rating scale administered more than once a year can provide pre/post growth comparisons, often on one rating scale sheet.

The most authentic results are obtained when assessments are based on several observed incidents that occur naturally within the classroom over a period of time; this is in contrast to a testing process in which children are pulled aside and asked to perform. These naturally occurring incidents are best remembered when they have been preserved as running records or anecdotes.

Individual rating scales may compile large amounts of information, usually categorized by developmental areas. Discerning practitioners do not simply file those completed forms in the child's portfolio and wait for the end of the year to reassess. Instead, when evaluations are complete, they analyze each form, look for patterns, compare it with other records, and plan follow-up observations or experiences as the year progresses.

Guidelines for Constructing Rating Scales.   Although well-designed rating scales are available, a teacher may not be able to find an existing scale for a selected area of concern. For instance, Francine (a primary grade teacher) would like to evaluate reading stages—specifically, the extent to which the children demonstrate the characteristics of the various stages.

It is useful for teachers to know the characteristics of each stage as this would help when observations are being made of children's reading behavior, especially when

Rating scales may provide one form of literacy assessment.

selecting methods and materials which will support children's learning in the most effective way at any stage. (Cutting, 1989, p. 15)

To fashion her own scale, Francine begins by studying the guidelines in Box 7.1. Constructing a rating scale requires her thoughtful preparation.

With an understanding of the guidelines, Francine proceeds. For this subject she chooses the graphic rating scale; its visual clarity will facilitate ease in use. She decides on four descriptors. Figure 7.4 is her hypothetical and incomplete scale based on the stages from *Getting Started in Whole Language* (Cutting, 1989).

Graphic scales, like the one created in Figure 7.4, are uncomplicated and seem time-efficient; however, "the apparent simplicity of ratings hides the complexity and opaqueness of the process of judgement in which the observer is involved" (Fassnacht, 1982, pp. 131–132). Choosing descriptors that are clear, objective, comprehensive, and free of observer bias can be a tedious and often complex task, even for a seasoned researcher.

Box 7.1
Designing a Rating Scale

1. Select an appropriate topic.
2. Research the topic in libraries and classrooms.
3. Identify clear and distinct items to be rated. Reject ambiguous terms. Select terms that can be interpreted the same way by all observers.
4. Design a recording form.
   - Choose the rating scale that best suits your needs, preferences, and subject matter: graphic, numerical, or category.
   - Assign clear meanings to the scale descriptors. Be careful that the descriptors do not overlap.
   - Choose the number of descriptors that gives an accurate picture of each item.
   - Be aware of the *error of central tendency*. If an odd number of descriptors is chosen, observers may tend to rate in the middle. Exercise caution or use an even number.
5. Pilot test the first-draft rating scale and make any necessary corrections.

If, as a classroom teacher, you choose to use an already-constructed instrument, be sure to check it against the given guidelines. Many available rating scales are poorly constructed. Using such an instrument could produce faulty judgments and conclusions.

Integration of Developmental Theory and Observation

Preschool Example.   During the preschool years, good programs assist children in mastering such self-help skills as dressing, toileting, cleaning up materials, etc. A child's sense of autonomy is developed through the young child's acts of independence, self-assertion, and decision-making (Hendrick, 1992). Let's explore how children develop autonomy when the teacher uses observations in assessment and planning.

Treasured Times Preschool has established a policy that all parents must attend four parent education sessions per year. One session covers Erikson's stages of emotional development with an emphasis on the preschool years. Another session trains the parents in anecdotal record keeping. Consequently, the parent volunteers in Billy Ray's room were well equipped to help him gather anecdotal records in the area of autonomy. He assigned different children to

Emergent Literacy Rating Scale

School/Grade:

Date: Time:

Observer: Child/Age:

Instructions: Circle the rating that applies.

Early Emergent Reading

Uses memory of story to "read" it again

| Always | Frequently | Rarely | Never |

Uses pictures cues

| Always | Frequently | Rarely | Never |

Uses language cues

| Always | Frequently | Rarely | Never |

Emergent Reading

Relies on memory as major cue in reading

| Always | Frequently | Rarely | Never |

Knows content and pages of familiar book

| Always | Frequently | Rarely | Never |

Uses key words from the text to retell story

| Always | Frequently | Rarely | Never |

Predicts and confirms story elements from picture cues

| Always | Frequently | Rarely | Never |

Begins to identify the relationship between the spoken word and the printed word (such as pointing to words, searching for key words, matching one spoken word with one printed word)

| Always | Frequently | Rarely | Never |

Early Reading   To be developed in the same manner as above

Fluent Reading   To be developed in the same manner as above

Figure 7.4.   Rating scale example (partially developed).

Source: From *Getting Started in Whole Language* by B. Cuttting, 1989, San Diego, CA: The Wright Group. Copyright © by the Wright Group. Adapted by permission.

each of the volunteers on the days they helped. Before long many anecdotes had been logged for all of the children.

Billy Ray also contributed anecdotes and running records to each child's portfolio. Using this observational data bank and his memory of perceived behavior, Billy Ray was able to fill out an autonomy rating scale for each of the 12 children in his class; Figure 7.5 offers the results for a child named Rosey. How could this rating-scale information help Billy Ray promote Rosey's optimal growth? What suggestions for follow-up plans are in order?

INTERPRETING THE DATA   To begin with, Billy Ray compares the children's rating scales, looking for threads of similarity. His group, overall, is quite capable and acts with autonomy. On occasion, boots or new jackets require assistance; that's understandable. From the rating scales Billy Ray can see that all of the children appeared to have difficulty remembering hand washing. He will investigate that tomorrow!

Organized classroom materials foster autonomy.

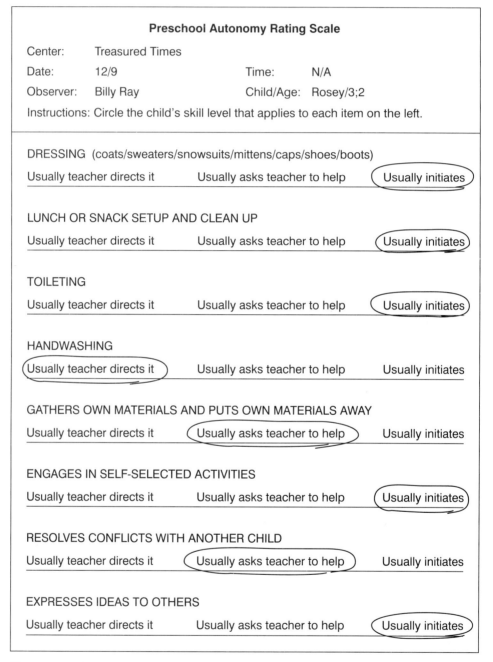

Preschool Autonomy Rating Scale

Center: Treasured Times

Date: 12/9   Time: N/A

Observer: Billy Ray   Child/Age: Rosey/3;2

Instructions: Circle the child's skill level that applies to each item on the left.

DRESSING (coats/sweaters/snowsuits/mittens/caps/shoes/boots)

Usually teacher directs it   Usually asks teacher to help   (Usually initiates)

LUNCH OR SNACK SETUP AND CLEAN UP

Usually teacher directs it   Usually asks teacher to help   (Usually initiates)

TOILETING

Usually teacher directs it   Usually asks teacher to help   (Usually initiates)

HANDWASHING

(Usually teacher directs it)   Usually asks teacher to help   Usually initiates

GATHERS OWN MATERIALS AND PUTS OWN MATERIALS AWAY

Usually teacher directs it   (Usually asks teacher to help)   Usually initiates

ENGAGES IN SELF-SELECTED ACTIVITIES

Usually teacher directs it   Usually asks teacher to help   (Usually initiates)

RESOLVES CONFLICTS WITH ANOTHER CHILD

Usually teacher directs it   (Usually asks teacher to help)   Usually initiates

EXPRESSES IDEAS TO OTHERS

Usually teacher directs it   Usually asks teacher to help   (Usually initiates)

Figure 7.5.   Preschool rating scale for Rosey.

Billy Ray singles out Rosey's rating scale (Figure 7.5) for further study. He notices that Rosey "engages in self-selected activities" but "asks for assistance in gathering and putting away materials." He asks himself, "Why the dichotomy?" Billy Ray would like to encourage Rosey's full autonomy. The next item reads "asks for assistance in conflict resolution." This behavior, suitable for a child of Rosey's age, will continue to develop. Billy Ray plans to keep ongoing anecdotes to ensure that conflict resolution remains an observational priority. In particular, he will watch for times when Rosey is successful on her own.

FOLLOW-THROUGH PLANS   Billy Ray surveys the classroom environment and keeps Rosey in mind as he thinks about a 3-year-old's abilities. He immediately spots a possible deterrent to individual autonomy. Although Billy Ray has organized and labeled the block center and a parent helper recently arranged the housekeeping center methodically, Rosey's favorite centers (the art and reading areas) are not so serviceable. Billy Ray resolves to add a help-yourself art shelf so that Rosey and others can independently select and put away materials of their choice.

Billy Ray assembles a low shelf to hold materials that need minimal supervision, such as crayons, markers, paper, scissors, paste, paper punch, yarn, and magazines. He invites Rosey to help him arrange the beginnings of the newly assembled help-yourself art shelf; for better success, they start out with only a few items on the shelf. Rosey eagerly points out the best place for the markers and the paper. A few weeks later, Billy Ray expands the number of the materials on the shelf, puts each item in a marked storage container with its picture, and invites Rosey to arrange them. He can see that she has no hesitations. As time passes, Rosey popularizes the usage of the help-yourself art shelf and seems to adopt a personal interest in cleaning up this area.

In the reading corner Billy Ray's class has an extraordinary number of books; unfortunately, they are shelved in disarray. To promote autonomy in this area, Billy Ray classifies many of the books into a few popular topics. For instance, all animal books get a red piece of tape on the binding and are filed in the red-painted section of the bookshelf. Billy Ray puts an animal picture on the front of the red section and so on, until the color/picture coding is complete. Now finding and returning books is much easier. Billy Ray puts another child, who also had difficulty initiating cleanup, in charge of this center. Using the information drawn from a rating-scale evaluation, this teacher improved the classroom environment so that several children were able to become more autonomous over the course of the year.

Primary Grade Example.   Rating scales can be used at any time throughout the year. Some teachers prefer to use the same scale at several different intervals, dating each mark. Melana used the teacher-designed graphic rating scale during the third week of school (see Figure 7.6). She wanted to assess current work habits so that she could begin to form a comprehensive picture of each child, thus enabling her to plan and meet individual needs better. Figure 7.6 is a

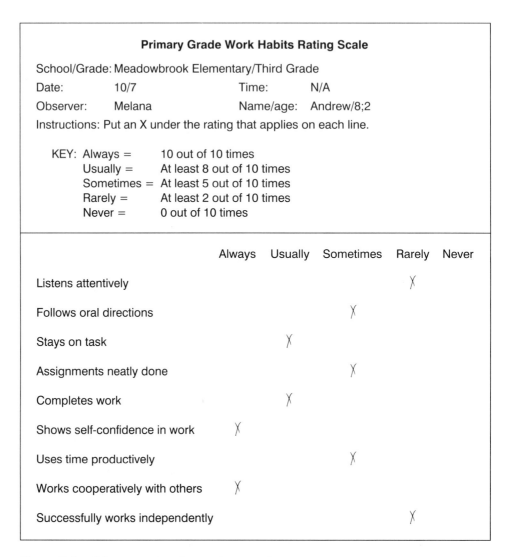

Figure 7.6.   Primary grade rating scale example.

completed rating scale for a child named Andrew. As you read this figure, be aware of your initial interpretations. Do you think this teacher is aware of the *error of central tendency*?

INTERPRETING THE DATA   After analyzing the ratings of Andrew's work habits, what did you infer about his classroom behavior? Did you picture a child who is out of his seat often or constantly talking with other children? Or perhaps you saw him as being confused and needing to ask other classmates what to do on assigned work. Might Andrew be a typical example of a "problem kid"?

Andrew's teacher, Melana, is aware that a serious danger of labeling is inherent in using rating scales as a final evaluation of children. Melana's approach was to use the rating scale as a beginning point in assessing, understanding, and planning. Andrew's inconsistent ratings raised immediate questions. How could Andrew usually complete his work yet have trouble listening to directions and working independently? Melana had based her ratings on her grade book and her memory of his classroom behavior. She was aware of Andrew's inattention and excessive talking, but he seemed to complete most of his work satisfactorily. What was going on?

Melana checked the anecdotes in Andrew's portfolio; several recorded Andrew's eagerness to contribute terrific ideas to class discussions. Melana had also noted that he is often a leader in group projects. He is well liked by his classmates and is frequently chosen first in team games. He shows a definite strength in social development. To gain a more accurate picture, Melana pulled together all the information she had recorded during the first 3 weeks. She reviewed her grade book once again. It documented another strength—finished work and excellent understandings. Included in Andrew's portfolio, however, is the result of a recent test, *The Reading Style Inventory* (Carbo, 1983), which evaluated Andrew's learning style as visual/kinesthetic. That means his best channels for processing information are through his eyes and body. The test also revealed that Andrew's ears are his weakest processing channel. No wonder he rarely appeared to listen and had trouble following oral directions! The rating scale marks began to make sense to Melana.

FOLLOW-THROUGH PLANS   The teacher-constructed rating scale helped Melana gain a more precise image of Andrew's work habits, but it also led her to explore other pertinent observations. She was then ready to plan teaching/learning strategies based on Andrew's individual needs. The following are Melana's plans:

- *Direction Giving*: Stand by Andrew or have eye contact when giving short oral directions. Write lengthy directions on the board. Have a student read the written directions a second time aloud. Underline the key words in the directions.
- *Work Improvement*: Label assignments in grade book OD or WD (oral or written directions). In those two columns keep a tally of times Andrew's papers were neat and not neat. See if there is a relationship between written direction-giving and neat work. Perhaps he hurries after he has had to spend time figuring out what to do, usually by asking others.

The issue of Andrew's productivity and independent work was difficult for Melana. She did not want to squelch Andrew's gregarious personality and his natural leadership skills. She wanted to encourage this strength as she helped him develop the weak area—independent work. How to do that was the task at hand. After much thought, Melana came to the conclusion that her teaching strategies seldom allowed for partner learning. From her past experience she thought that the highly social children were more comfortable when they were able to share new insights with other children.

Melana had prided herself on having a quiet classroom despite all of the times she had to remind Andrew to quit talking. Looking back in Andrew's portfolio, she found some anecdotes of incidents when Andrew seemed so excited from reading about science in his self-chosen books that he shared newfound information with the child next to him. Perhaps if she gave Andrew a specific time he could count on each day to have conversations, he would grow toward using independent work time appropriately. Melana developed her plans further as follows:

• *Group Work*: Set up daily cooperative reading experiences. Using small groups, plan activities in which the children could read favorite stories to each other, share stories they had written, or discuss story characters they were reading about. Suggest that the shared reading groups, especially ones whose members are kinesthetic learners, develop skits or puppet shows together.

Oh yes, the whole picture was becoming very clear to her now. She had not allowed the children enough social exchange; Andrew was trying to meet his own need. She felt fortunate that it was early in the year and that she had uncovered a necessary adjustment in her teaching strategies. So, where else could she adjust?

• *Math Tasks*: Andrew showed a special interest in math. Melana did not want to miss the opportunity to reinforce Andrew's critical-thinking skills. In addition to the present small group instruction and independent work in math, Melana decided to add a box full of "brain teasers." At first, the activity would be part of the group math work. Eventually, the teasers would be made available for children to work on in pairs when they had finished their independent work. Melana would reserve a portion of one bulletin board wall for children to share their analytical projects.

Melana saw a definite change in Andrew's work habits almost immediately when he was given written instructions and more time to work cooperatively. Melana had conferred with Andrew, and they discussed the new plan before its inauguration. Andrew liked the idea of written directions and suggested that the paired reading experience follow the independent reading time. He told Melana that occasionally he wrote stories or had an idea that he just had to tell someone during independent work time.

After another 6 weeks Melana repeated the rating scale. All of Andrew's marks were in the *always* or *usually* columns. Melana was satisfied with Andrew's progress and with the new learning environment. Not only were Andrew's strong social needs supported, but according to her latest class rating scales, children who were somewhat withdrawn were beginning to take a more active part in cooperative work times.

What other ideas can be added to Melana's beginning plans? There rarely is just one right way! The sky is the limit as long as the plans effectively fit the child's needs and are integrated with the teacher's style.

Applications

Strengths and Limitations.   Rating scales and checklists share many strengths. Like checklists, rating scales require less time than do other observational methods. With high classroom demands and hectic schedules, teachers appreciate the simplicity of these two methods. Rating scales and checklists can be based on memory and can therefore be completed at the teacher's convenience. Both methods are relatively easy to mark and require no special training. These orderly forms also offer a developmental summary for parent conferences.

In the early childhood classroom, rating scales are especially useful to assess multiple characteristics within a given area. Unlike the checklist, which records only the presence or the absence of a characteristic, the rating scale allows the observer to measure the degree or frequency of behavioral characteristics. We have already looked at how an instrument assessing autonomy can quickly give a detailed picture, thus allowing the teacher to compare children within the classroom or to evaluate one child. "Convenience and efficiency are primary reasons for the widespread use of rating scales" (Witt, Heffer, & Pheiffer, 1990, p. 368).

The many advantages of rating scales, however, are often overshadowed by the disadvantages. As Figure 7.4 illustrates, constructing a rating scale with clearly defined, objective items and descriptors can be challenging. Designing a scale with choices that adequately represent the observer's true assessment is yet another feat. Even when an observer has designed a rating scale, the observer is asked to pigeonhole the evaluation by using limited, preselected choices on the rating scale continuum, thereby sometimes restricting an accurate response.

This limitation reminds me of the recent discussion at my house following the "eggplant soup dinner." I love to experiment making new kinds of soup once a week. We've enjoyed my adventurous culinary practices—until I made the eggplant soup. That soup was memorable! I asked my husband how he would rate it. "On a scale of what?" he asked, having been highly schooled in research. "Oh, 1 to 3," I answered, trying to decide if I'd ever make it again. "I'd prefer more choices; I'll use 1 to 7," he countered as he continued to develop the following scale:

1. Would cause sickness
2. Wouldn't eat it unless starving
3. Was tolerable
4. Just average
5. Would choose to have it occasionally

6. Would enjoy having it several times a month

7. Wow! I'd tell everyone about it. A true culinary pleasure.

I listened with delight and thought of the abbreviated rating scale I use on all my recipes.

1. Crowd pleaser

2. No comments

3. No clean bowls

I refer to the shortened scale to decide whether the dish is worth making again. I would find the seven-point system time-consuming and cumbersome. (Just in case you are curious, my husband rated the eggplant soup a 4 on his scale. I gave it a 3 on my scale; I wouldn't make it again!) So you see, each rater can have a preferred scale. If you don't construct your own scale, however, you are asked to make a choice that may not be as representative of your evaluation as you would like.

Forced choice is the most common frustration and a grave limitation of rating scales. To counteract this restriction, many teachers use spaces between the items for written comments.

Another limitation is the influence of observer bias. For instance, an observer may rate a child who has well-developed language skills as a leader or the observer may rate a child as uncooperative because the child's older sibling was. This bias, which is known as the halo effect, was discussed in Chapter 5.

> The *halo effect* refers to the tendency for an assessment of the characteristic of a person to be influenced by another characteristic or by a general impression of the person. Thus, a positive general impression could lead to more favorable ratings, and, a negative impression, to less favorable ones. (Goodwin & Driscoll, 1980, p. 126)

If the characteristics being rated are unclear or too complex, the halo effect may be unavoidable.

Finally, rating scales do not tell the conditions that surround the evaluation. The skills, behaviors, or conditions being rated are lifted out of their context, thus leaving an overall evaluation of isolated items. If rating scale assessments are coordinated with running records or anecdotal records, however, they become a useful summary for planning and conferences.

Action Project 7.1

Practice in Using a Rating Scale

Design a rating scale that evaluates impulse control in the early childhood classroom.

- Review the guidelines for construction.
- Refer to Chapter 2 or a child-development textbook for background information.
- Select your rating scale design and construct your instrument.
- Guard against observer bias.
- Pilot test the rating scale.

With the newly constructed rating scale in hand, locate a preschool or K–3 teacher who is willing to work with you and try out your observational instrument. Share your results in class.

Points to Remember

Because they are fast and easy to use, rating scales are popular with teachers. Rating scales are also versatile; the basis for marking rating scales can be direct observations or impressions of perceived behavior. To use rating scales accurately, however, teachers must be vigilant in avoiding the error of central tendency and the halo effect. Use caution!

Many rating scales come ready-made for the early childhood classroom; however, some teachers prefer to construct their own. This chapter reviews design alternatives and offers guidelines for success for teachers who wish to create their own scales.

When used for children, rating scales can be helpful in making overall assessments for diagnosing individual needs, facilitating conferences, and charting growth over time.

Think About . . .

When Billy Ray evaluated the rating scales on preschool autonomy for his class (Figure 7.5), he was interested in yet another child, Kirby. He wondered why Kirby (4;1) usually required a teacher's help to express ideas to others. Billy Ray wanted to discover those circumstances that motivate Kirby to ask for help and those that were conducive to his autonomous communication. Billy Ray was also curious about how other children responded to Kirby's communication.

Think about the requisite elements of an observation to meet Billy Ray's interests. When you turn the page to Chapter 8, you will study an observational method designed to explore the antecedents and consequences of an event.

Observing the Development of Individual Children by Using ABC Narrative Event Sampling

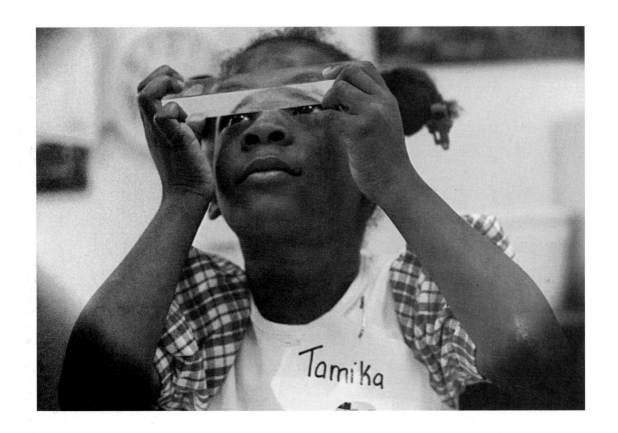

The review of rating scales typically leaves the observer interested in the dynamics behind particular items; the teacher in the Chapter 7 Think About section, Billy Ray, is no exception. Mulling over the assessment of Kirby's (4;1) autonomy, he wants to probe the reasons why this child "usually asks teacher to help" when expressing his ideas to others. The observational method introduced in this chapter will allow Billy Ray to learn about Kirby's communication abilities within their natural contexts.

Two forms of event sampling are studied in *Through the Looking Glass:* ABC narrative event sampling and tally event sampling. This chapter introduces the ABC narrative event sampling format for investigating the causes and consequences of an event. The study of causes will help Billy Ray identify the situations that encourage Kirby in his attempts to express his ideas and those that hinder this process. The study of consequences focuses on what follows: how others respond to Kirby and what kinds of feedback his communications evoke from his peers. In other observational investigations, observers may wish to uncover the frequencies of events; in such cases, the tally event sampling format discussed in Chapter 10 can be used.

Overview of Observing Using ABC Narrative Event Sampling

Description. Wright (1960) contributes to the general understanding of *event sampling* with this apt definition: "Event sampling singles out naturally segregated behavioral events . . . and records these events as they arise and unfold" (p. 75). In Kirby's case, "expressing ideas to others" is an event to examine because it represents a complete behavior. Through event sampling, the observer studies events in their everyday contexts and collects enough of them to draw conclusions.

Event sampling permits the observer to collect data about the targeted behavior in a time-efficient manner. An observer is not able to see every event of interest, but a sample of observations over a limited period should represent the behavior. Billy Ray cannot observe all of Kirby's communications even for a day (he wouldn't get anything else done), but he can observe enough of Kirby's communications to feel comfortable in allowing his collection to represent the entirety. Thus, the collection of observed events is a sample of all of Kirby's communications.

Observers using event sampling are ready to record an event whenever it naturally occurs over a limited period. Think about the logistics of exploring children's difficult separations from their parents; perhaps there is prolonged clinging and crying. The observer must be ready to record in the mornings when this event naturally occurs. In this case the observational period might conclude 10 minutes after the school day has begun, and the teacher may choose to collect a sample of observations over a week or two. To consider a teacher's classroom-management methods, on the other hand, the recording sheet must be kept handy throughout the day and the observer must remain ready to focus on management events as they arise. If the events occur frequently, an adequate sample might be accumulated in 4 or 5 days.

The above information is applicable to event sampling methods in general, and the following is a specific event sampling method. Bell and Low (1977) present a straightforward method of observing naturally occurring events: the *ABC narrative method*. Although their method is not the only means of collecting narrative qualitative data for event sampling, its clear organization and ease of use make it worthy of special attention. The ABC method concentrates the observer's attention on the antecedent event (*A*), the behavior or event itself (*B*), and the consequence of the event (*C*). Therefore, the event is seen in the context of what came before and what followed. Reflect on how well this observational method will meet Billy Ray's needs in his exploration of Kirby's independent communications.

Now consider a few more examples. A teacher concerned about a child who grabs toys organizes an ABC recording form around what preceded the grabbing, the event itself, and what immediately followed. Another teacher, who comforts crying children every morning after their parents leave, decides to describe several children's separations, the smooth as well as the difficult, in hopes of revealing successful and unsuccessful separation patterns. This teacher also uses the ABC event sampling form, which records how the parent–child pairs enter the classroom, how they say good-bye, how the child responds to the parent's departure, and the teacher's initial interaction with the child. A primary grade teacher who is concerned about a child's seemingly random cruel remarks (e.g., "I knew you'd get that one wrong!"), prepares an ABC narrative form to investigate what prompts the remarks and how the victim of the remark and others respond. The ABC form can be used to examine a wide range of problems.

Take a few moments to suggest appropriate events to study through the ABC narrative event sampling approach. Choose behaviors or events within their naturally occurring contexts—items that you could follow from their roots to fruition.

Student Activity 8.1 _____

Topics for ABC Narrative Event Sampling

List three topics that may be appropriately studied by ABC narrative event sampling in the early childhood classroom. Remember that this method is useful when you want to observe an event carefully in context. You will be searching for what prompts the event and what follows.

Examples:

- Wandering and unoccupied behavior
- Disruptive behavior
- Tattling behavior

1.

2.

3.

Purpose.   When the goal of observation is to uncover the causes and effects of a behavior, the ABC narrative approach to event sampling is an excellent method. Suppose a child throws several temper tantrums over the course of each day. The teacher wants to explore these events in search of a possible pattern or explanation. At this point, the teacher does not write an anecdotal record about one tantrum because the goal is to evaluate the processes of many tantrums. Nor does the teacher prepare items to observe (as in checklists and rating scales) because of uncertainty about the key elements in this child's process of temper tantrums. The narrative approach to event sampling is the observational method of choice because it allows the teacher to remain unrestricted by a prepared form with predetermined categories and free to observe the natural unfolding of the temper-tantrum events.

Let's step back for a moment and take a look at the forest rather than the trees. Why do we care about understanding the cause of an event? Many child guidance books offer creative and practical solutions to common behavior problems and are not concerned with their causes; however, if teachers assume, for example, that there is one best way to respond to a temper tantrum, they close the door on the opportunity to respond to children as individuals at their own developmental levels with their own strengths, interests, family histories, limitations, and personalities.

There are many possible causes of temper tantrums. For some children, temper tantrums might result from fatigue from long days in day care, insecurity upon the arrival of a new baby in the family, or anxiety over the recent separation of the parents. The tantrums might be vents of frustration for young children whose language development does not yet adequately serve their needs to communicate. There are probably other situations that prompt young children to release their emotional tension—usually at the most inopportune times! Knowing what is behind individual children's temper tantrums allows teachers to reevaluate the 5:00 p.m. activities at a day care center, promote sociodramatic play with a child experiencing a new baby at home, increase the emotional support of a child under stress, and help verbalize the feelings of the 2-year-old with little language. The point is that teachers explore causes of events in order to devise appropriate and helpful responses for a particular child.

Guidelines for ABC Narrative Event Sampling.   After deciding on an appropriate event to study, the observer prepares a sheet of paper with the typical heading of information at the top and four columns below labeled *Time, Antecedent Event, Behavior,* and *Consequence.* This format is presented in Figure 8.1.

The ABC narrative event sampling method is an effective means of understanding behaviors within their natural contexts.

ABC Analysis

Center or School/Grade:

Date: Time:

Observer: Child/Age:

Behavior:

Time	**Antecedent Event**	**Behavior**	**Consequence**

Figure 8.1.   ABC narrative event sampling recording form.

The observer keeps the recording sheet on a clipboard close at hand to record the event under scrutiny whenever it is observed. Occasionally, an observer might miss seeing the antecedent event; if so, he or she continues to record the time, behavior, and consequences. This happened to Gabrielle, the observer in Figure 8.3, and she used an ellipsis (. . .) to indicate the gap of information. She hopes that the remaining information, in conjunction with the observations of many complete events, will still add up to the "big picture."

Integration of Developmental Theory and Observation

Preschool Example.   Rachel is a quiet and shy 4-year-old girl who has posed no problems for her teachers, Sal and Pam. Several anecdotal observations focusing on Rachel during large- and small-group activities and directed outside games describe a cooperative group member. In November (when the classroom of 24 children is running smoothly), however, the teachers begin to pay more attention to Rachel's behavior during free-choice times. She typically stays with an activity for no more than 10 minutes and wanders the room until a new activity is suggested. Rachel rarely makes anything to take home; when she does, her artwork appears rather simple, like something a younger child could have accomplished. Sal, who is most familiar with Rachel, takes responsibility for observing Rachel's

ABC Analysis

Center: Peach Hill Nursery School
Date: 11/8   Time: 8:15–9:15 a.m.
Observer: Sal   Child/Age: Rachel (4;3)
Behavior: Wandering around room, unoccupied

Time	Antecedent Event	Behavior	Consequence
8:15	Rachel arrives with Mom. Mom kisses her good-bye.	Wanders around room for 15 minutes, watching children.	Alex says, "Want to play cars with me?" Pushes cars on block area carpet for 6 minutes.
8:40	Watches the noisy arrival of the bus kids. Pam (teacher) says, "OK, free-choice time. Find something to do."	Watches Daisy and Chloe hang up jackets and rush off to house area.	Turns attention back to kids entering room.
8:46	Sal (teacher) says to Rachel, "You need to get started now."	Walks slowly around room with no expression on her face, looking carefully in each area.	Goes to art area and rolls play dough with rolling pin for 4 minutes. Looks around classroom more than at her play dough.
8:54	Puts play dough away.	Walks slowly to edge of manipulative area and watches Pam (teacher) and 3 kids.	Pam (teacher) says, "Would you like to join us? Here are some Bristle Blocks." Rachel focuses on stacking blocks for 5 minutes.
9:13	Pam leaves area.	Rachel stops building and watches other kids. She smiles at Betsy.	Betsy smiles back and asks, "Want to play with play dough?" Rachel nods. They leave the blocks on the floor and head toward the art area.

Figure 8.2.   ABC narrative event sampling form: Preschool example.

wandering behavior. The ABC form in Figure 8.2 is kept on a clipboard in the classroom for 2 days; included in the figure is a portion of the data collected.

INTERPRETING THE DATA   At the end of the second day of observation, Sal and Pam read over the event descriptions on their ABC event sampling form. They are disheartened to see that in Rachel's first hour of school on 11/8 she did virtually nothing. She was not intently involved with materials or people, and she did not initiate activities or interactions. She responded agreeably to suggestions from Pam, Alex, and Betsy as if she had no plans or ideas of her own. The events recorded on 11/9 are similar. Sal and Pam worry that Peach Hill Nursery School is not optimizing this 4-year-old's development.

The 2-day sample of observations documents Rachel's wandering and unoccupied behavior during free-choice times both inside and outside the classroom. Sal and Pam recall that during the more structured times, such as circle or story, Rachel shows interest and willingly participates in the activity. They suspect that they did not notice her behavior during free-choice time during the first 2 months of school because she is such a cooperative group member.

FOLLOW-THROUGH PLANS   Sal and Pam feel bad for having overlooked Rachel's consistent wandering and unoccupied behavior during free-choice times, but they concentrate their energies on the future. They put the data to use and develop several strategies for helping Rachel focus her attention and learn more from her encounters with materials and other people. Below are three summaries drawn from the ABC event sampling form and the teaching strategies they prompted in Sal and Pam.

Summary of observation: Sal and Pam realize that neither of them personally greeted Rachel and that she responded positively to friendly overtures from Alex and Betsy.

Strategy: Sal will come over to greet Rachel when she arrives and tell her about special materials out in the various areas.

Summary of observation: Pam announced when it was free-choice time and said, "Find something to do"; Sal told Rachel that it was time to play and to get started. Perhaps Rachel has no clear understanding of her options or of what is expected of her during free-choice time.

Strategy: When Sal greets Rachel, he will remind her that during free-choice time, she can choose her own materials and friends to play with. He will also stay with her until she gets started. He might walk around the classroom with her to help her make her choice.

Summary of observation: The data show Rachel worked superficially with materials (e.g., pushing cars, rolling play dough). Perhaps she is not comfortable enough with other children to focus on her activity, or perhaps she has not had much experience in working with many of the materials available at Peach Hill Nursery School.

Strategy: Betsy will join Sal's small-group time so that the new friendship between Rachel and Betsy can be fostered.

Strategy: Outside, the teachers will plan optional group games to provide some enticing structure for Rachel and encourage her to play with other children.

Strategy: Once during each free-choice time, Sal will work next to Rachel with the same materials to model new ideas. He will be careful to build from her initial activity. For example, when she chooses play dough, he might roll out lots of snakes and see if Rachel is interested in shaping them into objects like bowls, log houses, or other ideas she might have.

Strategy: Sal will use small-group times to explore many uses of familiar materials to widen Rachel's experience with objects. He suspects that he has overlooked the importance of exploration for other children as well. For example, he might plan an activity to explore print making with Bristle Blocks and other small manipulatives. Dipping the objects in paint to make prints on paper, pressing them into clay to form imprints, or making rubbings with crayons and paper are all options. Another day, the children might use Bristle Blocks for building. They might first stick them together flat on the table, then form a high tower, and next build enclosures. These activities might be done individually and then in a group so that one huge flat surface, tower, and enclosure are put together. Sal would offer the children a variety of small counting animals to go inside their buildings. Sal will plan many small-group times that encourage the children to explore materials, make things with them, and then pretend with them.

Strategy: Sal and Pam will reuse their ABC event sampling form on Rachel in 2 weeks to observe her progress. They expect to see more focused behavior during free-choice time.

The ABC event sampling method proved to be productive for Sal and Pam. It allowed them to observe in detail a problem of which they had only vaguely been aware. Sal's recordings of the event in context evidenced noteworthy consistencies in the child's behavior. Instead of limiting the observer's attention to the wandering and unoccupied behavior, the ABC method provided a means of observing which classroom situations prompted Rachel's wandering and what followed. The teachers took advantage of the data collected to plan strategies to enhance Rachel's development. Data collected on a different child's unfocused behavior during free-choice time might well have shown different patterns, thereby suggesting the trial of different teaching strategies.

Primary Grade Example.   Gabrielle teaches first grade and is nearly fed up with Adam's disruptive behavior. Although she knows that she has an ample reserve of surface patience, she is wearing thin inside. Some mo. nings, she notices herself dreading to face Adam again.

At the end of a dismal week, Gabrielle promises herself to keep an ABC narrative event sampling form close at hand beginning on Monday. She worries she will neglect the observation once she is involved in teaching, but she is motivated to try. Her reprimands, pleas, and light punishments have been to no avail. Figure 8.3 contains a representative portion of the data Gabrielle collected over the next week. (Recall that Gabrielle uses an ellipsis [. . .] to indicate a gap in the information collected.)

INTERPRETING THE DATA   By Friday lunchtime, Gabrielle can stand the suspense no longer. Anxious to confirm her growing suspicions nourished by her data collection, she eats at her desk and rereads the seven pages of event descriptions. The data are voluminous, and she tries to think of some ways to make them manageable.

Gabrielle experiments with sorting Adam's disruptions into categories to look for possible patterns. She finds four times during the school day that account for the bulk of Adam's disruptions: math time, the end of story time, sustained silent reading time, and group math games. Then she begins to do some figuring. First she counts up all of Adam's observed disruptions over the course of the 4½ days of observation and finds the sum to be 38. She tallies the disruptions in each category and lumps the remaining six into an *other* category. Finally, she divides each category sum by the total number of disruptions (38) to find its percentage of total disruptions. For example, she divides the 17 math-time disruptions by the 38 total disruptions to get .45 or 45% of the total disruptions. (Notice that Gabrielle is doing some quantitative analysis with the qualitative narrative data.) The results, displayed in Figure 8.4, would have surprised Gabrielle on Monday before she began her data collection.

Before Gabrielle began to gather data on Adam's disruptive behavior systematically, she would have predicted that the disruptions occurred at an even pace throughout the day. She is excited because this is not the case and feels rewarded for her week-long observation efforts. Now it is time to search for the meaning behind the data.

Gabrielle considers the high proportion of disruptions during math activities and realizes that disruptions during math time or group math games account for 55% of the total; she wonders if this is an important clue. Had Adam's disruptiveness commenced and accelerated as math became more difficult? The grade book documents his initial average and then declining grades, and she makes a note to review his next math test personally. (Parents correct most of the children's math tests and save Gabrielle time, but now she wishes she were more familiar with her students' specific strengths and weaknesses. With 32 first graders in her class, this is a difficult task.) She forms a hypothesis that Adam's

ABC Analysis

School/Grade: Jefferson Elementary/First Grade
Dates: 10/16 to 10/20   Time: Various
Observer: Gabrielle   Child/Age: Adam/6;7
Behavior: Disruptions

Time	Antecedent Event	Behavior	Consequence
8:20	…I had just started the math lesson.	Pokes neighbor (Marcus) with pencil.	Marcus squirms, then laughs aloud. I say, "Excuse me, Adam."
8:22	…Math lesson.	Pretends to draw on back of Marcus' shirt (uses eraser).	Marcus yells, "Hey!" I say, "*Please*, Adam, pay attention."
8:25	…Math lesson.	Grabs Marcus' eraser.	Marcus wrestles his eraser back. I ignore.
8:27	I demonstrate a subtraction problem on the board.	Adam is under his desk when I turn around.	I send Adam to the time-out desk isolated at the side of the classroom.
11:45	I regretfully close *Matilda* by R. Dahl and say we are out of reading time for today.	Moans loudly and argues, "Oh come on, come on Mrs. Ambleson. Just a little more, *please*. We can be late for lunch; come on, *please*. The lines are too long anyway."	I say, "I'm sorry; we'll read more tomorrow," and dismiss the class for lunch.
12:40	…Sustained silent reading time; OK for 5 minutes. Reads *Frog and Toad* for umpteenth time.	Puts head and arms down on desk and rolls into Marcus.	Marcus rolls back. I say, "Sit up please, boys."
12:43	…Sustained silent reading time continues.	Cups chin in hands and stares across at Rayme.	Rayme glares and whispers harshly, "Stop it, Adam." Sianna and Noriko join in the scolding. I send Adam to the time-out seat.
1:30	Adam is cooperative in "7-up." I announce "Around the World" (math game) and ask for a volunteer.	Throws eraser in air and goes on floor to retrieve it.	I say, "You won't get a turn, Adam, with that kind of behavior."

Figure 8.3.   ABC narrative event sampling form: Primary grade example.

Adam's Disruptions (10/16 to 10/20)		
Time	Number	Percent of Total Disruptions
Math time	17	45
End of story time	5	13
Sustained silent reading	6	16
Group math games	4	10
Other	6	16
	38	100

Figure 8.4.   Understanding ABC event sampling data.

disruptions during math are connected to his tentative (at best) understanding of the subject matter; disturbances are Adam's ticket out of math.

The disturbances during story time and sustained silent reading time encourage Gabrielle to turn her attention to Adam's reading interests and abilities. Judging from his pleas for story time to continue, Adam relishes a compelling story. Unfortunately, this appreciation is not being satisfied by his choice to read the same book (however good) over and over. Perhaps Gabrielle can build on Adam's interests and excellent reading ability and decrease his disruptive behavior in the process.

In the privacy of her classroom, this thoughtful, reflective teacher lays aside her pride and wrestles with the quality of her responses to Adam's disruptions. "How indecisive I've been!" Gabrielle moans. She admits that her reprimands are neither meant nor taken seriously; she has not acted like a teacher who expects her directions to be followed. "When did I give up?" Gabrielle wonders.

FOLLOW-THROUGH PLANS   As Gabrielle thinks about her next step, she feels heartened by her many options. She needs to do more sleuthing to determine Adam's particular math weaknesses. She plans to do more spot checking of children's daily math assignments to be sure they are on the right track or clear up confusion before frustration and failure set in. Confident in her ability to teach math, Gabrielle is certain she can effectively reduce Adam's errors. She suspects that Adam's problems center around subtraction, and she begins to plan next week's math using manipulatives to allow the children to experience subtraction concretely.

How wonderful that the ABC narrative event sampling observation renews Gabrielle's awareness of Adam's interest and strengths in reading. Adam loves Arnold Lobel's endearing characters Frog and Toad, and Gabrielle knows there are other literary characters who can also win Adam's heart. Edward Marshall's

Careful study of the data leads to appropriate follow-through plans.

George and Martha are two characters who might fit the bill, as well as Elsie Fay from *Troll Country* a bit later. She will also browse through some Steven Kellogg books to check the reading difficulty and keep *The Beast in Ms. Rooney's Room* series by Patricia Reilly Giff in mind for later in the year. She is excited by the superb store of authors just waiting for Adam's discovery.

Gabrielle resolves to reevaluate her classroom control and to begin this process with Adam (hopefully a manageable task). She will consider the reason behind a disruption before criticizing a child. If she had practiced this strategy, she might have picked up Adam's math discomforts earlier. Gabrielle also examines Adam's long complaint when story time had to end at 11:45 a.m. Whether or not she or Adam likes it, Jefferson Elementary School runs on a schedule. She realizes, however, that her abrupt dismissal did not acknowledge Adam's feelings of regret. She might have said that she understood his wishes to continue but that lunchtime was not something they could choose to skip or delay. On Monday she will ask Adam to keep an eye on the clock and let her know when she has to stop reading for lunch; sharing in the responsibility for keeping the class on schedule might be a profitable experience for him. Gabrielle will continue to look for these types of experiences to help children build self-control rather than relying on a time-out desk.

On Monday's plan Gabrielle schedules time for a class discussion about classroom rules; it is obviously time to revisit this issue. Her goal is for the children to brainstorm suggestions for classroom rules. When they talk about why rules are important, Gabrielle will make them aware of how the welfare of the classroom depends on the actions of individuals. The children can imagine the resulting chaos if everyone talks at once or throws erasers in the air. The rules will be evaluated and a reasonable list posted in the classroom. Gabrielle hopes that this group experience will help the children perceive the rules as less arbitrary and more compelling. As Gabrielle relaxes during the last few moments of her lunch break and savors her feelings of accomplishment, she warmly remembers her college class on observation: time and study well spent.

Applications

Now let's move on to an activity that asks you to solve the puzzle of an event. In Student Activity 8.2, you will be studying the clues of a child's behavior in order to zero in on observations that generate responsive and appropriate teaching strategies.

Student Activity 8.2
Narrative Event Sampling: Acquisition of a Second Language

You are the teacher of a child who has recently arrived in the United States with her family from Hong Kong. During the first week, the child said nothing; thereafter, she began to speak occasionally in Chinese. Toward the end of her third week, you notice Lin speaking a word or two in English. You are very excited and resolve to keep an ABC narrative event sampling form to observe the situations that seem to promote Lin's attempts to speak English.

Study the following ABC data to identify events or situations that seem conducive to Lin's learning and speaking English. Then write down specific summaries of observations that lead to specific strategies. For example, after observing that Lin smiled and quietly said "hi" to Marion, you plan to encourage that friendship by putting their snack place mats next to one another.

ABC Analysis

Center: Where the Kids Are
Date: 4/26   Time: 8:30–9:00 a.m. (free-choice time)
Observer: Robbie   Child/Age: Lin/3;10
Behavior: Lin attempts to speak English.

Time	Antecedent Event	Behavior	Consequence
8:30	Marion arrives with her mother and is holding a stuffed bear. Lin stares at the bear.	Lin smiles and says "hi" softly and without eye contact.	Marion smiles back and goes to the house area.
8:40	Lin stands near the house area watching Marion and Carlota feed their bears at the table.	When noticed by the girls, Lin raises her arms and asks a question (It sounds like "Bear?").	Carlota says, "Lin, what?" Lin does not answer. All look confused, and Lin moves away.
8:55	Max (teacher) is mixing sand and water with children in the sand area to make molds. Lin wanders to the outskirts.	Max says, "Lin, would you like to play with us?" Lin smiles broadly and says "yes" in a loud, clear voice.	Lin hesitantly approaches a vacant space next to Damon, a quiet 3-year-old. She works with the sand molds with silent enjoyment and concentration.

Summary of observation:

Strategy:

Summary of observation:

Strategy:

Summary of observation:

Strategy:

Strengths and Limitations.   The primary value of the ABC narrative event sampling method is to study a behavior in the context of its antecedents and consequences. Observers use this method to explore an event as it naturally unfolds from its causes through its outcomes. The ABC method promotes the exploration and understanding of the relevant features of an event.

The ABC method also heightens awareness of children as individuals. It focuses attention on a unique person in the midst of often complex circumstances. The ABC method looks at events with a movie- rather than with a still-camera lens; there is no stop-action photography here. A problem is viewed as a process with prompting conditions and results. Such scrutiny allows observers to respond with individualized strategies.

The care with which an event is analyzed can also be a drawback because the ABC method requires time and commitment. It can be a burden for overextended teachers or those who lack support in the classroom. The observer requires time to observe the event in progress and record data. This is true of all observational methods and is not so much a limitation as an admonition to teachers to work observational time into their daily schedules.

The ABC method is best used by observers with keen eyes and who strive toward objectivity. Subjective observers with predrawn conclusions will easily shade their observations from the truth. The ABC method will illuminate an event for those who have the skills and vigilance to look.

Action Project 8.1
ABC Narrative Event Sampling

Return to the list of appropriate ABC narrative event sampling topics in Student Activity 8.1. If you teach, try out one of the examples in your classroom. If you do not teach, arrange a visit to a preschool or elementary school to practice the ABC method. After collecting your narrative data, analyze them and write down appropriate follow-through plans. Remember, to gain more than a superficial understanding of the method, you must try it out.

Points to Remember

The ABC narrative event sampling format allows the observer to study specific behaviors of individual children; these behaviors may (e.g., Adam's disruptiveness) or may not (e.g., Lin's preliminary attempts to speak English) be problematic. The purpose of this observational method is to reveal behaviors in the contexts of their antecedents and consequences. The observer using the ABC format yearns for enlightenment; the goal is not to document or assess individual children's development but to understand patterns of behavior. Responding to the unique yield of qualitative data, the observer plans supportive teaching strategies.

Think About . . .

Sal and Pam are extremely pleased with the results of Rachel's follow-up ABC narrative event sampling observation. Rachel's wandering and preoccupied behavior during free-choice time has decreased markedly. The teachers are eager to share Rachel's overall progress with her parents during a scheduled conference. Consider additional information that Sal and Pam might have accumulated about Rachel's development since September: running records, anecdotal records, checklists, and rating scales. Think about various ways teachers can organize their observations and how they can effectively communicate the results to children's parents.

CHAPTER 9

Child Portfolios and Parent Conferences

Recall with affection some of the children you've met so far in this text:

- Annie, who seized the yellow road grader for reasons unknown, in Chapter 1
- Thienkim, who withdraws from interactions with other children, in Chapter 4
- Matthew, whose exquisite language far exceeds developmental norms, in Chapter 5
- Gilberto, as yet unable to alternate feet when climbing up and down stairs, in Chapter 6
- Andrew, whose work habits are unproductive, in Chapter 7
- Rachel, who wanders, in Chapter 8

Each of these children sings with individuality; each is unique and multifaceted in development. They will blossom in supportive early childhood classrooms, and most have at least one parent or guardian who wants and needs to know how they are progressing in school.

The trained early childhood professional keeps comprehensive observational records for all children to accurately record and report their progress and to plan activities that nourish their development.

> Teachers need to develop a coherent picture of individual children based on their observations and knowledge of child development. . . . They must make use of chance behaviors observed in a natural setting and must continually revise and update their view of each child as new events occur. (Phinney, 1982, p. 16)

This semester or quarter, you have begun your training in observation. So far, you have learned how and when to use five observational methods that focus on individual children. In addition, you have had classroom practice in applying these methods. When you move into a teaching role in an early childhood classroom, however, the observational treasures will have limited value unless records are systematized.

The goal of this chapter is to answer the question posed in the Think About section at the end of Chapter 8: how can teachers organize their observations, and how can they effectively communicate the results to children's parents? You will become acquainted with options in organizing bountiful classroom observational records and sowing the seeds for successful parent/teacher partnerships. The first part of this chapter discusses designing and personalizing organizational systems, selecting system components, and finding time to keep records. The second part of the chapter presents the topic of parent/teacher conferences—preparation, content, and leadership. Although the teacher-in-training cannot apply this information immediately and comprehensively, this chapter develops tools to direct professional growth.

Overview of Child Portfolios

Throughout the year early childhood teachers may complete running records, anecdotal records, checklists, rating scales, and ABC narrative event samplings for each of their students. Occasionally, a tally event sampling or time sampling (Chapters 10 and 11), usually recorded for groups, is kept for a single child. As a result, early childhood teachers gather a great deal of documentation over the course of a year. Some of these records note specific developmental milestones. Some records are used immediately to plan activities and determine teaching strategies. Other records are saved to illustrate points during parent conferences or develop Individual Education Plans (IEP) and Individual Family Service Plans (IFSP). All records are used to understand the overall developmental progress of each child.

With mounds of observational records, an organizational challenge is at hand. This challenge can be as overwhelming as filing income taxes is to some people. Organizing, however, doesn't have to produce anxiety if the teacher uses a workable record-keeping system. Remember, the point is to organize early childhood records for simple access, not to store the records away as we do with our tax records.

Let's look at the payoffs from using systematized observational records. First, an efficient record-keeping system retains and orders documents of each child's developmental growth; it is a priceless memory bank, easily accessed by the teacher. In contrast, unorganized observations become an explosion of papers piled high or tossed into a file folder or desk drawer. Consequently, records are time consuming and difficult to access. Second, an organized storehouse of observations allows for smooth, consistent planning of classroom activities that respond to individual needs. Masses of unorganized observations often result in abandonment of planning to meet individual needs; curricula become haphazard or uniformly prescribed for all children. And third, with systematic record keeping, teachers have abundant information at their fingertips and can prepare for conferences expediently and confidently. In summary, organizing observations is essential for first-rate teaching!

Description.   A record-keeping system is a specified procedure used to organize the many observations written by the teacher throughout the year. One teacher compares record-keeping systems to financial portfolios: a list of an investor's securities. Early childhood record-keeping systems, listing records of development, are certainly portfolios!

An orderly portfolio system acts as a frame within which to assemble all the puzzle pieces. Once the teacher has chosen or created an arrangement for keeping records, all of the children's records are stored in like fashion. The system allows the teacher to collect as much observational information on each child as is wanted; the system also allows the teacher to arrange this information in logical order and to protect the child's privacy.

Two possible designs for record-keeping systems are described below. The farsighted teacher-in-training will explore and compare the systems, noting the advantages and disadvantages of each. Time spent in examining workable systems provides the foundation for determining a preference and, eventually, a confident choice once the teacher is inside the classroom. On the other hand, experienced teachers may have other ideas that have worked for them. There is much room for additions, improvements, and diversity.

Notebook or File Box System.   Records for 12 or 15 children can be housed in a 3-inch, three-ring binder or a few large 5-by-8-inch file boxes. These two systems are treated together because their internal organizations are the same; they differ only in the teacher's preference for the outer container (notebook or file box). Using either the notebook or the file box system, the teacher arranges classroom observations using the major developmental areas discussed in Chapters 2 and 3: *cognitive, psychosocial, physical,* and *creative.* (The order of the areas makes no difference as long as they are consistent within the system.) The notebook or file box is sectioned off by index tabs into the traditional developmental areas for each child. (Valuable space is saved if the child's name and birth date are placed on the first tab with the title *Cognitive.*)

First index tab:	Child's Name and
	Birth Date
	Cognitive
Second index tab, indented:	Psychosocial
Third index tab, indented:	Physical
Fourth index tab, indented:	Creative

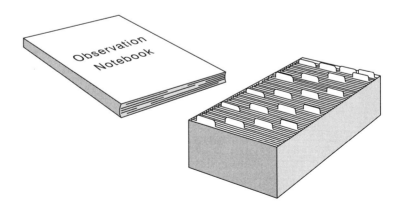

In order to conserve space, instead of using a blank page or index card for each section, put an index tab on the first observation page or card you put in each section. This advice will help when managing 60 or more index tabs! In addition, color coding the index tabs proves to be time efficient.

Not all teachers choose to use the traditional developmental areas presented above. Because of the monumental importance of language during the preschool years, many preschool teachers prefer to have a separate index for it. Other teachers choose to include language development under the cognitive index. Some teachers prefer to have a separate index for perceptual development; others cover this aspect of development under *cognitive* and *physical*. The primary grade teacher may want to subcategorize cognitive development by using color-coded pages or cards for reading, math, and other subjects.

Regardless of how the categories are selected, all observations can be filed behind the corresponding index tab in notebooks or file boxes. In fact some observations may be duplicated and filed behind more than one section (e.g., an easel painting that shows creative, cognitive, and/or fine motor advances). Each separately filed observation is dated and filed in chronological order. This method of organization simplifies filing and retrieval.

Some teachers think the file box system is more convenient than the notebook system because file boxes kept on the desk top are always within reach. One primary grade teacher, a proponent of the file box system, sought to facilitate collecting and filing of observations. She made a simple 3/4-length smock with two big pockets just the size of the file cards she was using; that way, she could keep a pen and several empty file cards handy for writing her daily observations.

In the primary grades, teachers may also use smock pockets to keep handy cards with the checklists of skills in math and reading. The file box system is simple to use because all of the cards are the same size and fit behind the index dividers.

The notebook system would be the best choice for teachers who prefer to write observations on a clipboard, a pad of paper, or on large peel-off labels. In addition, notebooks are often the choice if the school uses developmental checklists, assessments, or inventories that fit nicely in a notebook but are too bulky for a file box. Teachers who use these forms have high regard for the versatility of notebooks.

File Folder System.   An alternative record-keeping system is the use of individual file folders. For each child in the class, the teacher labels a file with the child's name and birth date. (Alphabetizing the folders permits quick reference.) Inside each file are four recording sheets (Figures 9.1 or 9.2) that contain the following headings: *Cognitive, Psychosocial, Physical,* and *Creative.* Take a minute to familiarize yourself with the samples of preschool and primary grade recording sheets. Each of the four boxes represents one entire page in each child's file folder. Color coding the recording sheets is an effective organizational strategy.

Page 1

Cognitive Development

Representation	Seriation/Number
Language	Memory
Flexible thought	Spatial relations
Perspective taking	Problem solving
Classification	Other

Entry 1—Date. Anecdote
Entry 2—Date. Anecdote
...and so forth with each entry
on the $8\frac{1}{2}$-by-11 inch pages

Page 2

Psychosocial Development

Attachment/Separation	Gender identity
Self-concept	Fears
Play	Impulse control
Aggression	Other

Entry 1—Date. Anecdote
Entry 2—Date. Anecdote
...and so forth with each entry
on the $8\frac{1}{2}$-by-11 inch pages

Page 3

Physical Development

FINE MOTOR:	GROSS MOTOR:
Grasp/manipulate	Run
Fasten/unfasten	Hop
Use of scissors	Jump
Insert/remove	Skip
String/lace	Gallop
Other	Balance
	Climb
	Other

Entry 1—Date. Anecdote
Entry 2—Date. Anecdote
...and so forth with each entry
on the $8\frac{1}{2}$-by-11 inch pages

Page 4

Creative Development

Two-dimensional art	Music
Three-dimensional art	Dramatic play
Block play	Other

Entry 1—Date. Anecdote
Entry 2—Date. Anecdote
...and so forth with each entry
on the $8\frac{1}{2}$-by-11 inch pages

Figure 9.1. Preschool anecdotal recording sheets using subcategories.

Anecdotes are written on these sheets (or stuck on, if the teacher uses peel-off labels); relevant information available to the teacher is filed behind the appropriate sheets, including running records, checklists, rating scales, ABC narrative event samplings, primary grade reading inventories, other observations, samples of the child's work, and cross-references for photographs and videotapes

Page 1

Cognitive Development

Representation   Classification
Language   Seriation
Logical thought   Memory
Perspective taking   Other
Subject areas

Entry 1—Date. Anecdote
Entry 2—Date. Anecdote
…and so forth with each entry
on the $8\frac{1}{2}$-by-11 inch pages

Page 2

Psychosocial Development

Self-concept   Gender identity
Play   Peer relationships
Stress   Moral reasoning
Other

Entry 1—Date. Anecdote
Entry 2—Date. Anecdote
…and so forth with each entry
on the $8\frac{1}{2}$-by-11 inch pages

Page 3

Physical Development

FINE MOTOR: GROSS MOTOR:
Use of tools   Run
Uniformity of letters   Hop
  and numbers   Skip
Eye–hand   Jump
  coordination   Throw/catch
Other   Balance
                        Other
                        Other

Entry 1—Date. Anecdote
Entry 2—Date. Anecdote
…and so forth with each entry
on the $8\frac{1}{2}$ -by-11 inch pages

Page 4

Creative Development

Two-dimensional art   Music
Three-dimensional art   Drama
Block building   Writing
Other

Entry 1—Date. Anecdote
Entry 2—Date. Anecdote
…and so forth with each entry
on the $8\frac{1}{2}$-by-11 inch pages

Figure 9.2.   Primary grade anecdotal recording sheets using subcategories.

(more on this later in the chapter). Please note that licensing regulations and educational standards in many states require each child's medical forms and personal information to be filed separately in a central office. If permitted, however, the competent teacher takes time to review these files, summarizing pertinent information for classroom records, and stores this information in each child's folder. A fifth recording sheet, labeled *General Data,* can be added.

The recording sheets in Figures 9.1 and 9.2 provide a flexible organizational framework. For teachers who prefer a more detailed and thorough system, the subcategories listed under each of the four developmental areas can be used. (Many of the subcategories are the growth indicators described in Chapters 2 and 3.) When you begin teaching, you may want to add or delete categories. Teachers using specific observational systems can modify the recording sheets. For example, those using the *High/Scope Child Observation Record* (High/Scope Educational Research Foundation, 1992a) may want to coordinate their record keeping by substituting that record's six developmental areas for the traditional ones shown in Figure 9.1 and using the letter items presented in the *Child Observation Record* for subcategories. The purpose of the subcategories is to present the teacher with a quick check-off system to ensure that records have been gathered in all domains of development, thus giving an expansive picture of the child's developmental progress. As the teacher records an entry for one of the major developmental areas, a check is made next to the appropriate subcategory on the top of the sheet. For example, if the teacher observed a child who was fearful when the fire fighter visited the class, the anecdote would be recorded on the sheet headed *Psychosocial Development* and one check made before the subcategory of fears. Because of their own interests and strengths, teachers may collect observations that concentrate on certain areas and subcategories of a child's development and neglect others.

> Do you have a tendency to be drawn to the most verbal children in your group, the children who help others solve problems, or the children who never break program rules? Observational assessment will point out to you on a day-by-day basis how much or how little you know about all the children in your program. (High/Scope Educational Research Foundation, 1992b, p. 4)

By adopting a detailed system that provides check-offs for observational entries, a teacher can merely glance at the sheets to see if the total picture for each child has been captured.

Practicing teachers report that using the anecdotal recording sheets with subcategories is a major support to the teaching process. The built-in organization of recording sheets (with other observations appropriately filed behind one of the four developmental headings) saves precious hours when studying growth patterns, planning activities, and conducting conferences.

When using the file folder system, choose the appropriate size of file to ease the potential storage problem. Large file folders are recommended if unwieldy representations, like easel paintings, are to be included in portfolios. The file folders, regardless of size, can be conveniently stored and transported, if necessary, in a plastic carrying case obtained from the local stationery shop.

Comparison of Record-Keeping Systems.   Three different management schemes for organizing and storing observations in children's portfolios have been shown: notebooks, file boxes, and file folders. A system tailored to meet personal teaching needs will be concise, orderly, and workable; study the advantages and disadvantages of the three systems compared in Figure 9.3.

What system initially strikes your fancy? Ask experienced teachers what type of portfolio system works best for them and why. Perhaps the school you choose to work in already has a system in place; if so, you may only need to experiment with modifications to suit your individual preferences. If you are selecting the system, however, you may want to try out several types of systems and then base your decision on your own needs. You may want to mix components of two systems. For example, if you prefer the notebook system but like the recording sheets from the file folder system—simply replace the four development index tabs in the notebook with the recording sheets. There are endless possibilities. Don't be in a hurry. Use the first 6 months to create a serviceable system; remember that it must work for you or you won't use it. A usable record-keeping system is one of the early childhood educator's most prized possessions!

Guidelines for Designing a System.   At this point you may have some ideas of your own for keeping your records organized. Below are some helpful hints.

- Choose a portfolio format that accommodates all methods of observation: running records, anecdotes, rating scales, checklists, and samplings.
- Check the format for ease in filing and planning.
- Label one index tab for each child. Arrange sections behind each name using major developmental areas. To save tabs, write the first area label on the child's name tab.
- Use color coding whenever advantageous.
- If the system does not include space for samples of children's work, determine how those will be filed and stored.
- Choose a system that protects confidentiality.

Advantages

Notebook	File Box	File Folders
Durable	Durable	Least amount of storage space
Easy to transport	Quick filing on desk top	Compact and comprehensive recording sheets
Held in place with rings	Cards fit in pockets for mobility	Expandable
Easy storage	Ease in planning	Planning at a glance using recording sheets
Expandable		Large files hold over-sized student papers
Versatile		Easy to transport
Quick-reference indexes		

Disadvantages

Takes more time to file using rings	One box per 5 to 7 children	Papers are loose in file
Difficult to sort for planning	Cannot fit all records in file box	
Cannot store children's oversize work	Cannot store children's work	

Figure 9.3.   Advantages/disadvantages of record-keeping systems.

- Understand that parents have legal access to all school records on their children. This law promotes an open-door policy and facilitates parental involvement in informed decision making.

There are many ways to organize and store observations rather than haphazardly collecting them in one big file folder for the entire class. Without a filing system, those valuable observations will serve little use in planning and conducting conferences.

Finding the Time.   Students may ask, "Where do classroom teachers find the time to do record keeping? Isn't it terribly time-consuming?" Do not be thrown off by initial perceptions. Compare the teacher who saves priceless time when developmental records are housed systematically with the college student who saves time in studying for exams when all the class notes are organized, easy to read, and pertinent. Tailor-made record-keeping systems are time efficient.

By examining programs, you may be able to make time-saving modifications and identify time that can be used for record keeping. Moving away from curricula that rely heavily on planning product art frees time needed to file observations and make plans based on emerging individual needs. Teachers are also freed up in

There are many ways to systematize records; here are two.

class when product art gives way to creative art; teachers do not have to spend time ensuring that children correctly duplicate the product. Many K–3 teachers report that when less time is devoted to direct teaching and more time is devoted to experiential learning (employing developmentally appropriate curricula), observational/recording moments are plentiful. In addition, many preschool programs compensate their teachers for an additional planning hour each day so that they can record, file, and plan, and teachers working at day care centers can use nap time for record keeping. Primary grade teachers have planning time built into their contracts. And don't forget, we live in the age of technology. A voice-activated computer may eventually become the record-keeping system of choice.

Flexibility and commitment are the cornerstones of effective daily observations. Teachers rely on their own rhythm and class happenings when gathering observations on children's growth in the areas of cognitive, psychosocial, physical, and creative development. From day to day new observational opportunities surge, rarely at the same time each day. Most teachers (depending on class size) strive to collect an average of one or two anecdotes a week for each child, along with the use of other observational methods. An average means that there will be times when more growth is occurring for one child and the teacher will want to capture many incidents for that particular child for several days. Perhaps 6 or 7 days may go by before another significant happening is recorded for that same child. Systematic observation enables teachers to tune into the unique ebb and flow within their classrooms while viewing each child's development clearly and totally.

Novice teachers, however, may need to establish a daily rhythm. To avoid the "I tried it once and it didn't work" syndrome, consider an observational routine using a specific focus.

We realize the process may seem a bit overwhelming to busy caregivers at first; but by beginning with spontaneous observations and gradually introducing regular planned

Observations	Recording/Filing
As children first arrive (see Jeffrey's and Thienkim's running records in Chapter 4, Lin's ABC event sampling in Chapter 8)	Before children arrive
During center time, free-choice time, or independent work time (see anecdotes in Chapter 5, Rachel's ABC event sampling in Chapter 8)	During center time, free-choice, or independent work time if others are present to assist the children
At snack time and lunchtime (especially good for psychosocial anecdotes)	During lunchtime
During outdoor time (see Miette's running record in Chapter 4, Evan's running record in Chapter 5)	During planning time or nap time
When children have departed (see checklists and rating scales in Chapters 6 and 7)	While children are at recess
When trained parent helpers are in the classroom (see Rosey's rating scale in Chapter 7)	After children depart

Figure 9.4. Examples of observation and recording opportunities.

observations, by focusing observations on only a few children at a time, and by scheduling time—to interpret the observations, the assessment process can be manageable. (Leavitt & Eheart, 1991, p. 9)

Figure 9.4 describes specific observational and recording times that teachers have reported as successful. These examples are offered as possibilities, not rigid schedules.

Overview of Parent Conferences

Parent conferences are scheduled appointments for teachers and parents to share their concerns about and support of the growth of these parents' children. Whether the conference is the traditional fall/spring event or if it has been specially called to discuss a child's specific problem, the attitude of partnership prevails.

> Schools must recognize and applaud the home as the foundation of the child's learning. Teachers must make every effort to bridge the gap between home and school. Effective communication between teachers and parents can and will bridge the gap. (Lawler, 1991, p. 89)

The teacher plays a key role in the development of the partnership. A positive tone is maintained and leadership is provided by a teacher who is prepared and trained. Read on to see how the teacher who has made comprehensive observations, filed them in a usable manner, and periodically reviewed them plans for a conference confidently and proficiently.

Conference Preparation and Content.   The child's developmental level and the educational program guide the conference content. For example, the content of a conference with a day care toddler's parent(s) is very different from that of a conference with a primary grade child's parent(s). Likewise, the conference content for various programs within the same age-range may be based on different overall goals, thus influencing the content (e.g., the emphasis of the conference content for a child in a Montessori program may differ from that for a child in a Head Start program).

Regardless of the program type, the teacher begins to prepare for the conference by filling out a conference form for each child (see Figures 9.5, 9.6, and 9.7). The summary form is based on the running records, anecdotes, rating scales, checklists, other observations, and work samples systematically stored in the child's portfolio. The prepared form establishes a focus for the conference.

The next three figures supply a structure for compiling the developmental information to be shared at the conference. The first one, Figure 9.5, is based on Leavitt and Eheart's (1985) caregiver responsibilities for reporting a comprehensive assessment of infants and toddlers. While reading through it, consider the young 2-year-old's need for active exploration, movement, a supportive environment, and predictable routine (Bredekamp, 1987).

School's Name
Conference Form

Name: Age: Date:

1. Daily routine. (Describes the child's behavior in such tasks as self-help skills and
   arriving and departing.)

2. Interest inventory. (Specifies what activities the child chooses to play with, such
   as water, sand, manipulatives, etc.)

3. Developmental summary. (Using the areas of cognitive, motor, language, social,
   emotional, and creative development, the teacher summarizes the child's overall
   developmental pattern. The emphasis is on what the child can do and how the
   child does it in comparison with previous assessments and general developmental norms.)

4. Typical day. (A written description is given of the child's typical day, thus allowing the parent to see the child in total.)

Figure 9.5.   Sample infant/toddler conference form (condensed in size).
Source: From *Toddler Day Care: A Guide to Responsive Caregiving* (pp. 7–8) by R. L. Leavitt and
B. K. Eheart, 1985, Lexington, MA: Lexington Books, D. C. Heath. Copyright © 1985 by D. C. Heath.
Reprinted with permission.

In contrast to the infant/toddler conference form, the half-day preschool
conference form emphasizes the developmental summary. Most parents of children in half-day programs are familiar with the typical day. Many parents stay
and observe on various occasions. Several have the luxury of helping out in their

children's classroom. However, all-day child development programs for children 2 to 5 years of age will want to include a description of the typical day in their conference reports. In the sample preschool form (Figure 9.6), the teacher provides developmental information based on classroom observations and fills out the teacher's portion before the conference.

School's Name   **Fall Conference**

Our Fall Conference is for sharing information, concerns, and goals.

Child's Name: Age: Date:

Socio-Emotional
      Teacher—
      Parent—
      Goals—

Physical
      Teacher—
      Parent—
      Goals—

Cognitive
      Teacher—
      Parent—
      Goals—

Creative
      Teacher—
      Parent—
      Goals—

Teacher's Signature _____

Parent's Signature _____

Figure 9.6.   Sample preschool conference form (condensed in size).
Source: Courtesy of L. Way, Pacific Preschool, Laguna Niguel, California. Copyright © 1992 by L. Way. Reprinted with permission.

School's Name
Conference Form

Name: Age: Grade: Date:

Cognitive: Covers the academic areas of reading, writing, math, science, social studies, health, language, listening/speaking. Also includes problem-solving abilities, logical thought, classification, seriation, memory, and perspective taking.

Psychosocial: Includes personal and social development, such as peer–adult relations, impulse control, motivation, self-concept, gender identity, and moral reasoning.

Physical: Discusses both gross and fine motor development. Includes child's abilities in physical skill development.

Creative: Includes music, art, creative writing, block play, and creative dramatics.

Figure 9.7.   Sample primary grade conference form (condensed in size).

Primary grade conferences traditionally have centered around a report card concentrating on the child's subject matter proficiency and school behavior. Developmentally appropriate curricula have, however, become increasingly implemented in K–3 classrooms. In these classrooms teachers and parents are concerned with the child's comprehensive growth and development. At conferences the graded report card is replaced or augmented with a more expansive reporting form (see Figure 9.7). The National Association for the Education of Young Children (Bredekamp, 1987) guidelines for developmentally appropriate practices for K–3 make the following suggestions for evaluations:

- No letter or numerical grades are given during the primary years.
- Children's progress is reported to parents in the form of narrative comments following an outline of topics.
- A child's progress is reported in comparison to his or her own previous performance and parents are given general information about how the child compares to standardized national averages. (p. 75)

Figure 9.7 suggests a developmentally appropriate conference form for the primary grade years. The teacher summarizes the child's development in all four areas, drawing on the child's portfolio of observations and work samples. A well-designed record-keeping system pays high dividends when you are preparing conference forms!

Getting Started.   Even though "a conference provides you and parents with time to share information and perceptions" (Feeney, Christensen, & Moravcik, 1991, p. 414), it is the teacher's responsibility to facilitate productive communications. How is that done? It's accomplished by understanding the main purposes of a conference: listening, sharing, and strengthening the parent/teacher partnership as it relates to the children's growth and development.

Now let's look at how a conference is generally carried out. The teacher begins the session by setting a positive tone—discussing an outstanding strength the child possesses or a recent accomplishment. Here are two examples:

- It's a real joy to see how Keara has grown in her ability to use words to solve problems independently. We've worked very hard on this. She seems so much more confident in this area at school. What do you see at home?
- Omar has such well-developed motor skills. I often observe his agility and coordination when he runs, hops, and skips. He's a great skipper. I've noticed recently that he doesn't seem to have the interest in the trikes that he used to. I think he's ready to try a two-wheeler; what do you think?

The opening positive statement does not have to be a monumental achievement. For the child who seems "lacking in strengths," the teacher looks for the small positives, such as attendance, grooming, a special interest, a hobby, or a family trip or excursion that the child talked about. The discussion of the child's overall development can begin in any area as long as it is positive.

After the teacher breaks the ice by setting a positive tone and inviting interaction with the parent, the discussion continues via the content of the conference form (see Figures 9.5, 9.6, and 9.7). The teacher, well prepared with examples of pertinent anecdotes and samples of the child's work, leads the parents through an informal conversation on all areas of the child's development.

Throughout the conference the teacher asks the parents if they've noticed similar or the same developmental strengths or weaknesses that may need to be addressed. Many times, parents relate stories that correlate with what the teacher has seen at school. Sometimes parents are surprised and report that their child is different at home. The teacher listens attentively and jots down the parents' input on the form. The teacher can then summarize joint concerns; together, the teacher and parents can establish specific goals.

Teachers and parents bring their own perspectives to the conference table, interpreting the child's growth through their own observational prisms. Together, they look through the looking glass, often doubling the visibility. The conference is a collaboration; it sets in place the desired home/school partnership.

Supporting Documentation.   Effective conferences require sharing of observations to augment the summaries. The trained teacher also selects samples of the child's work (e.g., drawings, stories, primary grade math or writing papers) to illustrate various topics on the conference form. For example, the teacher may present a painting or a collage that shows the child's ability to represent or a child's unfinished math assignments as evidence of weak work habits. Parents appreciate documentation in the form of children's work samples and can more clearly understand their children's developmental advances or impediments when samples accompany the written summaries.

Another way to widen the perspective and document written comments is to present audiotape, videotape, or videodisc records and photographs (Evertson & Green, 1986). The use of instant photographs is demonstrated by a teacher who tells about Juanita, a child who always responded with, "I don't know," when her parents asked her what she did at preschool:

> During the parent conference I brought out some photos of Juanita's science discoveries using magnets and balances along with photos of her block-building feats, and her favorite dramatic play scenario—the office. Her parents were delighted to see her emerging science interest and her active classroom participation. Those pictures were worth a thousand words!

Not to be overlooked in the early childhood classroom is the appropriate use of videotapes. The use of the video camera to film children at work in the classroom can offer parents an enlightening and rewarding view of their child. A videotape can be useful in clarifying a child's strengths and weaknesses or portraying developmental progress. For example, video clips can be chosen to show a toddler's growing ability to interact with other children. In a preschool or primary grade conference, video clips can highlight leadership skills. Let's look at how one teacher integrated videotapes into a conference.

> I once taught a 4-year-old, Bethany, who was precocious in her artwork. By the second or third month, Bethany ventured out into the block area, where she became as interested in pursuing social contacts as in building. Her time in the art area declined, and she took less time and care with her projects. Unfortunately (from my perspective), her parents grew increasingly dissatisfied with the "quality" of work Bethany brought home from preschool!
>
> My verbal explanations of Bethany's change in pursuits were not as effective as a videotape of Bethany during free-choice time in persuading her parents that her time was being well spent. Once they recovered from their initial surprise and disappoint-

ment (remember, their expectations were not being met), they began to appreciate how hard Bethany was working to expand her social networks. In the short term the videotape lessened the parents' anxieties about unproductive time in preschool and, in the long run, helped to allow Bethany the needed time to achieve a balanced life at school.

Videotapes and other recording media can provide important insights during the parent conference. Parents value the opportunity to see their children on their own and leave the conference with a broadened understanding of the educational program.

Guidelines for Parent Conferences

1. *Preparation.* Treat each child individually. Carefully review observational records in portfolios. Write each child's developmental summary on a conference form. Choose items to discuss, such as children's work, photos, and anecdotes. Organize.

2. *Planning.* Set a time that is convenient for the teacher and the parent(s). Aim for an approximately 20-minute session. Invite the parent(s).

3. *Setup.* Arrange a comfortable place for the parent(s) to wait. Provide adult-size chairs and a table with reading materials. Early childhood magazines, class photo albums, or stories children have dictated or written help early arrivals pass the time. A pitcher of ice water or a pot of coffee is always appreciated.

4. *Appointment.* Start the conference on time! Keep track of the time so that others are not inconvenienced. During the conference be friendly, positive, and open. Listen and exchange views. Keep your purpose in mind. Develop goals with the parent(s) on the basis of shared information. Send home a copy of the conference form with the parent(s).

5. *Follow-up.* Make a phone call, send a note home with the child, or informally chat at departure time to keep the lines of communication open. Schedule another conference or make a home visit if a concern requires additional attention. Let your sincere interest be known; continue to build partnerships!

Guidelines for Using Videotapes During Parent Conferences

1. *Know the equipment.* Valuable conference time will be wasted if the teacher cannot work the equipment efficiently.

2. *Plan the program.* Select which tape clips of each child to show and know where to find them. Carefully preview each tape and record the counter numbers of each clip.

3. *Utilize videotapes to make substantive points to parents.* Videotapes can illustrate how children work in school, their interests, their strengths, and so forth. Think about each selection and how you want to use it during the conference. Planning time will be shortened if the video clips depicting more than one child are cross-referenced in each child's portfolio.

4. *Present a balanced view of each child.* Try to show parents at least two clips of their child to document the variety of activities and experiences that are part of early childhood education. Remember that the clip may be short yet effective.

The diagram of the cycle of observing, recording, planning, evaluating, and communicating represents the process that surrounds conferences. The base of the triangle inside the circle represents shared parent/teacher support for the developing child.

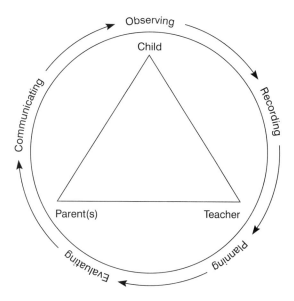

This cycle is repeated over and over throughout the year. After the teacher has pulled together and written down the child's developmental information for the parent conference, the teacher can quickly analyze the child's positive attributes as well as limitations. The teacher will then be ready to discuss, listen openly, and help set mutual goals.

During a responsive and supportive conference, parents readily furnish additional information, new insights, and suggestions. Their perspectives help give the teacher the broadest possible view of the child. As parents and teachers share their own perspectives of the child's abilities and developing abilities, a valuable partnership is created. Throughout the year this partnership is developed by keeping the lines of communication open and staying in touch. The parents, the teacher, and most of all the child benefit from the cycle of observing, recording, planning, evaluating, and communicating.

Applications

To exemplify the conference process, let's get acquainted with Toby (4;8). Before the conference day, Toby's teacher compiled the conference form summaries using the observations from Toby's portfolio; the documents in Toby's portfolio are displayed in Figure 9.8. (This portfolio is unusually large for the end of October because of the teacher's present focus on Toby's pressing developmental needs.)

14 *anecdotes* representing physical, cognitive, psychosocial, and creative development dated as follows:
    9/9, 9/14, 9/15, 9/17, 9/18, 9/25, 9/28
    10/1, 10/5, 10/8, 10/12, 10/13, 10/21, 10/23

2 *running records* (one inside and one outside) dated 9/11 and 9/16, each 5 minutes

ABC narrative event sampling on group entrance dated 9/21 to 9/24

COR (Child Observation Record) *rating scale* completed 10/26 based on above
records

1 *video clip* of outside play

Figure 9.8.   Portfolio documents.

    With the purpose of the conference in mind (to enhance the teacher/parent
team approach by listening, discussing, and sharing joys and concerns regarding
Toby's developmental progress), read through the summary and begin to answer
the following questions. What topics would you, as a teacher, be sure to discuss
with his parents at the conference? What would be your tentative plans and goals
for Toby? Conference dialogue will ultimately determine joint goals; however,
effective teachers come prepared with some possible goal suggestions. Student
Activity 9.1 will give you an opportunity to make some preconference goal suggestions based on the information in Figure 9.9.

    Toby was chosen specifically to demonstrate how a teacher can use a positive
tone throughout the conference report to relate important and difficult developmental information. This year, the last year before kindergarten, will be a critical
year in Toby's growth. His parents are already aware of many of their child's abilities and talents as well as his limitations (remember that this child is 4;8). Toby's
teacher knows that a collaborative parent/teacher effort to establish joint goals
will serve Toby's best interest.

Student Activity 9.1
Suggestions for Teacher Goals

    The goals recorded on each child's conference form are jointly set by the
teacher and the parent(s) during the conference. The teacher, however, prepares for the conference by writing (on a separate piece of paper) some ideas
for possible goals that address strengths and weaknesses.

    After reviewing Figure 9.9, answer the question on page 207 as if you were
Toby's teacher.

Seaside Developmental Center
Fall Conference

Name: Toby   Age: 4;8   Date: 10/16

Physical
Teacher: In large-motor skills Toby shows confidence and thoroughly enjoys running, jumping, and climbing—all executed with ease and coordination. His movements are smooth and controlled; he is an excellent ball handler. He demonstrates strength and agility in all large motor activities.

Toby's interest in small motor tasks is limited to working with manipulatives such as puzzles and an occasional visit to the art table. He has not yet established hand dominance; he picks up art tools (crayons, brushes, chalk) or puzzle pieces with either his right or left hand.

Parent:

Goals:

Cognitive
Teacher: Toby has a large vocabulary and complex sentence structure; his language is rich. He likes relating what he knows to new information. When participating in a group, he asks thoughtful questions and has creative ideas.

Through language he demonstrates representation, classification, and seriation. He exhibits admirable recall abilities daily.

Toby loves books. He spends some of each morning's free-choice time in the language area.

If asked, Toby can print his name with either hand when a model is provided. He counts using 1:1 correspondence up to 12.

Parent:

Goals:

Figure 9.9.   Completed preschool conference form *(continued on next page).*
Source: Courtesy of I. Andrews, St. Margaret's Preschool, San Juan Capistrano, California.
Copyright © 1992 by I. Andrews. Adapted with permission.

Psychosocial

Teacher: Toby shows no fears and is inquisitive, curious, and adventurous. Directing his exuberance when he is interacting with other children is his biggest challenge. He is often "out-of-bounds," engaging in rough play and frequent outbursts of anger when playing with other children. Children have already begun to avoid and reject him in their play. Guidance and close proximity to adults offer support as he learns to use his words to tell his friends when he doesn't like what is going on.

Entering a group poses a particular problem for Toby. During the first weeks of school Toby chose to enter groups by force—knocking down structures, throwing sand, etc. Toby and I have begun to work together in this area. As a first step, I have assured him that I can tell he wants to play with others and when he wants help, he should come and tell me. As his trust grows, he seeks my help more often. He seems to be pleased with his few (at this point) successes.

Toby focuses the longest on solitary self-selected tasks. He is proud of his mastery of puzzles. He is interested in books and tabletop number games. He is very cooperative when engaged with an adult one-on-one or with a small group on a directed task.

Parent:

Goals:

Creative

Teacher: At this point Toby's creative ability is displayed primarily in his verbal skills and dramatic play. For limited periods of time he engages in positive role play (e.g., pizza man or daddy). As his psychosocial skills develop, his ability to display his creativity will blossom.

Parent:

Goals:

Figure 9.9.   Completed preschool conference form *(continued).*

What are your initial preconference goals for Toby?

Physical goals:

Cognitive goals:

Psychosocial goals:

Creative goals:

To implement successful conferences, the teacher must be skilled in writing goals and summaries. Student Activity 9.2 offers practice in writing summaries.

Student Activity 9.2
Writing Summaries

It is time to prepare for fall conferences at Eighth Street Elementary. The teacher thoughtfully fills in the conference form (Figure 9.9) to discuss Keo's (5;3) development. The teacher praises Keo's gregarious personality, which is loved by all. The teacher also applauds Keo's adeptness in large motor development. The teacher is concerned, however, about Keo's preoccupation with superhero figures; Keo's compelling interest interferes with other kindergarten activities. The teacher also discusses Keo's limited fine motor skills.

Using the form from Figure 9.9, imagine that you are Keo's teacher preparing for a fall conference. Write the psychosocial paragraph addressing Keo's attraction to superheroes. Be positive, clear, and concise when conveying this information.

Eighth Street Elementary
Fall Conference

Name: Keo   Age: 5;3   Date:

Psychosocial:

Action Project 9.1

Evaluating Record-Keeping Systems

Option 1

Choose three schools that serve the age group you are interested in (2- to 8-year-olds). Call ahead and request *blank* copies of their observation sheets, record-keeping sheets, and conference forms. If each school can meet your need, stop by and pick up the forms. (If a school cannot meet your request, choose another that can.) Upon examination of your collections from three schools (a skeleton portfolio), answer the following questions by writing down your findings.

- What information about each child do the various forms collect, and what information do they omit? How are they similar and different?
- Do the forms meet the guidelines given in this chapter for designing your own system? If not, what modifications would you suggest?

Option 2

Visit one school that serves children of the age you are interested in (2- to 8-year-olds) and that uses written observations. Obtain *blank* copies of the observation sheets, record-keeping sheets, and conference forms. Make an appointment and discuss them with a teacher or teachers at the school. Learn how the sheets and forms are used at that school. Find out what the teacher(s) considers the benefits and drawbacks of the samples you've collected. Write down your findings.

Points to Remember

A serviceable record-keeping system promotes efficiency and confidentiality in filing observations, enables the teacher to tailor activities to individual needs, and helps the teacher prepare for parent conferences. Successful systems are tailored to meet the teacher's and program's needs. Teachers may design their own systems, modify others' systems, or use one presented in this chapter (file boxes, notebooks, or file folders).

An effective record-keeping system expedites planning for parent conferences. Prudent teachers prepare for parent conferences by filling out conference summary forms using the information collected in the children's portfolios. The teacher provides the guiding hand in conducting conferences that are positive, supportive, and sharing. Together, the parents and the teacher build a partnership that ensures optimal progress for the child.

The organization necessary for record keeping and conference preparation requires teachers to prioritize their use of time; record keeping may seem overwhelming at first. Using a record-keeping system, however, is much like following the directions to a new destination—at first the instructions appear complex, but once you're on the road, the path is clear and simple to follow. The going becomes smooth and direct when teachers utilize systematic organization.

Think About . . .

At the end of each week, the teachers at Canyon Primary School set aside time for individual class evaluations and general planning for the next week. They record and file observations in well-used portfolios. On these Friday afternoons, they spend the bulk of their planning time rereading observations, identifying emerging patterns, and planning appropriate activities and teaching strategies.

Today in Room 3, one team of teachers is pondering how to stimulate more divergent thinking during class discussions. The teachers are disturbed because observational records in many of the children's portfolios describe quick, short answers during discussions of important topics. As the teachers brainstorm further, attention turns to their own teaching techniques. They begin to suspect that the way they lead discussions, specifically the types of questions they ask, could contribute to the recorded responses. The teachers decide to observe how often they ask questions that promote divergent thinking and extend language as opposed to questions that elicit one-word responses. What observational method could these teachers use to explore their own question-asking patterns over a 2-week period?

PART III

Observing Children, Teachers, and Interactions in the Early Childhood Classroom

CHAPTER 10

Observing Children and Teachers at Work by Using Tally Event Sampling

Laughing, sharing, problem solving, mixing, pouring, building, running, reading, writing, drawing, discovering—observations in the early childhood classroom usually focus on behaviors of *individual children*. In Chapter 9's Think About section, however, you were asked to select a method to observe how *teachers* could explore their own question-asking patterns. The time has come to broaden our observational scope by expanding the subject of our observations to include more than one person; the looking glass widens.

As you puzzled over the question in the Think About section and searched your current knowledge for an appropriate observational method, you may have thought about using a checklist to observe and examine whether the teachers asked more questions that promote divergent thinking than questions that elicit a one-word response. A checklist would be a good choice if the observers wanted to document only the presence or absence of the two types of questions and if they were observing only one teacher at a time. The Canyon Primary teachers, however, wish to investigate, analyze, and compare teachers' questioning patterns on more than one occasion. In essence these teachers want to evaluate one aspect of their teaching methodology—question asking. In order to obtain the information requested in the Think About question, we will explore a new method—tally event sampling.

Overview of Observing Using Tally Event Sampling

Description.   Chapter 8 introduced an event sampling method used to study causes and effects of individual children's behavior: ABC narrative event sampling. This chapter presents another event sampling method: *tally event sampling*. Observers use this method, "a topic-centered approach" (Evertson & Green, 1986, p. 182), to determine how often an identified behavior or situation occurs. Using a structure called a *grid* for data collection, tally event samplings "record every occurrence of preselected response categories over a specific observational period" (Hutt & Hutt, 1970, p. 67). The observational period provides a representative segment of the topic known as a *sampling* (just as the ABC method did). These two methods, then, differ in purpose, form, and data produced. The ABC narrative approach yields qualitative data, whereas the tally approach provides quantitative data.

The two Canyon Primary teachers discussed in Chapter 9's Think About section ultimately chose tally event sampling to find out the number of times each of them asked an *open question* (a question that promotes divergent thinking and extends language) or a *closed question* (a question that elicits a one-word response). With this method, the observer inscribes one tally mark each time one of the two types of questions is asked by a teacher during a group discussion. The tally marks are recorded on a grid that organizes and simplifies the potentially cumbersome task of observing several subjects (teachers) and recording abundant

Tally Event Sampling of Teachers' Open/Closed Questions

School/Grade:

Date: Time:

Observer: Teachers:

                                                              Children:

Event: Open questions—have many possible answers that allow the child
                    opportunity to expand and explain. (O)
                    Closed questions—have one correct answer. (C)

Instructions: Make one tally mark in the appropriate column each time a teacher
                     asks a question during specific discussion times.

Discussion Time	Science		Social Studies		Math		Shared Reading		Small Group	
Teacher / Question	O	C	O	C	O	C	O	C	O	C
Xavier										
Nadia										

Figure 10.1. Tally event sampling: Teachers' questions.

data (questions asked). Figure 10.1 exhibits the grid developed by the Canyon Primary teachers.

This form may be expanded vertically to include additional teachers and horizontally to include other subjects. For preschools, room areas or activities can be substituted for the subject categories. This tally form enables the teachers to summarize and compare their overall patterns of open or closed questioning throughout the day. The results will undoubtedly promote conversation among these teachers about the value and implications of open and closed questions during class discussions. In addition, the teachers may discuss how this same process could be used to observe other categories of questions; one example would be the types of questions from Bloom's taxonomy (1985b).

The tally approach can be used to examine a wide range of topics and is versatile because of its flexibility in subject choice. For example, the observer can measure the frequency of events involving *one person* (e.g., a teacher's repeated use of classroom management techniques or the number of times a child is out of her or his seat during work periods), events involving *groups* (e.g, teachers' questioning patterns or children's use of *power language*—profanity or other offensive words [e.g., *shut up*]), or events involving *interactions* (e.g., children's language exchanges). Let's look closely at an excellent example of using tally sampling to observe child–child interactions (see Figure 10.2). Watson, Omark, Grouell, and Heller (1981) present a system for recording "who spoke Spanish . . . to whom within a classroom" (p. 126).

Watson et al. (1981) note that teachers and aides could be added to the list for a more comprehensive classroom picture of verbal interactions in Spanish. Information from this event sampling might help teachers in a bilingual classroom pair children for collaborative apprenticeship (peer teaching).

In a multilingual classroom the teacher might want to know the prevalent language interactions in order to promote friendships, mutual respect, and language development. The grid would specify the senders and receivers of messages as in Figure 10.2 and also the language used; language codes (e.g., *J* for Japanese) would be substituted for tally marks. Perhaps the data would show that one child converses only in Japanese with other Japanese students. On the basis of this information, the teacher might want to pair this child with a Japanese

---

Tally Event Sampling of Language Interactions

Center:

Date: Time:

Observer: Teacher:

                                           Children: Juan, Mary, Tony, Alberto,
                                                        Dan, Rosalia

		Receivers				
Child	Juan	Mary	Tony	Alberto	Dan	Rosalia
Juan						
Mary						
Tony						
Alberto						
Dan						
Rosalia						

(Senders)

Figure 10.2.   Tally event sampling: Language interactions.

Source: From *Nondiscriminatory Assessment: Volume I—Practitioner's Guide* by D. L. Watson, D. Omark, S. L. Grouell, and B. Heller, 1981, San Diego, CA: Los Amigos Research Associates. Copyright © 1981 by Los Amigos Research Associates. Reprinted by permission.

buddy who is also comfortable speaking English (Watson et al., 1981). Both children will profit from this arrangement.

Keep in mind that tally event sampling can be used to record various overt (observable and apparent) behaviors occurring infrequently or with moderate frequency. What about events that occur rapidly, incessantly, or with very high frequency? Those require yet another method, which is explained in Chapter 11.

What recurring events or behavior would teachers want to examine? Think about appropriate topics that can be observed using the tally event sampling method.

Student Activity 10.1
Tally Event Sampling Topics

Identify four topics that could be studied using tally event sampling.

Examples:
- Frequency children use selected methods to obtain the teacher's attention
- Frequency of teachers' use of direct method instruction

1.

2.

3.

4.

Purpose.   Tally event sampling is most useful for teachers when they want to know how frequently an event (an identified behavior or incident) occurs. Employing this approach, teachers can quickly and easily obtain unbiased information to be used in planning or revising teaching strategies, activities, and materials. For example, one teacher concerned with meeting individual needs was interested in exploring how often each child used various methods to gain teachers' attention. With these data the teacher could analyze possible preferences. The tally approach would furnish the requisite data.

Teachers can use tally sampled data to monitor developmental changes and the effectiveness of teaching strategies. Suppose a preschool teacher, Noi, who is exasperated with a child's use of power language, uses tally event sampling to check the child's frequency of power language use before and after intervention strategies. In the first tally sampling, this child used power language an average of nine times a day. (Noi expected 40 times!) As Noi sets into practice a plan to help the child control this behavior, she knows that a behavior change may be a long and difficult process. Because the use of power language particularly irritates Noi, it seems as if no progress is being made. After 2 weeks of concerted effort, however, Noi again samples the child's use of power language and finds that it has diminished to an average of twice a day! Encouraged by the positive and objective results, she continues the corrective practices and looks forward to continued progress. Another power language sampling is planned for 3 weeks later.

Teachers are often shocked at the findings of tally event sampling, especially in the area of teacher and child behaviors. Particularly in large classrooms, teachers' perceptions of classroom behaviors are easily distorted. With objective information procured from the samplings, however, teachers can analyze patterns and plan for adjustments. Responding to the recorded data can facilitate, enrich, and promote an exceptional early childhood environment.

Recording Time.   A common concern for observers using the tally approach is how to gather information over the entire day. After all, the early childhood classroom is bursting with activity. How can a teacher collect data on one topic all day or perhaps over several days?

Questions regarding the time are important. Kerlinger (1986) offers this advice: "The investigator who is pursuing events must either know when the events are going to occur and be present when they occur, as with classroom events, or wait until they occur, as with quarrels" (p. 492). The teacher keeps the form close at hand for the duration of the sampling period and records marks whenever the event occurs. The length of the sampling period is determined by the event studied, specifically how long the teacher thinks it will take to gather enough data for a representative sample. For instance, the teacher may record daily for a week when sampling aggression in the classroom but only for a few days when sampling direct teaching methods. Remember, tally marks are made on the recording form only when the event occurs. Tally event sampling, a shortcut observational method, is simpler than many of the narrative methods. Tally event sampling requires little teacher time once the form has been designed.

Guidelines for Constructing and Using Tally Event Sampling Instruments.   Tally event sampling users may design an instrument to suit their observational needs. To ensure that the resulting grid can be used objectively to collect the necessary quantitative data and produce valid information, however, certain ordered steps must be taken.

Box 10.1 presents an overview to assist the process of devising instruments and interpreting the results. The process is divided into the steps outlined in Box 10.1; each point in the box is explained in the next section of this chapter.

To illustrate this process, two examples follow. The preschool example demonstrates how to design an instrument to measure how often children display classification. The primary grade example asks you to participate in constructing an instrument to research the question "Do teachers call on boys more often than girls?"

Box 10.1
Designing and Using a Tally Event Sampling Instrument

1. Select an appropriate topic, and formulate an observational question.
   - Define the event.
2. Research the topic in the library and classroom. Review what others have already done in the selected area.
3. Identify clear and distinct categories.
   - Generate sets of categories, vertical and horizontal.
   - Operationally define each set of categories.
   - Select a system: sign or category.
   - Decide if category codes are needed.
4. Design a recording form. Use a heading and a grid.
5. Pilot test the instrument, and make needed corrections.
6. Establish inter-rater reliability.

Steps in Interpreting the Results

1. Use recording forms to gather the data. Compile all collected data onto one sheet when possible.
2. Analyze the data (see Chapter 12).

Formulate Follow-Through Plans

1. Plan appropriate activities, environment changes, interventions, and teaching strategies on the basis of the data analysis.

Integration of Classroom Situations and Observation

Preschool Example.   The scene for the six-step process of designing a tally event sampling instrument unfolds as follows. Molly, a preschool teacher, and her class of 12 children have just returned from a *pocket walk*. While sitting in a circle on the floor, the children enthusiastically take the collected treasures from their pockets and pile the items in front of themselves. Molly is not surprised to see that everyone has collected several rocks. As the children explore, compare, and discuss their finds, Molly can see that rocks are the most numerous. She decides to capitalize on their interest and moves around the circle, stopping to chat about rock texture with some and about similarities and differences with those who are already sorting. She suggests that the children might like to group similar rocks together. The children complete the project with various arrangements.

Having studied child development, Molly knows that classification ability develops gradually, is linked to maturation and direct experiences with manipulative materials, and is tied to school readiness. The pocket walk activity has spurred her interest in systematically investigating classification experiences in her classroom. Specifically, she would like to ask, "How often do the children in this classroom use materials for classification during free-choice time?" Molly reviews the possible observational methods and chooses the most appropriate one—tally event sampling. The process of designing a tally event sampling instrument is set in motion.

STEP 1   With her observational topic selected and her question clearly stated, Molly completes Step 1 by defining the event so that it is open to only one interpretation.

Classification—the ability to sort objects into classes and subclasses according to their similarities and differences.

STEP 2   Choosing the proper categories (components of the chosen event) requires Molly to research the topic. She checks child development books,

Exploring likenesses and differences enhances children's classification abilities.

Makes graphic collections: the child's arrangement is based on his or her unique pictorial groupings rather than logical groupings. For example, the girl doll goes with the car because she likes to drive; the boy doll goes with the wagon because he fits in it.

Sorts by identity: the child groups identical objects together. In the example, identical cups, bowls, and plates are sorted into separate groups.

Sorts by similarity with errors: the child attempts to group similar objects according to one attribute but makes one or more errors in grouping. For example, the child sorts various square and rectangular blocks by shape but is not entirely correct.

Sorts by similarity: the child groups similar objects according to one attribute. For example, blocks are correctly sorted by shape: cylinders, triangles, and arches.

Sorts and re-sorts: the child can sort and re-sort objects in more than one way. For example, the child sorts buttons into groups with one, two, or four holes. Then the child might re-sort the buttons by shape.

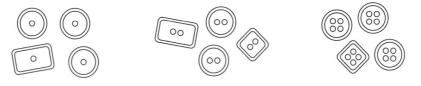

Figure 10.3.   Types of classification.

curriculum books, and journal articles in the library and selects *Young Children In Action* (Hohmann et al., 1979) to use as a reference for developing categories. She also observes children and teachers involved in classification activities and reflects on her own experiences in this area.

STEP 3   After careful review and consideration, Molly chooses her first set of grid categories (types of classification exhibited by young children, Figure 10.3) and supplies operational definitions. Operational definitions explain the categories by "specifying the activities" (Kerlinger, 1986, p. 28).

The use of a category or sign system is determined while categories are being chosen.

Category System	**Sign System**
Categories must be mutually exclusive; each category is distinct and separate from the others.	Categories must be mutually exclusive; each category is distinct and separate from the others.
AND	BUT
Categories must be exhaustive; a category is listed for every possible observed behavior. Nothing is left out.	Categories do not have to be exhaustive. Allows the observer to select only pertinent categories.

For classification activities of preschool children, Molly's five selected categories do not include preclassification skills or the more advanced classification levels exhibited by older children. Therefore, what system did Molly choose for her first set of categories?

Molly enlarges her data collection by looking in each area of the classroom for children's classification activities. She wants to know if classification opportunities are available to the children who play in the same area time and time again. For example, if a child regularly explores activities in the science area, are there diverse classification opportunities available and do children use them? What about all the other classroom areas? To include this information in her grid, she creates a second set of categories. She considers her choice of systems, sign or category, and decides on the following room areas:

- Blocks
- Art
- Dramatic play
- Music
- Manipulatives

- Language arts
- Science

When other possible classroom areas are considered, like those in the Montessori classroom, the above list of areas is not exhaustive. Molly selected the sign system for the first set of categories (classification activities) and the second set of categories (room areas).

Molly quickly notes that codes are in order. The category descriptors are long (e.g., sorts by similarity with errors), and having to continually reread lengthy descriptors may cut down on efficiency. Codes take up less room on the recording sheet, thus leaving more space for data recording. Therefore, using a code to represent each of her classification categories is advantageous. She could use abbreviations, letters, numbers, or symbols. She settles for the efficiency of letters; they will serve to jog her memory if necessary:

G: Makes graphic collections
I: Sorts by identity
S/E: Sorts by similarity with errors
S: Sorts by similarity
S/R: Sorts and re-sorts

When codes are used, the observer tries to memorize them before going into the classroom to observe. In the construction of the form, however, Molly includes the code meanings in her heading for quick reference. Code definitions ensure that others can use and understand the form; they may be printed in the heading or, if lengthy, on a separate sheet or on the back.

STEP 4   Molly is ready to construct the grid and fills in the heading on the tally event sampling form. She uses a scratch sheet of paper to try out different grid-arrangement patterns. Taking the size of the paper into account, she places the shortest set of categories (types of classification) along the top and the longest set (classroom areas) down the left side of the recording sheet so that all of the categories can fit on one sheet.

The tally event sampling grid for classification is complete with the matrix that displays the intersection of the two sets of categories. The grid is placed below the heading and definitions (Figure 10.4).

STEP 5   To check that the form is efficient, is easy to use, and collects the desired information, Molly tests her instrument while visiting another classroom on an in-service day. For her abbreviated pilot test she systematically observes seven areas.

Molly is reasonably pleased with the organization of the instrument. She would, however, like to keep track of who initiates the classification activities she observers: children or teachers. Therefore she adds the subcolumns—*child initiated*

Tally Event Sampling of Preschool Classification Activities

Center:

Date: Time:

Observer: Teacher:

                                               Children:

Event: Classification—the ability to sort objects into classes and
                          subclasses by their similarities and differences.

Classification Codes: G = sorts by graphic collections, I = sorts by identity,
                          S/E = sorts by similarity with errors, S = sorts by
                          similarity, S/R = sorts and re-sorts.

Classification Activity / Area	G	I	S/E	S	S/R
Blocks					
Art					
Dramatic play					
Music					
Manipulatives					
Language arts					
Science					

Figure 10.4.   Tally event sampling preschool example: Classification activities.

(*CI*) and *teacher initiated* (*TI*) (see Figure 10.5). She also adds a space for comments at the bottom. Molly makes the required corrections on the instrument grid and once again tests her instrument. This time, she is satisfied that the instrument will enable her to collect data to answer her complex and more specific observational question: how often and in which centers do the children in Room 8 use materials for classification during free play time, and who initiates the classification?

Tally Event Sampling of Preschool Classification Activities

Center: University Heights Children's Center
Date: 2/16 to 2/24   Time: 9:00–9:50 a.m.
Observer: Al   Teacher: Molly
                                    Children: Twelve 3- to 4-year-olds

Event: Classification – Ability to sort objects into classes and subclasses by their similarities and differences.

Classification Codes: G=sorts by graphic collections, I=sorts by identity, S/E=sorts by similarity with errors, S=sorts by similarity, S/R=sorts and re-sorts.

Initiator Codes: CI=child initiated, TI=teacher initiated.

Instructions: Make one tally mark in the appropriate box each time a child exhibits classification in one of the seven classroom areas.

Classification	G		I		S/E		S		S/R		
Initiator / Area	CI	TI	CI	TI	CI	TI	CI	TI	CI	TI	
Blocks	I		++++ II		I		III				(12)
Art			++++				III				(8)
Dramatic play			++++								(5)
Music											(0)
Manipulatives	I		III				IIII				(8)
Language arts											(0)
Science	II						II			I	(5)
	(4)	(0)	(20)	(0)	(1)	(0)	(12)	(0)	(0)	(1)	

Comments:
  Blocks: all CI-I at cleanup
  Music was not available for 4 out of the 7 days.

Figure 10.5.   Tally event sampling preschool example: Classification (data).

STEP 6   The final step in instrument construction, the inter-rater reliability check, is executed using paired observers. Molly enlists the help of Al, a fellow student from her early childhood curriculum night class. Together, they observe the same two classroom areas for 20 minutes, each using the revised tally instrument (as in Figure 10.5). When the observation time is complete, they check for consistency in what they recorded.

Inter-rater reliability is a measure between two or more observers resulting in a percentage that indicates the amount of agreement; exact agreement is 100%. Molly and her partner compute high agreement (96%). (Chapter 12 explains the process for computing inter-rater reliability.) The high percentage indicates that these two observers are likely to produce similar results in different situations. If inter-rater reliability were low, Molly would reevaluate the instrument to clarify categories or definitions or provide the observers with additional training.

INTERPRETING THE DATA   Al agrees to observe and collect classification tallies in Molly's preschool classroom for 7 days, recording each area for one day from 9:00 to 9:50 a.m. The results have been compiled onto one form (Figure 10.5) for manageable analysis.

Molly draws several conclusions from the quantitative data. Adding the tallies down the columns summarizes the types of classification activities the children performed. How often the classification activity was initiated by the teacher or by the child can be compared by adding the results in the *CI* and *TI* subcolumns separately. The classification activities in the various areas can be compared by totaling the tallies across the rows.

Molly surveys the results and formulates the following questions:

1. What can be done to stimulate more classification activities, particularly at the S/E and S levels? (Think about the gold mine of opportunities in the dramatic play area.)
2. Are materials available for classification in the language arts area; if so, why aren't they being used?
3. Why were classification activities teacher initiated only in the science area?

FOLLOW-THROUGH PLANS   Molly is troubled by her lack of initiation. Is she so preoccupied with redirecting children, answering questions, and solving problems that she seldom initiates classification? As she thinks about it, she realizes that she doesn't know when to intervene and what to do to initiate classification activities.

Molly brings up her problem in her night class and finds that other students share her anxieties and hesitations about teacher initiation. The class members come to the conclusion that the anxiety stems from not knowing what to do, even when the right moment is identified. Responding to the students' concerns, the professor gives a few examples and asks the students to form discussion groups to complete the following two tasks: (1) Define and brainstorm ideas of teacher initiation. (2) Prepare to share one example related to classification with the class. The students came up with the following:

Definition: Teacher initiation involves asking questions, providing needed materials and experiences for individual children and groups, and seizing treasured teaching moments to model.

Teacher Initiation Examples

Modeling classification. In the block area Jacob (4;2) has been making roads for several days. He has built an extensive road system and has also used cars and trucks in his play. The teacher notices that he seems to be at a standstill and chats with Jacob about how he has created the roads and where he used small, medium, and large blocks. The teacher then asks, "Shall we make some garages for your cars and trucks?" Jacob smiles and nods eagerly. "We'll make some little ones and big ones. Let's see what goes in each garage," the teacher says as they begin to build.

Asking questions or making comments that recognize classification. The teacher, while noticing a child's easel paintings, encourages the child's interest by saying, "How terrific! You've made a lot of circles on your paper. I see different sizes. You've arranged them in groups on your paper." This might help the child to notice that he's put big circles along the bottom and small circles along the top.

Asking questions to help children identify attributes that can lead to classification. In the science area the teacher explores the characteristics of rocks by using open-ended questions that fit the activity, "How do the rocks feel to you? Safa says the gray rock is smooth. Let's see if we can find some that are bumpy." The teacher may want to help the children explore other attributes—color, shape, effects of water on rocks, weight, or buoyancy.

Providing materials for classification. In the dramatic play area the teacher observes children reenacting the field trip to the post office by folding papers to make envelopes. The teacher asks if the children would like to add mailboxes. They choose to make mailboxes out of shoe boxes with their names on them. Mail delivery becomes a classification activity as the children sort and deliver the envelopes.

Molly returns to her classroom with confidence and a new understanding; she is ready to plan specific follow-through plans based on the observed data.

In addition to her plans to model classification, encourage representation, ask questions, and provide materials, Molly goes to the children's files to read observational records concerning classification. She finds running records, anecdotal records, and checklists to enrich her understanding of individual children. She notes the type of classification activities the children have exhibited. She also notes which children have no records relating to classification. Follow-through plans can now be made to incorporate specific classification activities into Molly's program.

Do teachers call on boys more than girls?

Primary Grade Example.   Lee, the principal of Fitzgerald School (grades K–3), provides dynamic leadership through effective use of staff meetings. In today's meeting, Lee guides a discussion on two articles, one in *Time* (Ostling, 1992) entitled "Is School Unfair to Girls?" and the other in the *Los Angeles Times* (Lindgren, 1992) entitled "Sex Bias in Class? Few Teachers Raise Hands." After many opinions about the articles have been shared, the principal shows some prerecorded videotape clips of teachers in the classroom. Lee directs the teachers to look at whom the videotaped teachers call on when questions are asked. He points out that even though all teachers intend to be unbiased and perceive themselves to be unbiased when choosing either a girl or a boy to call on, gender fairness is an area that "you constantly need to monitor" (Guerin, cited in Lindgren, 1992, p. B1). The teachers begin to wonder if subjective factors can creep into their intentions to choose children equitably.

Much discussion is generated by the teachers about their own personal experiences with gender fairness in their classrooms. One teacher, Cathrina, suspects that the subject being taught may produce unconscious biases (e.g., subscribing to stereotypes of boys being better and more interested in math than girls). She suggests that a classroom study could help raise consciousness. Another teacher, Giancarlo, thinks that teachers may call on boys more often than girls just to manage the class; in his experiences, boys have often been the eager hand wavers. He is interested in finding out whether girls raise their hands as often as boys do and whether teachers call on children of one gender more often than on those of the other.

*Student Activity 10.2*_____

Construction of a Tally Event Sampling Instrument

In this activity you will have the opportunity to apply your understanding of tally event sampling. Your task will be to design an effective grid to collect the requested information for the Fitzgerald School teachers.

Let's return to the teachers' meeting for more details. The team of teachers decides to gather data to analyze the gender distribution of student responses to teachers' questions in their school. (The principal is enlisted to collect the data on the instrument designed by the teachers.) The teachers choose tally event sampling to determine how many times girls and boys raise their hands in response to teachers' questions and the relative frequency at which each teacher calls on boys or girls. In order to compare the results, the data will be collected during shared reading time in each classroom.

Having agreed on the event and determining that no event terms need to be defined, the next step is to develop the categories. The following categories are chosen:

Hand raisers: girls/boys
Teacher calls on: girls/boys

Using the categories defined above, construct a grid and fill in the skeleton form in Figure 10.6.

_____

INTERPRETING THE DATA   After the pilot test of the grid and measurement of inter-rater reliability, the data can be collected and examined to further the teachers' objective understanding of gender fairness at their school. The staff will have a precise picture of the gender-related question-and-answer patterns by asking the following types of questions.

- Does one gender in an individual classroom account for a disproportionate share of hand raisers?
- What is the relationship between the gender of hand raisers and the gender of those who are chosen?
- What is the difference between the number of *boy* responses and the number of *girl* responses?
- Do individual teachers have gender-preference patterns?
- Are there changes that the entire staff wants to work on?
- Are there teachers who seem to be gender equitable and could act as role models for teachers who may want to improve in this area?

```
┌─────────────────────────────────────────────────────────────────────┐
│                    Tally Event Sampling of                          │
│            Gender Distribution of Student Responses                  │
│                                                                     │
│  School/Grade:                                                      │
│  Date:                              Time:                            │
│  Observer:                          Teachers:                       │
│                                     Children:                        │
│  (Fill in definition(s) if any are needed.)                         │
│  (Fill in codes and meanings, if any are used.)                     │
│  Instructions:                                                      │
│  ─────────────────────────────────────────────────────────────     │
│  (Fill in horizontal categories, and then add vertical lines        │
│   between categories.)                                              │
│  ─────────────────────────────────────────────────────────────     │
│  Teacher 1                                                          │
│  ─────────────────────────────────────────────────────────────     │
│  Teacher 2                                                          │
│  ─────────────────────────────────────────────────────────────     │
│  Teacher 3                                                          │
│  ─────────────────────────────────────────────────────────────     │
│  Teacher 4                                                          │
│  and so on listing the primary grade teachers                       │
└─────────────────────────────────────────────────────────────────────┘
```

Figure 10.6.   Tally event sampling: Gender distribution of student responses.

Suppose the data show that the teachers called on girls 28 times during shared reading but called on boys 46 times; thus, the girls answered questions 38% of the time and the boys answered questions 62% of the time. The hypothetical data also show that the girls raised their hands 10% less often than the boys did. This staff is astounded and disturbed by these overall comparisons. As a group, they examine individual teacher scores and find that the boy-choice trend is fairly equally distributed throughout all the classrooms. The teachers continue their investigation by sampling during other times of the day—including math time and the introduction of a new unit, using small and total class groups. Comparing the responses during different curriculum times provides information about consistency in gender choices during the entire day. Additional data will help the teachers draw sound conclusions. With a broad understanding the teachers can then develop strategies to foster gender equity.

The results of this gender inquiry may also lead to additional teaching strategies beyond calling on boys and girls equally; the teachers may consider checking gender access to computers, providing girl and boy models of achievement in every area, balancing feminine and masculine language usage, and monitoring children's reactions to others' mistakes. Striving to eliminate biases and audit gender equity adds another dimension, or perhaps for some a renewed awareness, to the teacher's role. In this instance the consciousness raising was generated by observations made through tally event sampling.

Applications

Strengths and Limitations.　　The greatest strengths of tally event sampling are efficiency and simplicity. Making tally marks takes little time. The form can be kept nearby on a clipboard or condensed to fit on a 5-by-8-inch card and kept in a pocket until complete. Event sampling "possesses 'time economy', in that the observer can often work at other tasks while waiting for a particular event to occur" (Bell & Low, 1977, p. 73). Tally marks can easily be collected, even in the busiest of classrooms.

The quantitative data collected through tally event sampling can be compared and analyzed quickly and objectively. The preschool classification example afforded a beginning experience.

> Quantitative analysis involves converting information to numbers—the number of times a person spoke in a group, the number of correct responses to specific questions, or the number of words in a composition. (Brause & Mayher, 1991, p. 136)

Chapters 11 and 12 discuss quantitative analysis further.

The versatility of this approach provides for observations of one teacher or child, but more often for groups of teachers, children, or their interactions. Tally event sampling can be used with a wide variety of moderate or infrequently occurring topics. Think back through the chapter examples; this method can be used by teachers for concerns about individual classrooms or by entire staffs for identified events schoolwide. Using event sampling to improve teacher effectiveness or the school environment is a potent way to build teamwork.

The major limitation of tally event sampling is that recording frequencies takes the behavior out of context. The tally approach does not record what takes place before or after the event. The cause of the event is not identified in tally event sampling. Its function is limited to recording how often an identified event occurs.

Action Project 10.1 _____

Preschool/Kindergarten Tally Event Sampling: Motor Development

Many educators believe that children develop gross motor skills on their own if the equipment is available (although it is usually only available outdoors). According to Miller's study of preschool children's motor development (as cited in Poest, Williams, Witt, & Atwood, 1990), however, "children allowed to play in well-equipped motor play areas scored significantly below normal in motor development compared to those provided with planned motor activity centers and guided movement experiences" (p. 4).

Suppose the teachers at Center X have observed that children often use the climbing structures for dramatic play and the tire swing (with little motion) for socializing. As a preliminary step before designing a planned motor development program, the teachers need an objective understanding of how the children are using the outside equipment. Their task, then, is to determine how often each child in the center uses the outside equipment for motor development or for other purposes. The data collection will require specific information regarding what other uses the children have for the equipment. For this action project you are invited to construct a tally event sampling grid on which these teachers may record the requested information.

Action Project 10.2 _____

Primary Grade Tally Event Sampling: Positive and Negative Self-Evaluations

The topic of self-esteem has been of interest to educators, parents, developmental psychologists, criminologists, social scientists, religious leaders, and politicians. For example, California state assemblyman Vasconcellos "has inspired 5 states and nearly all 58 counties in California to set up self-esteem task forces" (Adler et al., 1992, p. 51). The California task force explored the importance of self-esteem in relation to personal and social responsibility. Likewise, teachers are also interested in promoting the development of children's self-esteem (feeling good about who you are).

> Children who perceive themselves as loved, valued, worthy, and competent develop healthy self-esteem. As children's interactional opportunities expand, self-evaluations naturally occur. Healthy self-esteem assures that these evaluations weigh more heavily on the positive than on the negative side. (Black et al., 1992, p. 228)

In this activity you will explore one aspect of self-esteem: how children speak about themselves. You are to collect data on each child's self-evaluation by listening and recording tally marks every time a child makes a positive or negative statement about himself or herself. There are 25 children and one teacher in your classroom. Design a tally event sampling instrument to measure the frequencies of this psychosocial behavior. Determine the sampling period. Then speculate on the possible implications for teaching.

Points to Remember

Teachers appropriately select the tally event sampling observational method when they want to determine how frequently an identified event occurs. This simple and orderly technique allows the observer not only to look at individuals (a child or a teacher) but also to move into another observational area—observing groups (children, teachers, and adult–child interactions).

Tally event sampling data are collected with instruments that are either predesigned or created by teachers to respond to their immediate interests. This chapter has enumerated the steps for devising appropriate instruments.

The quantitative data from the tally observations can easily be analyzed and appropriately used to examine chosen behaviors, classroom strategies, curricula, or environments.

Think About . . .

You would like to observe what teachers do and say in the classroom. Your collections would include:

Teacher Verbalizations	Teacher Behaviors
Gives new information	Prepares materials
Gives directions	Adds materials
Comments	Models new ideas
Asks questions	Presents materials
Gives praise	Observes children
Gives encouragement	Instructs by direct method
Gives salutations	Cleans up/picks up
Criticizes	Unoccupied
Talks with other adults	

What problems might be encountered if tally event sampling is used to observe teacher verbalizations and behaviors in a busy classroom? The answer to this question will pave the way for investigating our last observational method.

CHAPTER 11

Observing Children and Teachers at Work by Using Time Sampling

At the end of Chapter 10, you thought about using the tally event sampling method to observe what teachers do and say in the classroom. After reviewing the 17 categories listed in the Think About section, you may have thought of additional behaviors or verbalizations you would like to include. The resulting observational project, however, is much too daunting, so you decide to pare it down. Now imagine it is free-choice time in an early childhood classroom and you are collecting data just on the following teacher verbalizations using the tally event sampling format.

Teacher Verbalizations
- Gives new information
- Gives directions
- Comments
- Asks questions
- Gives praise
- Gives encouragement
- Gives salutations
- Criticizes
- Talks with other adults

Erma Bombeck could most likely write a humorous, true-to-life profile of your weary hand and frazzled mind. Tally event sampling is not a practical means of studying events that occur in quick succession; you could probably not keep up with everything teachers say for any length of time. Fortunately, there is a more feasible observational method to apply in this case, one "that appears to be indigenous to research in child development" (Wright, 1960, p. 93).

Overview of Observing Using Time Sampling

Sampling. In order to tally *everything* teachers say, observers would require virtually perfect listening and memory skills for on-the-spot tallying or the use of tape recorders or video cameras to record the verbalizations for later coding. Even so, some verbalizations simply may be inaudible to the human ear or the tape recorder. Therefore, a sample, or subset, of teacher verbalizations is studied. This viable alternative to tally event sampling, *time sampling*, samples what teachers say on many occasions and lets the data represent the typical behaviors under investigation. Let's think about an analogy for a few minutes to explore the meanings of sampling and samples.

Imagine that the quality-control manager of a cereal company wants to know what proportions of pretzels, peanuts, and cereal are in a mix it sells and requests your careful assistance. Of course, you cannot count every piece in the thousands of boxes that are filled in the factory even in a single day. As an alternative, you place a $2\frac{1}{2}$-lb empty coffee can under the filling chute on the packaging line and count all these pieces to calculate the percentages of pretzels, peanuts, and cereal. You allow the ingredients in the can (the sample) to represent the ingredients in all boxes of this product (the population).

Consider a few potential problems. First, you are concerned about the size of the sample, in this case the coffee can. You want to collect enough of the mixture to feel confident that your sample is representative of the bin. You know the coffee can would just about fill one small box of the mixture, whereas a smaller sample, say a handful or even a cupful, might be unrepresentative just by chance. A coffee can is large enough that chance (random) conglomerates of ingredients (e.g., a bunch of peanuts) even out.

Because the can was filled from the same packaging line as the product boxes, you are confident that the ingredients in your sample have been as well mixed as those in the boxes. Suppose, instead, you had drawn your sample from the top of a large bin feeding into the filling chute. If the peanuts were poured into this bin first, the pretzels second, and the cereal last and the ingredients were not mixed, your scoop from the top would contain only cereal and would therefore be unrepresentative. Or suppose the mixing was only cursory at the top of the bin; your scoop would still be unrepresentative. You are reassured by knowing your sample comes straight from the filling chute.

You also evaluate possible subjectivity in your work for the cereal company. If you had allowed yourself to scoop out the sample yourself, your selection might have revealed your personal biases. Imagine these scenarios. You want the cereal company to put in more of your favorite ingredient, so you purposely look for a no-peanut place to scoop. This unrepresentative sample will help make your case for adding more peanuts. Or suppose you are a loyal employee of the company and are tired of hearing complaints that there aren't enough pretzels in the mixture—so you just happen to aim your scoop toward the bunch of pretzels in view. Your data will show them! Therefore, in the interest of accuracy and objectivity, you place your coffee can under the filling chute and let the machine pour in a random sample of ingredients.

Now back to observational projects in the early childhood classroom; the same problems apply. You have to be careful to observe enough examples of the behavior(s) under study to ensure that your sample is representative. You have to collect data from a well-stirred pot—consider time of day, activities, and the people in the classroom. And you must be careful that your own views, predictions, and wishes don't get in the way of collecting a truly *representative sample*. With this knowledge you can follow Kerlinger's (1986) definition: "a 'representative sample' means that the sample has approximately the characteristics of the population relevant to the research in question" (p. 11).

If you fail to collect a representative sample, the results may lead you to incorrect conclusions. For example, the observation of teacher verbalizations pertains to the entire school day and all teaching adults in the classroom. If you observed only 20 consecutive verbalizations, you might not draw a representative sample. If you only assessed teachers' verbalizations during the first half hour of school, you might conclude that the teachers spend an inordinate amount of time giving salutations. If you only observed small-group activities, you might erroneously conclude that teachers never talk to each other. And if you only observed your least favorite teacher, you might see an imbalance of criticizing. Such problems are compounded if you trap yourself in several of these pitfalls. Let's now learn how to maximize the yield of useful and accurate information using the time sampling method.

Description.   The unique component of time sampling is the use of predetermined units of time (time samples) to guide the observer's attention throughout the observational period. There are two major methods of specifying the time sampling units. In one, the time unit stipulates how long the observer observes and records before moving on to the next object of concentration (e.g., 30 seconds). In the other, the time unit stipulates the observational period (e.g., 20 seconds), and a separate time unit stipulates the coding time (e.g., 10 seconds).

The observer using the time sampling observational method depends on an easy-to-use recording grid to study a clear set or sets of defined categories. Categories primarily describe behaviors (e.g., child verbalizations, social play, teaching strategies), but categories describing characteristics (e.g., age, gender, subject matter) may also add useful information. A group is the usual focus of inquiry (children or teachers), and in this case, the time sampling format allows the observer to systematically shift attention from individual to individual.

Time sampling can yield quantitative data about the group as a whole (e.g., the incidence of types of play in a preschool classroom) and about individuals (e.g., the predominance of individuals' play types). The observer might, for example, wish to consider an individual teacher's or child's verbalizations within a classroom. Through the examination of children's and teachers' behaviors, the observer may also evaluate the effectiveness of the program and environment.

Purpose.   Time sampling observations are used for methodical investigation of behaviors that occur in rapid succession (e.g., teacher verbalizations). The procedures of time sampling help the observer collect representative data. The observer may then draw conclusions from the time samplings and use these conclusions to learn more about children and to refine her or his teaching strategies, the curriculum, or the environment. Time sampling can be a systematic and efficient observational method.

Guidelines for Constructing Time Sampling Instruments.   The thoughtful construction of time sampling instruments can produce the means to study rapidly occurring behaviors. The steps discussed in this section are summarized in Box 11.1.

Box 11.1
Designing a Time Sampling Instrument

1. Select an appropriate topic, and formulate an observational question.
2. Research the topic in libraries and classrooms.
3. Identify clear, distinct categories.
   - Generate sets of categories, vertical and horizontal.
   - Clearly define the categories.
   - Select a sign or category system.
   - Decide if codes are needed.
4. Design a recording form.
   - Use a heading and grid.
   - Specify the time sampling units.
   - Plan to collect the data in the form of tallies or durations.
   - Plan the observational schedule.
5. Pilot test the instrument.
6. Establish inter-rater reliability.

The selection of an appropriate topic to study is the first step in using time sampling. The topic should focus on overt behaviors that occur rapidly. For example, the types of children's play are *overt behaviors* because the observer can easily see if children are playing alone or with others and, with a bit more attention, if they are merely playing next to one another or truly engaging in cooperative play. The causes of children's derogatory comments about other children on the playground are often inapparent to an observer and are therefore inappropriate for time sampling. Utilizing the time sampling method, observers have studied such diverse topics as thumb sucking by infants, friendships, and teacher responses to children (Wright, 1960).

Time sampling is appropriate for observing behaviors that occur frequently. When a behavior occurs at least every 15 minutes, time sampling is suitable; behaviors occurring much more frequently necessitate this method. For example, teachers may verbalize so frequently that only time sampling methods can manage such an incessant flow of data. If, on the other hand, an observer wants to learn more about teachers' introductions of new materials into the classroom, a time sampling schedule that specifies 1 minute of observing and 30 seconds of coding might not yield any data at all; the only instance of a teacher introducing new materials might occur during the coding period. This behavior occurs infrequently enough that the topic would be better handled by tally event sampling. Now take a few moments to generate a short list of topics appropriate for the time sampling observational method.

Student Activity 11.1 _____

Appropriate Topics for the Time Sampling Observational Method

List three topics that can best be studied through the time sampling observational method. Remember that the behaviors to be observed must be overt and occur rapidly. You may include topics focusing on children and/or teachers.

Examples:
* Preschool children's uses of culturally diverse materials
* Primary grade teachers' classroom-management statements
* Number of words in children's sentences

1.

2.

3.

After choosing time sampling for the topic at hand, the observer formulates an observational question. A clear question specifies a manageable portion of the topic to observe and eases subsequent instrument construction. For example, a teacher who is interested in the use of a well-stocked dramatic play area may ask, "How do children use culturally diverse materials in the dramatic play area during free-choice time?"

Library research time, classroom observation, and the application of previous experience help the constructor of a time sampling instrument investigate the topic and identify the precise categories to be observed. The categories of behaviors or characteristics should be mutually exclusive, but they may represent a sign or category system, whichever provides the most appropriate information. Once selected, the behaviors should be clearly and operationally defined so that any user of the instrument interprets them in the same way. Parten's (1932) clear definition of parallel play from a classic time sampling study provides a fine example:

> *Parallel activity*—The child plays independently, but the activity he chooses naturally brings him among other children. He plays with toys that are like those which the children around him are using, but he plays with the toy as he sees fit, and does not try to influence or modify the activity of the children near him. He plays *beside* rather than *with* the other children. There is no attempt to control the coming or going of children in the group. (p. 250)

If definitions are lengthy, they are usually printed on a separate sheet or on the back of the recording form so as not to take up valuable space. Definitions are reviewed and memorized in advance of the observation so that once in the classroom the observer will need to refer to them only for occasional reminders or clarifications. The observer decides whether or not to use codes for the categories to be observed; the answer should be *yes* if the labels are long or cumbersome and would take up needed space on the recording form.

Working with well-defined categories, the observer is ready to design a recording form. Space is provided at the top for the traditional heading. Then categories (e.g., types of play with culturally diverse materials: exploration, representation, dramatic play) are listed horizontally near the top of the grid or vertically down the left side of the page, where there is more room. The other category (e.g., materials) may be posted in whichever space remains, lines are drawn horizontally and vertically to mark off the two sets of categories, and a grid is completed as in Chapter 10. In many studies the observer also wants to know the identity of the children, materials being used, and other information, so additional organization and detailing may be necessary.

On paper, the most difficult task in constructing a time sampling instrument is specifying the time sampling units. To create a feasible schedule that produces the requisite information, the observer must do some pilot testing. Previous experience and best guesses may help, but the greatest aid will be trying out the time sampling schedule under real conditions. Important elements to consider are how many individuals and how much detail are to be observed and coded. Some systems may allow the observer to observe and record within a single time unit without overlooking data. More complex systems, however, require separate time units to observe and code in order to eliminate the risk of missing behaviors while recording. For example, the pilot testing of a detailed instrument might provide the feedback that 30 seconds of recording time are needed after the 20 seconds of observation. There is no substitute for this hands-on experience.

The observer considers the type of time sampling data that will best answer the observational question. Theoretically, time sampling forms that generate checks or tallies or record the duration of the observed behaviors may be constructed (Medley & Mitzel, 1963). In practice, however, most observers reject the checks option because they want to learn more about the behaviors under study than simply if they are present; if not, then a checklist is a more straightforward method of choice. Simple checks on a time sampling form yield a minimum of information, so this method is best discarded in favor of the richer yields of tallies and durations.

If the observer is interested in the frequency of behaviors, it is worthwhile to record tallies; for example, a teacher might be interested in how often culturally diverse materials are used in exploratory versus representational play. As an alternative, the observer may choose to monitor the duration of each observed behavior with a stopwatch to answer questions about the proportionate time of the behaviors (e.g., time of teacher talk versus student talk in a K–3 classroom). Instructions may also be given to combine tally- and duration-recording as in Figure 11.1.

Once the observational and coding time units are in place, a judgment needs to be made about how long to observe and during which parts of the day. If a study focuses on teachers' behaviors, the observer will sample their behaviors during all parts of the day and an abundance of data may be collected within a week. Note, however, that the high mental concentration necessary for observation may urge the observer to visit the classroom at various times over the course of several weeks rather than a whole day per visit; the goal may be to observe each time period (free play, snack, circle time, outside time, etc.) three times. If, on the other hand, a primary grade teacher's math instruction techniques are examined, the observer would collect data only during math time but on several different occasions.

The instrument is now ready for pilot testing so that its strengths and weaknesses may be explored. After adjustments are complete, the observer establishes inter-rater reliability (detailed in Chapter 12) in preparation for data collection in a real classroom.

Integration of Classroom Situations and Observation

Preschool Example.   Blocks and preschool go together like apple blossoms and spring, and of course, there are good reasons why blocks are a staple of early childhood centers. *The Block Book* edited by Elisabeth Hirsch (1990) will renew an appreciation of the many experiences blocks provide.

The presence of blocks in a classroom, however, does not guarantee that children use them and learn from them. Teachers are responsible for organizing blocks and making them accessible to children, providing additional interesting materials to use with blocks, and extending children's work with blocks. The potentials of blocks are endless, but skilled teachers are required to fulfill them.

A child care director bought a copy of *The Block Book* at a convention of the National Association for the Education of Young Children, read it on the trip home, and began wondering about the specific ways teachers interact with children in the block areas in her center. She sketched out a time sampling instrument (Figure 11.1) to help her systematically observe her staff's teaching strategies in the block area. Why did the director select time sampling as an observational method? You can answer this now; think about the frequency and type of behaviors to observe, and you will be on your way.

The director decided to use a sign system when selecting teacher behaviors to observe in the block area because she was not interested in tallying every possible behavior she might see. Rather, she was motivated to record those behaviors that support and extend children's block activities; her "other" category could serve as a catchall for unlisted behaviors. Therefore, she would mark a tally for each target behavior she saw during a 30-second observational time unit.

To collect some information about the duration of time teachers spent in and out of the block area, the director elected to circle the tally marks in the "not present in the block area" category when the teacher was not in the block area for all of the time unit. Thus, a circled tally mark would indicate that the teacher was not present in the block area for all 30 seconds of a time unit. A simple tally

Time Sampling of Teaching Strategies in the Block Area

Center:	Mesa Office Park Child Care	
Date:	11/15 to 11/17	Time: 9:30–10:30 a.m.
Observer:	Kemlyn	Free choice (7 centers available)
		Teacher: Evelyn, Dante, Mari
		Children: Twenty-four 4-year-olds

Instructions: Observe one teacher for 30 seconds and code for 30 seconds; rotate observations of teachers, and repeat throughout free-choice time. Mark tally for each behavior observed in the block area. Circle tally mark when teacher is "not present in block area" for an entire 30–second observational period.

Teacher / Behavior	Evelyn	Dante	Mari
Builds with child		⊤⊢⊤ ⊤⊢⊤ ⊤⊢⊤ ⊤⊢⊤ ⊤⊢⊤ IIII 29	
Offers materials		II 2	⊤⊢⊤ I 6
Encourages	II 2	⊤⊢⊤ ⊤⊢⊤ ⊤⊢⊤ I 16	⊤⊢⊤ ⊤⊢⊤ ⊤⊢⊤ ⊤⊢⊤ II 22

Figure 11.1.   Time sampling preschool example: Block area teaching.

would indicate that the teacher was not present in the block area for part of a 30-second observational time unit.

A few days after her return, the director told her child care teachers and assistants that she wanted to observe their block areas for the purposes of collecting information for future staff discussions. She observed three free-play periods

Behavior \ Teacher	Evelyn	Dante	Mari
Asks open questions	I 1	⟋⟋⟋⟋ III 8	⟋⟋⟋⟋ ⟋⟋⟋⟋ ⟋⟋⟋⟋ II 17
Models new ideas			
Observes	II 2		
Other	⟋⟋⟋⟋ ⟋⟋⟋⟋ IIII 14	III 3	I 1
Not present in block area	⓪⓪⓪⓪⓪⓪⓪⓪⓪⓪ ⓪⓪⓪⓪⓪⓪⓪⓪⓪⓪ ⓪⓪⓪⓪⓪⓪⓪⓪⓪⓪ ⓪⓪⓪⓪⓪⓪⓪⓪⓪⓪ ⓪⓪ II	⓪⓪⓪⓪⓪⓪⓪⓪⓪⓪ ⓪⓪⓪⓪⓪⓪⓪⓪⓪⓪ ⓪⓪⓪⓪⓪⓪⓪⓪⓪⓪	⓪⓪⓪⓪⓪⓪⓪⓪⓪⓪ ⓪⓪⓪⓪⓪⓪⓪⓪⓪⓪ ⓪⓪⓪⓪⓪⓪⓪⓪⓪⓪ ⓪⓪⓪⓪⓪⓪⓪⓪⓪⓪ ⟋⟋⟋⟋ ⟋⟋⟋⟋ III
	⓪ = 26 min	⓪ = 15 min	⓪ = 20 min

Comments:

Evelyn: "Other" — Lots of reminders about building rules, mediated minor quarrels, some empty praise ("How pretty!").

Dante: "What are you going to build next?"
"Where should I put my trade center?"

Mari: "I wonder if the little counting bears in the manipulative area would fit inside your 'teensy' houses."

Figure 11.1.   *(continued)*

in each classroom and compiled the data; Figure 11.1 presents the results from the 4-year-olds' room.

INTERPRETING THE DATA   The director, Kemlyn, observed one hour of free-choice time for 3 days. During each day, she rotated her observations from teacher to teacher and observed for 30 seconds and then coded for 30 seconds. Thus, in 60 total minutes of daily observation, she focused her attention on each of the three teachers for 20 minutes; of those 20 minutes, she observed for 10 minutes and coded for 10 minutes. Consequently, over the course of 3 days, she collected 30 minutes of data on each teacher.

Kemlyn was stunned to discover how infrequently children had the pleasure of a teacher's company in the well-used block area. During her 90 minutes of observation (30 minutes per teacher), she made circled tallies for 61 minutes. She was particularly dissatisfied with her observations of Evelyn, the head teacher. Evelyn knew that Kemlyn was observing the block area, and perhaps she felt uncomfortable about being observed and avoided the area (for 26 minutes). Perhaps her teaching skills in the block area are severely limited. It is also possible that as a head teacher she focuses on the children as a class rather than as individuals with unique strengths and interests. Whatever the reason, Kemlyn

Blocks offer children a wealth of experiences in the early childhood classroom.

realized that the head teacher in the 4-year-olds' classroom was not modeling effective teaching strategies in the block area.

On the other hand, Kemlyn was delighted to see Dante frequently down on the carpet building with the children. For example, on one day he was involved in planning and constructing an elaborate cityscape with two boys. He was generous with his encouragement and asked two open questions ("What are you going to build next?" and "Where should I build my trade center?"). Dante wrapped a block in aluminum foil to simulate reflective building materials and offered the roll of foil to the boys with the restriction that they could use it for only one building. The time sampling observations led Kemlyn to conclude that Dante enjoyed playing with the children but that his methods of extending children's activities in the block area were virtually nonexistent (he extended his own very well!). Kemlyn wanted Dante to be able to step back from his own involvement, observe the building in progress, and think about how he could best support the children's ideas. At present, the children were only following his lead.

Mari floated in and out of the block area during all three of Kemlyn's visits. Although she never stopped to build with a child or take a few moments for observation, she did ask open questions to inquire about what the children were doing, encourage their constructions, and offer additional materials (e.g., "I wonder if the little counting teddy bears in the manipulative area would fit inside your 'teensy' houses"). Mari seemed to support children intuitively in their activities, and Kemlyn hoped that her teaching skills would blossom with information and guidance.

Kemlyn was glad to have included the "other" and "not present in block area" categories; they helped her gain a broad picture of how the teachers spent their time. In the "comments" section, she recorded verbatim quotes and other specifics she wanted to recall. For example, she noted that most of Evelyn's "other" behaviors involved reminding children of the rules (e.g., height limits on buildings), mediating minor disputes about materials, and giving evaluative praise.

FOLLOW-THROUGH PLANS   The data from the 4-year-olds' classroom were fairly typical of the data Kemlyn collected in the other classrooms. Kemlyn speculated that there were two major factors behind teachers' inability to work effectively in the block areas at Mesa Children's Center:

1. *Teachers did not have the requisite knowledge to identify children's growth in the block area*. They did not know how building skills progress and what children might learn in the block area. Further, the teachers did not know how to interact with children in order to promote this growth.

2. *Teachers lacked observational skills*. Good observational skills should enable teachers to assess individual children's building interests and skills and then aid the formation of supportive strategies. In her center, however, Kemlyn observed that there were no systematic approaches to collecting information about children's growth in the block area. Kemlyn was pleased to observe all of the class-

rooms functioning rather smoothly. The lack of teacher time in the block area was not due to pressing management or supervisory concerns elsewhere.

Kemlyn decided to tackle the two parts of the block area problem through her biweekly staff meetings and continued education. For the first meeting, she called the local chapter of the National Association for the Education of Young Children to ask for a speaker recommendation. She requested a person who is knowledgeable about stages of block building and learning opportunities in the block area and who would be able to guide teachers in planning supportive teaching strategies. This meeting would provide much needed information for the teachers. Two weeks later, Kemlyn would follow up with a workshop on anecdotal record keeping as a means to begin the observational process. She made plans to videotape children working in the block area in each classroom; clips would provide the basis for integrating the speaker's information about block building into the classrooms and for practicing anecdotal records. Finally, Kemlyn contacted the early childhood education department at the local college for course information and began to consider how best to encourage her staff to continue professional training. Kemlyn enthusiastically anticipated collecting "new and improved" data on her time sampling instrument in 2 or 3 months.

Student Activity 11.2

Block Area Teaching Strategies in the Kindergarten, First-Grade, or Second-Grade Classroom

Pilot test the time sampling instrument on block area teaching strategies (Figure 11.1) in a kindergarten, first-grade, or second-grade classroom. Write down any modifications you would make. Remember, blocks are not the exclusive domain of children under age 5; their qualities extend far beyond.

Primary Grade Example.   A second-grade teacher, Jorge, was intrigued by his summer reading, *The Art of Teaching Writing* (Calkins, 1986), which sent his mind spinning with questions and ideas. He found the book well-stocked with thought-provoking commentary on the nourishment of children's writing, research and experience to back up the author's conclusions, and marvelous anecdotes selected from a wide diversity of children. Here are two jewels:

> Some [second graders] will quickly see that their lives are full of topics . . . "I think up topics all the time," Randalio explained to me. "If we have a beautiful Christmas tree, I think that I could write about it. If I'm playing car races with my friend, I think I could write about it. Choosing is the hard part." (p. 71)

If we can keep only one thing in mind—and I fail at this half the time—it is that we are teaching the writer and not the writing. If the piece of writing gets better but the writer has learned nothing that will help him or her another day on another piece, then the conference was a waste of everyone's time. It may have done more harm than good, for such conferences teach students to be dependent on us. (p. 120)[1]

Calkins advocates that the writing curriculum be driven by children and their individual interests, needs, strengths, and skill levels. Along with others, she contends that the art of teaching writing requires "high teacher input and high student input" (p. 163) to produce classrooms in which students can benefit from timely and supportive instruction without giving up their own excitement about writing. So although Calkins advocates that teachers should not be afraid to teach, she also cautions that they should "think carefully about the kinds of teacher input which will be helpful to our students" (p. 165).

After reading Calkins' book, Jorge was curious about the types of feedback he gives to his second graders. He formulated the observational question, "What types of input do I give to children during the writing process?" Jorge began to work on an observational instrument to evaluate his responses to students' writing.

First Jorge considered possible behaviors to observe during writing periods. Drawing on his reading and experience, he operationally defined the "teacher's input" in the following categories:

Teacher's Input

- *Listens*—Teacher listens attentively to a child. *Example:* "Mr. Mendoza, listen to the end of my story: 'Aren't you glad an ankylosaurus won't bother your plants?'" (Calkins believes that the strategy of listening helps children become more critical readers of their own writing.)

- *Encourages or praises descriptively*—Teacher is descriptive in his or her encouragement or praise so that the child understands the value of the writing. *Example:* "Your question at the end of your story gives the reader a connection to you. As your reader, I felt as if you were talking just to me."

- *Gives approval*—Teacher praises a child's writing while focusing on its worth, not its substance. *Example:* "What a neat idea!"

- *Gives information*—Teacher builds on a child's piece to help the child learn more about writing. *Example:* "I can see you had your reader in mind when you asked this question at the end of your story. Question-asking really gives the reader something to think about. A question can grab the reader's attention."

- *Suggests*—Teacher suggests a change or addition to the child's writing. *Example:* "Sometimes authors end their piece with a question to give the reader something to think about. Why don't you try it?"

---

[1] Reprinted by permission of Lucy McCormick Calkins: *The Art of Teaching Writing* (Heinemann Educational Books, Portsmouth, NH, 1986).

- *Directs*—Teacher directs a change or addition to the child's writing. *Example:* "This question at the end doesn't have much to do with your story. Either take it out or show more of a connection."
- *Corrects*—Teacher corrects a child's writing. *Example:* "This question at the end of your story needs a question mark."
- *Criticizes*—Teacher criticizes a child's writing. *Example:* "I think you forgot something at the very end of your story."
- *Asks question*—Teacher asks a child a question. *Example:* "What have you said so far in your piece?"
- *Answers question*—Teacher answers a child's question. *Example:* "Yes, it's fine to end a story with a question."

Jorge's reading also encouraged him to specify the categories of writing components on which a teacher might focus. A teacher's input might center around the content of the writing, the design (organization, flow) of the piece, or editing (paragraph structure, sentence formation/variety, word choice, or grammar and punctuation). Calkins encourages teachers to spend far more time focusing on the contents and designs of children's pieces than on editing. Jorge wanted his observational instrument to reflect these "focuses of teacher's attention" so that he could evaluate his priorities. Thus he generated a second set of categories and defined them as follows:

Focuses of Teacher's Attention
- *Content*—Teacher focuses on the subject matter of the child's writing. *Example:* "Your description of the frog on the ferris wheel makes me laugh!"
- *Design*—Teacher focuses on how the child has organized and shaped the piece (e.g., chronologically, thematically, snapshots), what the child emphasizes, and the pace of the piece. *Example:* "You told me so much about your dog by writing lots of little stories about her."
- *Editing*—Teacher focuses on the child's use of paragraphs, sentence structure, word choice, grammar, punctuation, or spelling. *Example:* "Listen to the suspenseful first sentence of your story: 'My most vived memore of my childhood was when I saw the misterys Zorf here is where my story begins.' I needed to pause and take a breath after 'Zorf.' You can put a period there to show your reader where the next sentence begins."

Next, Jorge began to think about how to put his observational instrument together. Knowing that teachers may speak continuously for short periods of time and realizing that an observer could not record or remember every statement, Jorge decided to construct a time sampling instrument to tally these rapidly occurring behaviors. He specified the time sampling units as 20 seconds for observation and 30 seconds for coding. The 20 seconds for observation would provide time to observe the content of the teacher's comments, and the 30 seconds for coding would allow time for accurate coding and movement around the classroom when there was difficulty in hearing.

To obtain a comprehensive view of the writing instruction methods in place within his classroom, Jorge planned to collect data during four writing lessons on different days. He designated the use of tallies on the recording sheet to document the frequency of each targeted teacher behavior. He rejected checks because he wanted to know more than if he just demonstrated a behavior once. He also rejected duration recording because of the impracticality of trying to record the duration of each statement; further, he was confident that the content of his messages to children, not the length of the messages, would be the key to his skills.

Jorge constructed the grid shown in Figure 11.2. He put the smaller set of categories (focuses of teacher's attention) along the top and the more numerous set (teacher input) down the side. Because there are many targeted behaviors, Jorge printed their definitions on an attached sheet for reference. He pilot tested the instrument in a colleague's class when his students were in music and found it to be satisfactory.

RECORDING PROCESS   Perhaps Jorge's obvious problem was that he would not be able to observe himself. He rejected using a tape recorder because he felt self-conscious on tape. Fortunately, Jorge is resourceful. He contacted the teacher-credentialing program at the area college and enlisted the help of a student, Faranak, in an observation class. Jorge explained the form and its purpose to Faranak, and during the primary recess, they observed a fourth-grade writing lesson and easily established inter-rater reliability. Faranak visited Jorge during four writing lessons and collected the data in Figure 11.2.

The observational method of time sampling can collect data on rapidly occurring behaviors—for example, a teacher's behaviors during a child's writing conference.

Time Sampling of Teacher's Behaviors During Writing Time

School/Grade: Longfellow Elementary/Second Grade

Dates:	3/6, 3/8, 3/13, 3/15	Time:	9:00–10:00 a.m.
Observer:	Faranak	Teacher:	Jorge
		Children:	28

Instructions: Observe teacher for 20 seconds and code for 30 seconds; repeat throughout writing period. Mark with a tally each teacher input in the appropriate box.

Focus of Teacher's Attention / Teacher Input	Content	Design	Editing	
Listens	///			3
Encourages/ praises descriptively	₸₸ ///	///	₸₸ ////	20
Gives approval	₸₸ /		////	10
Gives information	₸₸ ₸₸ ///		₸₸ ₸₸ ₸₸ /	29

Figure 11.2.   Time sampling primary grade example: Teaching writing.

INTERPRETING THE DATA   Together, Jorge and Faranak compiled the data from the four observations and totaled the rows and columns. Jorge was immediately critical of his emphasis on children's editing (42 inputs) rather than on the content of their writing (41) or the design of their pieces (3). He was also struck by how little he seemed to help children think about how they wanted to design their pieces, and he made no suggestions whatsoever. Although he was pleased to see that his encouragement outweighed his approval statements, he planned to reduce the latter even further. He could just hear himself murmuring, "Oh, good; that's very nice." Such empty praise gives children nothing to hold on to, nothing to help them appreciate the substantive qualities of their writing.

Focus of Teacher's Attention / Teacher Input	Content	Design	Editing	
Suggests				*0*
Directs			⌗ |||	*8*
Corrects				*0*
Criticizes				*0*
Asks question	||||		⌗	*9*
Answers question	⌗ ||			*7*
Comments:	*41*	*3*	*42*	

Figure 11.2.   *(continued)*

FOLLOW-THROUGH PLANS   Jorge's first plan is to have children read their stories more—to him and to each other in peer conferences. Thus, he will listen to children's stories and hear their underlying messages, hidden in intonation and expression and hesitation.

Frankly, Jorge needs to learn more about design issues. His students tend to write their stories chronologically, never varying from this pattern. At least Jorge wants to open their eyes to other possibilities. He is stimulated by Calkins' (1986) ideas:

> I hope teachers will continue to help children focus their topics and redefine and limit the boundaries of their subjects. . . . I also hope we will issue invitations to chil-

dren to experiment with the shapes and forms of writing. Our purpose should be not so much to help them produce well-ordered products but to invite them to try the groping, shaping, ordering activities that are such a part of writing. For young writers, "form" is more important as a verb than as a noun. (p. 145)[2]

Drawing on Calkins' book, Jorge plans to collect specific questions to ask and points to make on handy note cards. Jorge looks forward to inviting Faranak to check his progress in several months.

Your turn! Study the data in Figure 11.2 and plan some specifics in Jorge's quest to improve his teaching of writing. Remember that observational instruments are only good if they increase knowledge about teachers and children and lead the way toward developmental practices.

Student Activity 11.3 _____

Follow-Through Plans Based on a Time Sampling Instrument

Using the data in Figure 11.2, think about specific ways Jorge can improve his teaching of writing. Record your favorite three follow-through plans in the space below. You may wish to study box, row, or column totals.

Example: Encourage children to read their stories more frequently to Jorge and other children.

1.

2.

3.

Applications _____

Strengths and Limitations.   The time sampling observational method is adaptable to for various subjects (e.g., teachers or children, one or more than one) and can be an efficient and systematic means of observing rapidly occurring behaviors. A large number of observations can be collected in a short period of time with some confidence that the samples are representative. The data collected are

[2] Reprinted by permission of Lucy McCormick Calkins: *The Art of Teaching Writing* (Heinemann Educational Books, Portsmouth, NH, 1986).

quantitative and are therefore useful for computing, studying, and comparing frequencies. The observer can remain unobtrusive and does not interfere with the natural flow of events.

The limitations of time sampling revolve around the collection of quantitative data within predetermined units of time. The observer records frequencies but not qualities of events; therefore, the behaviors are not observed in context. Researchers further caution that time sampling may overestimate frequencies of behaviors and inaccurately record durations (Mann, Ten Have, Plunkett, & Meisels, 1991). The observer, as always, needs to match the information required with the most appropriate observational method and remember that the study of a topic through several observational windows is more complete than just through one.

Action Project 11.1 _____

Constructing a Time Sampling Form to Observe Stages of Children's Block Play

Appendix 1 in *The Block Book* (Hirsch, 1990) summarizes the stages of block building as described by Harriet Johnson:

Stage 1: Blocks are carried around, not used for construction. This applies to the very young child.

Stage 2: Building begins. Children make mostly rows, either horizontal (on the floor) or vertical (stacking). There is much repetition in this early block building.

Stage 3: Bridging: two blocks with a space between them, connected by a third block.

Stage 4: Enclosures: blocks placed in such a way that they enclose a space. (Bridging and enclosures are among the earliest "technical" building problems that children have to solve. They occur soon after a child begins to use blocks regularly.)

Stage 5: When facility with blocks is acquired, decorative patterns appear. Much symmetry can be observed. Buildings, generally, are not yet named.

Stage 6: Naming of structures for dramatic play begins. Before that, children may also have named their structures, but the names were not necessarily related to the function of the building.

Stage 7: Children's buildings often reproduce or symbolize actual structures they know, and there is a strong impulse towards dramatic play around the block structures. (pp. 101–104)

Construct a time sampling instrument to observe stages of children's block building. The tasks are as follows:

- State your specific observational question.
- Decide on labels or codes for each stage.
- Specify the observational and coding time units in your time sampling schedule.
- Determine how long you will observe during which portions of the day and over what period of time.
- Elect to use tallies or observe the durations of the behaviors. Consider the advantages and disadvantages of each.
- Construct a recording instrument; the following will get you started.

Stages of Block Building

Center:

Date: Time:

Observer: Teacher:

Definitions and Codes:

Instructions:

Stage / Child	Stage 1	Stage 2	Stage 3	Stage 4	Stage 5	Stage 6	Stage 7
Simon (3;1)							
Andre (3;8)							
And so on							

Comments:

Arrange to observe a preschool when children can use the block area. Test your instrument, and then answer the following questions:

- Were your definitions and codes clear, or were you unsure of how to code some behaviors?
- How did your sampling schedule of observational and coding time units work out?
- Do you need to make some adjustments? If so, describe.

Next, choose the data from two children to discuss. Begin by responding to the following questions:

- What stages of block building did each child demonstrate? Was one stage most descriptive of her or his play?
- If you were each child's teacher, how could you best support his or her block play?

Points to Remember

In this chapter the observational method of time sampling was introduced as a means of collecting representative samples of data on rapidly occurring behaviors. Examples demonstrated that time sampling is an appropriate means of investigating teachers' behaviors (e.g., interactions with preschool block builders and primary grade writers), and the preceding action project applied time sampling to the study of children's behaviors (e.g., stages of block building). Through the examination of children, teachers, and their interactions, observers can learn more about children's development, teachers' effectiveness, and the quality of the curriculum and the classroom environment. Time sampling lends itself to a quantitative analysis of data and is therefore best suited to topics in which the observer wants to compare frequencies.

Think About . . .

Think of a variety of classroom topics that may be of interest to you; recall in this chapter that a child care director was concerned about teachers' interactions with children in the block area and that a second-grade teacher wanted to evaluate his strategies of teaching writing. Consider topics regarding children's physical, cognitive, psychosocial, and creative development in the classroom. Also, consider topics regarding teachers' strategies, roles, and management approaches. Brainstorm several ideas you might wish to pursue. Now be selective; what one topic holds substantial interest for you?

CHAPTER 12

Designing Observational Instruments to Use in the Early Childhood Classroom

As an active reader of the previous chapters, you have probably raised some of your own questions about children and classroom processes—even without the prompt in the Chapter 11 Think About section. Because you will not always be able to rely on previously constructed instruments, you will need the observational tools and skills to respond to questions and problems that arise for you. This chapter is devoted to the process of designing and using an observational instrument to find answers to specific questions. Box 12.1 lists the steps in designing and using observational instruments.

Although the steps in Box 12.1 are presented in sequential order, observers may need to backtrack several times during the design process. For example, after specifying an observational question and doing some pilot testing, an observer may discover that the question is unclear and requires refinement. Later, after pilot testing the first draft of an instrument, the observer may need to rework some confusing definitions. Such backtracking is a valuable component of the design process; thoughtful observers frequently reevaluate previous work and remain open to productive adjustments.

The steps of designing an observational instrument are described in this chapter. Most terms are not defined because very little of the information is new. This chapter, rather, serves to synthesize the information presented in previous chapters. The steps may be applied to the design of a checklist, rating scale, tally

---

Box 12.1

Steps in Designing and Using Observational Instruments

1. Select an appropriate topic, and formulate an observational question.
2. Select an appropriate method of observation.
3. Research the topic in libraries and classrooms.
4. Identify clear, distinct categories.
   - Select a sign or category system, if appropriate.
   - Decide if codes are needed.
5. Design a recording form.
6. Pilot test the instrument.
7. Establish inter-rater reliability.
8. Collect data.
9. Analyze and present the data.
10. Interpret the data.
11. Formulate follow-through plans.

event sampling instrument, or time sampling instrument, but of course, an observer beginning with an observational question considers the workability of a greater variety of methods (i.e., running records, anecdotal records, and ABC narrative event sampling).

Select an Appropriate Topic, and Formulate an Observational Question

A serviceable observational topic is explicit and manageable rather than general and vague. For example, the term *teachers' attention-getting strategies* adequately suggests observable categories, whereas *imagination* does not. A productive technique of further narrowing the topic is to form a question to study. One question represents a workable initial focus and leads to a precise delineation of the specifics to be observed.

Attention-Getting Example.   Four observation students are interested in the topic of teachers' attention-getting strategies during transition times in the preschool classroom. They have noticed frequent problems when preschoolers are expected to change activities (e.g., from free-choice time to cleanup), and they hope to identify effective teaching strategies for these transitions. As a team, they devise a twofold observational question: how often do preschool teachers use various methods to capture the attention of children during transitions, and how effective are these methods? The observation students will investigate this question in three classrooms in only one preschool; therefore, they understand that their data will be applicable to specific classrooms but not to early childhood education in general.

Select an Appropriate Method of Observation

After formulating an observational question, the appropriate method of observation may be quickly apparent to observers, or they may need to evaluate the potential effectiveness of each method. This text presents the following methods:

- Running records
- Anecdotal records
- Checklists
- Rating scales
- ABC narrative event sampling
- Tally event sampling
- Time sampling

Observational questions may focus on children, teachers, programs, and environments. Each teacher has unique questions and concerns.

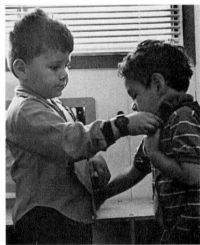

The choice is made on the basis of which method will best answer the observational question (Evertson & Green, 1986). In looking beyond an initial study, observers appreciate the benefits of viewing a question through a variety of observational lenses and may plan additional research drawing on other methods.

Attention-Getting Example.   The students review the observational methods they have studied. They quickly rule out the methods of running records, anecdotal records, and ABC narrative event sampling because these will not yield the quantitative data needed to answer their observational question. The students also reject checklists and rating scales; these methods will not produce the frequency data they want. The list of methods is effectively narrowed to tally event sampling and time sampling. A reassessment of their question helps them make the final choice. They know that transition times are not rapidly occurring events, so time sampling can be eliminated. The students want to be prepared and ready to observe transition times whenever they occur; tally event sampling is the observational method to choose.

Research the Topic in Libraries and Classrooms

Library research, classroom observation, and previous experience help identify the behaviors and characteristics that effectively answer an observational question.

Attention-Getting Example.   Each of the four observation students visits a different preschool classroom to observe transition times and record methods used by teachers to capture children's attention. Each also draws on personal experience with attention-getting strategies to add to the list. Then, as a group, they search the literature on early childhood education in their college library for additional attention-getting strategies they may have missed. Their efforts prove productive.

Identify Clear, Distinct Categories

Categories are clear and unambiguous, and they often must be defined. Depending on the scope of the focus, observers may choose a sign or category system, but in either case the categories must not overlap. Codes for categories may be specified to save space on the recording form.

Attention-Getting Example.   The observation students identify and define the following strategies for capturing children's attention:

Teacher's Attention-Getting Strategies
- *Chimes*—Teacher rings chimes or a bell.
- *Claps*—Teacher claps hands.

- *Lights*—Teacher turns lights off or off and on.
- *Directions/loud*—Teacher gives directions in a loud voice.
- *Directions/quiet*—Teacher gives directions in a quiet voice.
- *Questions/loud*—Teacher asks questions in a loud voice.
- *Questions/quiet*—Teacher asks questions in a quiet voice.
- *Counts*—Teacher counts aloud.
- *Raises hand*—Teacher raises hand in air.
- *Sings*—Teacher sings.
- *Music*—Teacher plays instrument or record/tape.

Because the students have either observed or researched the teaching strategies, they hope their list is complete. Nevertheless, they add an "other" category to provide the means to record additional, unanticipated strategies.

- *Other*—Teacher uses a different strategy.

Sharing observations from their exploratory classroom visits stimulates the students' interest in how teachers fit their attention-getting strategies to the ages of the children. Their initial hunch is that some strategies are more effective with younger children than with older children and vice versa. The students, who are interested in preschool classrooms, decide to include the following categories of age groups on their recording form; note how easily their form could be adapted for K–3 use by changing age groups to grades:

Age Groups
- *2- to 3-year-olds*—Classroom contains predominantly 2- to 3-year-olds.
- *3- to 4-year-olds*—Classroom contains predominantly 3- to 4-year-olds.
- *4- to 5-year-olds*—Classroom contains predominantly 4- to 5-year-olds.

The students are temporarily satisfied with the selection of categories to observe (teachers' attention-getting strategies and age groups).

Design a Recording Form

Recording forms begin with the heading used throughout this text; the heading includes the name of the center or school and grade, date, time of observation, observer, and person or persons being observed. Some forms require the definition of categories and/or instructions to the observer, and most observers appreciate space for relevant comments. The specific format of the remainder of the form must be compatible with the method used; for example, a checklist would

Preschool Teachers' Attention-Getting Strategies During Transition Times

Center:

Date: Time:

Observer: Teachers:

                                                  Children:

Event: Attention-getting strategies – Methods to gain others' attentiveness.

Instructions: Mark one tally in the appropriate box for each attention-getting strategy observed.

Age Group / Strategy	2- to 3-Year-Olds	3- to 4-Year-Olds	4- to 5-Year-Olds
Chimes			
Claps			
Lights			
Directions/loud			
Directions/quiet			
Questions/loud			
Questions/quiet			
Counts			
Raises hand			
Sings			
Music			
Other			
Comments:			

Figure 12.1.   Sample recording form design: Teachers' attention-getting strategies.

contain items preceded by check boxes whereas a time sampling instrument would be based on a grid recording sheet.

Attention-Getting Example.   The four observation students work together to design their recording form (see Figure 12.1).

Pilot Test the Instrument

Although an observational instrument may appear adequate on paper, the process of trying it out in a classroom is essential to assessing its workability. Taking time to make adjustments in and additions to an instrument streamlines the future collection of useful information.

Attention-Getting Example.   The observation students again venture into different preschool classrooms to try out their instrument and then meet to share feedback. They find their pilot testing experiences extremely valuable and constructive. Each student identifies effective aspects of the instrument as well as problem areas.

The major point of discussion surrounds the students' realization that their instrument does not provide the data to answer the second part of their observational question; their data do not reveal whether a particular teaching strategy was effective in getting the children's attention. One student reports observing a classroom in which the children ignored a teacher who gave directions in a loud voice. Everyone agrees that this effectiveness information is important to collect.

Further, there is some debate about whether all children must respond before a method is tallied; but the students agree that a tally should be earned if most of the children respond. The students also discuss how to code children responding the 3rd time a method is used, or the 4th, or the 10th! They concur that if a teacher has to use a method three times to get a response, the method is ineffective; therefore, they decide to code all ineffective responses together. The following are the codes for the children's responses (CR):

Children's Responses
- *CR-1*—Most children respond the first time the method is used.

- *CR-2*—Most children respond the second time the method is used.

- *CR-0*—The method is ineffective. Most children do not respond to the method at all or respond after the second time it is used.

The students' revised form may be seen in Figure 12.3.

Establish Inter-Rater Reliability

Observers and designers of instruments want to have confidence that observers agree about how to use the instrument; all observers collecting data with an instrument should produce consistent, accurate, dependable—in short, reliable—data (Kerlinger, 1986). To explore the agreement between observers when they observe the same setting at the same time, the percent agreement may be calculated to represent the level of *inter-rater reliability*. If the observers can demonstrate that their collected data are very similar, then they are ready to go out into various classrooms to observe on their own.

Agreement of at least 85% provides confidence in the accuracy of the data collected (Borg, 1987). If the instrument is not reliable between raters, the instrument itself may need adjustments or the observers may need further training. Typical causes of low inter-rater reliability are unclear categories or instructions and insufficient training of observers.

There are a few cautions about using percent agreement among observers as a measure of inter-rater reliability (Dooley, 1990). Sometimes instruments require observers to make such detailed distinctions among categories that agreement might be close but not exact. The percent agreement computation cannot take the degree of agreement into account. Other instruments have so few categories that high percentages can result by chance. Also, if the people being observed (e.g., teachers) are very similar, the percent agreement does not demonstrate the ability of the observers to make accurate judgments and distinctions. In these cases, a *correlation coefficient* is a better measure of inter-rater reliability than is percent agreement, but computation of a correlation coefficient is beyond the scope of this book. Estimating inter-rater reliability through the percent agreement calculation is sufficient for an initial evaluation of the clarity and effectiveness of observational instruments.

A straightforward formula to compute agreement between two observers ascertains their reliability (Boehm & Weinberg, 1987). The computational procedure is given in Figure 12.2 along with an analysis of some data. Columns for additional observers may be added on the right-hand side in order to compute the agreement among more than two observers, and rechecking the inter-rater reliability from time to time reevaluates observers' consistency over time.

Attention-Getting Example.   To begin the process of establishing inter-rater reliability, the observation students pair up to use their instrument for the first time. The data collected by two student observers in a classroom of 2- and 3-year-olds demonstrate the process of computing inter-rater reliability (see Figure 12.2).

The student observers' 78% agreement is unsatisfactory, and they discuss their use of the observation instrument with their instructor to identify possible problems. Catalina (Observer B) recognizes that her placement near the house area but away from the teacher did not facilitate diligent observation and further remarks that she was frequently distracted by the children's play. Here, the

Step	Category	Observer A (Mai)	Observer B (Catalina)
1. Record tallies in each category for Observers A and B.	Chimes (CR–1)	1	0
	Chimes (CR–2)	0	1
	Lights (CR–1)	3	3
	Directions/quiet (CR–1)	1	0
	Directions/quiet (CR–2)	2	2
	Questions/loud (CR–1)	1	1
	Questions/quiet (CR–2)	2	3
	Questions/quiet (CR–0)	1	0
	Sings (CR–2)	3	2
	Sings (CR–0)	4	3
2. Total the number of observations for A and B.	Total	18 +	15 = 33
3. Count the number of agreements in each category and total.	Chimes (CR–1)	0	
	Chimes (CR–2)	0	
	Lights (CR–1)	3	
	Directions/quiet (CR–1)	0	
	Directions/quiet (CR–2)	2	
	Questions/loud (CR–1)	1	
	Questions/quiet (CR–2)	2	
	Questions/quiet (CR–0)	0	
	Sings (CR–2)	2	
	Sings (CR–0)	3	
	Total	13	
4. Divide the total number of agreements by the total number of observations.		13 ÷ 33 = .39	
5. Multiply the quotient by the number of observers. This is the rate of agreement.		.38 × 2 = .78	
6. Multiply the rate of agreement by 100 to compute the percentage of agreement between observers.		.78 × 100 = 78%	

Figure 12.2.   Inter-rater reliability formula and computation.

causes of inadequate agreement lay with an observer—not the instrument. The two students try again and accomplish a 96% agreement. Having achieved competence and confidence in pairs, all four students meet in a child development laboratory school and observe from behind a one-way mirror to establish inter-rater reliability without disturbing the classroom at work. They achieve a reputable agreement of 94%.

Collect Data

A reasonable amount of data is collected to provide a fair sample of the behaviors being studied. Observers plan when during the classroom schedule to observe and how much data to collect. A clear observational question and a concise recording form facilitate data collection.

Attention-Getting Example.   The observation students want to observe entire preschool sessions (3 hours) in order to observe the teachers' attention-getting strategies during transition times accurately. They are faced, however, with myriad personal scheduling problems. As an alternative, each student arranges 3 hours of observation in each of the three classrooms. Over the course of 2 weeks, their scheduling allows the group to collect data in three classrooms (one at each age level) during all times of the session. This plan supplies a wealth of data because each student observes for a total of 9 hours. The data are compiled in Figure 12.3.

Analyze and Present the Data

The collected data may be analyzed through various procedures, and computer programs offer a multitude of shortcuts to this process. Observers select data analysis procedures that will provide information relevant to the observational question and present the data in a clear format. Then the observers will be able to interpret what the data mean for real children and teachers in real classrooms. An assortment of data analysis and presentation procedures is given below; not all of these procedures need to be used in any one observational study.

Frequencies.   Frequencies allow observers to answer questions about how often behaviors, events, or strategies occurred (e.g., How often did children quarrel during outside time? How often do children use materials for classification during free-play time?). To compute frequencies on a grid, row tallies or column tallies are simply added. Computing frequencies is a productive way to begin studying the data.

Preschool Teachers' Attention-Getting Strategies During Transition Times

Center: City View

Date: 4/15 to 4/26   Time: all morning sessions

Observers: Mai, Jesse, Catalina, Tritia   Teachers/   (2/3) Loidy/Noe
                                              Aides: (3/4) Tabitha/Zev
                                                          (4/5) Reggie/Meryl

                                              Children: approx. 16 per class

Event: Attention-getting strategies – Methods to gain others' attentiveness.
Instructions: Mark one tally in the appropriate box for each attention-getting strategy observed.

Age Group	2- to 3-Year-Olds			3- to 4-Year-Olds			4- to 5-Year-Olds		
Children Respond (CR) \ Strategy	1	2	0	1	2	0	1	2	0
Chimes	IIII	卌 IIII	卌 II (20)	卌 III 卌	卌 II 卌	II			
Claps		I	III					II	III
Lights	卌 卌 卌	卌 II 卌		卌 I 卌	卌 卌 卌 IIII	I			
Directions/loud	III	IIII	III	II	卌 III	IIII	卌 IIII	卌 III	卌 IIII
Directions/quiet	II	卌 I 卌	卌	III	卌 II	II			
Questions/loud	IIII	III	I	卌	卌 II 卌	III	卌 III	卌 卌	III
Questions/quiet	I	卌		II	卌 I				
Counts		I	III				III	卌 I	卌 I
Raises hand							卌 II	卌 I 卌	卌 卌
Sings	卌 I	IIII	I	卌 II	II	卌			
Music	卌 IIII	III	I	卌 I	卌 II 卌	IIII			
Other				I	II		I	卌	卌 I

47

Comments: 44   379

Figure 12.3.   Data: Teachers' attention-getting strategies during transition times.

ATTENTION-GETTING EXAMPLE   The observation students can easily determine how frequently each attention-getting strategy was used by computing the row totals and how quickly children in different age groups responded to these strategies by computing and comparing the column totals. Their recording form is somewhat complex because the students dealt with three age groups and three types of children's responses. At first, the numbers overwhelm the students, but they make sense of them by analyzing them one row and one column at a time.

Student Activity 12.1

Counting Frequencies of Observations

Working with the data presented in Figure 12.3, count the following frequencies. You may write the totals directly on the recording form.

1. *Attention-Getting Strategy Totals*—Count the total number of times each strategy was used by adding the tallies across each row. For example, add 4 + 9 + 7 + 13 + 12 + 2 to see that chimes were used 47 times in all classrooms.
2. *Children Respond (CR) Totals*—Count the total number of times the children in each age group responded the first time, the second time, or not at all or after the second time to attention-getting strategies by adding tallies down each column. For example, add 4 + 15 + 3 + 2 + 4 + 1 + 6 + 9 to note that the 2- and 3-year-olds responded 44 times the first time an attention-getting strategy was used.
3. *Strategy by Age Groups*—Count the total number of times a strategy was used in each age group. For example, add 4 + 9 + 7 to see that chimes were rung to get children's attention 20 times in the classroom of 2- and 3-year-olds. Write the *20* somewhere within these three squares.

Percentages.   Frequencies show the sheer magnitude of observed behaviors, but unlike percentages, frequencies do not lend themselves to easy comparisons. Observing that primary grade children make 53 visits to the science center over the course of a week does not produce useful information in isolation; however, computing the percentages of children's visits to all of the classroom areas begins to describe how the science center is used in the context of children's available choices. Percentages help put the data in perspective.

ATTENTION-GETTING EXAMPLE   Consider the category of attention-getting strategies. Suppose the student observers want to understand teachers' relative reliance on each of the strategies. Having already totaled the frequencies for the strategies, they divide each row total by the total number of observations (379)

Strategy	Frequency	Percentage
Chimes	47	12 (47 ÷ 379 × 100)
Claps	9	2
Lights	58	15
Directions/loud	50	13
Directions/quiet	30	8
Questions/loud	49	13
Questions/quiet	14	4
Counts	19	5
Raises hand	28	7
Sings	25	7
Music	35	9
Other	15	4
Total	379	

Figure 12.4.   Percentages of attention-getting strategies for all classrooms.

and multiply by 100 to compute the percentage. For example, the chime-ringing strategies were used 12% of the time by the teachers observed ($47 \div 379 \times 100 = .12 \times 100 = 12\%$). The percentages of attention-getting strategies are presented in Figure 12.4.

These percentages provide an overview of attention-getting strategies across all three age groups; the most common techniques were turning lights off and on, loud directions, loud questions, and ringing chimes. If the students combine the categories of singing (7%) and music (9%), however, they see that utilizing music in some way was the most common attention-getting strategy of all (16%).

The above percentages, which were computed from the combined data from all three classrooms, enable the students to make some general statements. Data analysis for individual classrooms, however, is necessary to provide individual teachers with the information they need to evaluate the prevalence and effectiveness of their own attention-getting strategies.

Student Activity 12.2 _____

Computing Percentages

Using the column totals, compute the percentages of how quickly children in various age groups responded to attention-getting strategies during transition times. For example, to compute the percentage of 2- and 3-year-olds responding the first time a strategy was used, divide the column total of first responses (44) by all responses by 2- and 3-year-olds (121) and multiply by 100. Fill in your calculations in the chart.

Percentages of Children's Responses (CR) by Age Group

Age Group	Frequency	Percentage
2- to 3-Year-Olds		
CR-1	44	36 (44 ÷ 121 × 100)
CR-2	53	
CR-0	24	
Total	121	
3- to 4-Year-Olds		
CR-1	49	32 (49 ÷ 151 × 100)
CR-2	79	
CR-0	23	
Total	151	
4- to 5-Year-Olds		
CR-1	28	26 (28 ÷ 107 × 100)
CR-2	42	
CR-0	37	
Total	107	

These calculations allow the students to specify how quickly children responded to attention-getting strategies in each classroom during transition times. For example, children in the classroom of 4- and 5-year-olds responded 26% of the time the first time a teacher used an attention-getting strategy, 39% of the time the second time the teacher used the strategy, and not at all or only after the second time 35% of the time. The students can also make comparisons across age groups. For example, older children paid less attention to the observed strategies than did younger children; the students noted the decline in CR-1 percentages from 36% in the classroom of 2- and 3-year-olds to 32% in the classroom of 3- and 4-year-olds to 26% in the classroom of 4- and 5-year-olds.

Student Activity 12.3 _____

Computing More Percentages

Continue working on the calculation of percentages; this time, compute the percentages of the various attention-getting strategies within each classroom. You have already computed the prerequisite frequencies in Student Activity 12.1. The calculations of these percentages will illuminate the relative reliance teachers of children of each age group placed on various attention-getting strategies. This activity will focus on the 2- and 3-year-olds' classroom, but you may certainly continue the computational process for the other two classrooms.

Percentages of Attention-Getting Strategies by Age Group

Age Group	Frequency	Percentage
2- to 3-Year-Olds		
Chimes	20	17 (20 ÷ 121 × 100)
Claps	4	3 (4 ÷ 121 × 100)
Lights	27	
Directions/loud	10	
Directions/quiet	18	
Questions/loud	8	
Questions/quiet	6	
Counts	4	
Raises hand	0	
Sings	11	
Music	13	
Other	0	
Total	121	

The observation students continue this process of computing the percentages of strategies used in the other classrooms to explore differences. They find, for example, that the teachers in the younger children's classrooms relied more on external signals (chimes, lights) than did the teachers of the 4- and 5-year-olds. This analysis could stimulate the teachers to talk about the comparative effectiveness of transition-time strategies in their classrooms.

Graphs and Tables.   Graphs and tables present data visually. Graphs represent a relation or relations in two dimensions (Kerlinger, 1986) and serve to highlight important results often embedded in the data on recording sheets. Tables also promote the clear presentation of information. A few options are reviewed below.

ATTENTION-GETTING EXAMPLE   The observation students want to dramatize the increasing noncompliance of children to teachers' attention-getting strategies as mentioned after Student Activity 12.2 and create the spike diagram depicted in Figure 12.5.

The graph visually represents the frequencies of children's responses to teachers' attention-getting strategies within each classroom. Keep in mind, however, that while frequencies report sheer numbers, they do not facilitate comparisons. The students want to be able to compare their data across classrooms and turn to the reporting of percentages.

Pie charts display percentages of data in sections of a circle. In Figure 12.6, three pie charts display the percentages of children's responses (CR) in each classroom to their teachers' attempts to get their attention; the teachers in each classroom can study the appropriate pie chart to evaluate their effectiveness. In

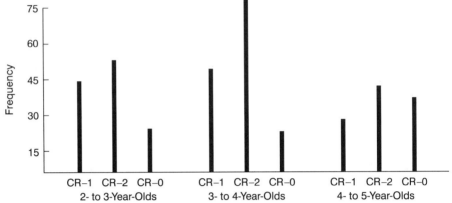

Figure 12.5.   Data presentation in a spike diagram.

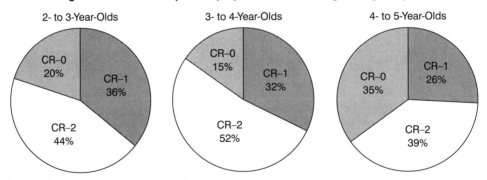

Figure 12.6.   Data presentation in pie charts.

addition, the pie charts may be compared. The students compare the percentages across classrooms and notice the teachers' increasing difficulty in capturing the children's attention as the children become older. These results lead to a profitable discussion of effective teaching strategies.

Data may also be effectively presented in tables. The observation students want to emphasize that loud directions were not nearly as effective as using music or lights in a classroom of 2- and 3-year-olds. They devise a table (Figure 12.7) and select the appropriate percentages to include.

The table presents data that show using music and lights to get the attention of 2- and 3-year-olds is more effective than giving directions in a loud voice.

Comparison of Effectiveness of Three Attention-Getting Strategies in a 2- to 3-Year-Old Classroom: Music, Lights, and Directions/Loud			
Children Respond (CR) Strategy	CR–1 (%)	CR–2 (%)	CR–0 (%)
Music*	63	29	8
Lights	56	44	0
Directions/loud	30	40	30

* The "sings" and "music" categories are combined.

Figure 12.7.   Percentages presented in a table.

Although the children never ignored the lights and rarely ignored music, they did ignore loud directions 30% of the time.

Conclusion.   The above methods of data analysis and presentation represent options for the observer; all need not be used. Additional methods might be helpful to some observers. For example, the analysis of some data may be enhanced by computing means (averages) or plotting changes in behaviors over time on a graph. Remember that the primary goals of data analysis and presentation are to use the data to answer the observational question and to present the information in clear, visual formats.

Interpret the Data

Uninterpreted data are of no use. After the data are collected, data interpretation is the next step in the process of designing and using an observational instrument.

Attention-Getting Example.   The observation students review their question: how often do preschool teachers use various methods to capture the attention of children during transitions, and how effective are these methods? The students focus on the first part of this question and compile the frequencies counted in Student Activity 12.1 to display in Figure 12.8.

The students examine the frequencies in the table and begin drawing specific conclusions. Do the same in Student Activity 12.4.

Frequencies of Teachers' Attention-Getting Strategies by Classroom			
Age Group / Strategy	2- to 3-Year-Olds	3- to 4-Year-Olds	4- to 5-Year-Olds
Chimes	20	27	0
Claps	4	0	5
Lights	27	31	0
Directions/loud	10	14	26
Directions/quiet	18	12	0
Questions/loud	8	20	21
Questions/quiet	6	8	0
Counts	4	0	15
Raises hand	0	0	28
Sings	11	14	0
Music	13	22	0
Other	0	3	12

Figure 12.8.   Frequency data presented in a table.

Student Activity 12.4

Interpreting the Data

Study the frequencies of teachers' attention-getting strategies in the three different classrooms (Figure 12.8). You may also like to draw from Student Activity 12.3 in which you computed the percentages of these frequencies in the classroom of 2- and 3-year-olds. State three conclusions based on the data. The following are examples:

• The teachers of the 2- and 3-year-olds relied mostly on lights (27), music (24), and chimes (20) to capture their students' attention during transitions.

- The teachers of the 4- and 5-year-olds used loud directions the most; teachers of the 2- and 3-year-olds used loud directions the least.

1.

2.

3.

Formulate Follow-Through Plans

Observation in the early childhood classroom provides information about children and teachers to evaluate current development and practices and to plan appropriate activities and adjustments. The detailing of follow-through plans is the culmination.

Attention-Getting Example.   The student observers are successful in offering the classroom teachers a wealth of clear and specific information about the use and effectiveness of their attention-getting strategies, and the teachers respond by planning some changes. For example, the teachers in the classroom of 4- and 5-year-olds want to reduce their reliance on loud directions, particularly after they checked the data in Figure 12.3 and realized how ineffective that strategy is.

Student Activity 12.5

Detailing Follow-Through Plans

Use the interpretations from Student Activity 12.4, and write appropriate follow-through plans for the classroom. For example, the teachers of the 4- and 5-year-olds plan to try some attention-getting strategies that they do not currently use. For the next week, they will ring chimes as a 5-minute warning before the end of free-choice time and sing to signal cleanup time.

1.

2.

3.

Action Project 12.1 _____

Designing and Using an Observational Instrument

Replicate the steps of designing an observational instrument as discussed in this chapter and exemplified by the four observation students interested in teachers' attention-getting strategies. Work with a few classmates and design a checklist, rating scale, tally event sampling instrument, or time sampling instrument to answer a specific question about children or classroom processes. Pilot test the completed instrument, and establish inter-rater reliability. Collect data in a classroom or classrooms (whichever is appropriate) to gain the experience of analyzing and interpreting real data. Finally, put the data to practical use and formulate follow-through plans. Be sure to refer to and follow all 11 steps presented in this chapter.

Points to Remember

Skilled observers have the freedom to select an observational question of personal interest and possible importance to a classroom in which they work. They have the tools and skills necessary to follow a question from the construction of an observational instrument through the creation of follow-through plans based on real data. The steps of this process, as detailed in this chapter, are as follows:

1. Select an appropriate topic, and formulate an observational question.
2. Select an appropriate method of observation.
3. Research the topic in libraries and classrooms.
4. Identify clear, distinct categories.
5. Design a recording form.
6. Pilot test the instrument.
7. Establish inter-rater reliability.
8. Collect data.
9. Analyze and present the data.
10. Interpret the data.
11. Formulate follow-through plans.

Think About . . .

When asked to think about an observational topic of interest, one student, Kirin, initially pursued a problem near and dear to her heart. As an aide in a preschool classroom, she encountered relentless problems in trying to get children's attention at the end of free-choice time. She wondered if the children didn't respect her because she was an aide or if she worked with exceptionally stubborn children. In any case, they seemed oblivious to her attempts to get their attention. Before Kirin got much of a start on her project, the head teacher rearranged the classroom and the transition problems disappeared! Was this a miracle, or might some classroom problems be solved by observing and evaluating the physical environment rather than by studying children's and teachers' behaviors in isolation? Think about this possibility in preparation for Chapter 13.

PART IV

Observing the Environment in the Early Childhood Classroom

Selecting Methods to Observe, Plan, and Enrich the Physical Environment

In simpler times when children attended one-room schoolhouses, teachers easily gained children's attention by tapping the ruler on the desk. From the discussion of teachers' attention-getting strategies in Chapter 12, it is apparent that modern schoolrooms are more diversified and teachers use many different methods to capture children's attention. The Chapter 12 Think About section asked you to look even further and consider whether such classroom problems could be solved by observing and evaluating the physical environment. For example, do teachers gain children's attention more easily in some room arrangements than in others? What are the potential attention-getting problems in a classroom with a 5-foot-tall room divider in the writing area and a book nook behind the piano? How could the placement of children's interest centers help or hinder the process? What impact does the physical environment actually have on teachers' ability to get the children's attention in a modern complex classroom? Some teachers endure unnecessary problems because they overlook the effect of the physical environment on teaching and learning. Once again, we gaze through the looking glass, but this time, the focus is on the setting itself.

This chapter, like Chapters 2 and 3, deviates from the format of the other chapters. The goal is to supply a knowledge base for environmental observation, an often overlooked but important observational subject. The first half of the chapter explores the major elements that produce a positive physical learning environment, both indoors and outdoors. The latter part of the chapter examines observational strategies used to assess the functional design of the physical setting. With a sound basis in observation, the teacher can assess how well the environmental elements support the educational process. If changes are warranted, the teacher can use the results of the observational data to make instructional decisions.

Indoor Environments

Recall a place in which you felt right at home the first moment you set foot inside. Perhaps it was a cafe or restaurant, your aunt's living room, your grandma's porch, a library corner, or a ski lodge. What did it look like? What made you feel so welcome?

Now think for a moment of places in which you did not feel comfortable—places that were cold, alienating, or unwelcoming. What did the uncomfortable rooms look like? What did those places have in common? Pause and identify specific factors that contributed to a sense of disfavor or uneasiness.

Our first reaction to a physical environment is emotional. Although the initial impression may be influenced by the purpose of the visit, the function of the facility, or the people within the space, the welcome feeling is fundamentally associated with the physical setting itself. All environments have the potential to enhance and support comfort levels.

Let's move the investigation into the early childhood classroom. Figure 13.1 illustrates portions of two different room arrangements for a specific preschool classroom. Take a moment to examine them. What observations can be made about these learning environments? What are your first impressions?

Now look more closely. Do the rooms welcome children's play? What can be said about the choice and locations of interest centers, boundaries, traffic flow, visual stimulation, accessibility of materials, equipment choice, and storage? Imagine a young child and then a teacher working and communicating in these two different arrangements.

The room arrangement in the top photograph in Figure 13.1 appears confusing and lacks an overall organizational plan utilizing area boundaries (e.g., block area, art area, manipulatives, etc.). Visualize this room with energetic children actively engaged in free play. Could a child move easily from one area to another?

Figure 13.1.   Two photographs of the same preschool classroom. *Top,* limited room arrangement; *bottom,* positive room arrangement.

Suppose two children were role-playing, dressed up in high heels and swishy dresses, cuddling their baby dolls wrapped in blankets. Imagine them clomping off to the grocery store. Using this scenario, three questions seem appropriate. Where could the market be? If the children could find an unoccupied area, could they get there without interfering with block builders, puzzle assemblers, or book readers? Also, where could a child go to be alone in this classroom? Some children arrive at school not quite awake and need a private wake-up place. Other children benefit from a few chosen moments away from groups, just as adults do.

Take a look at the visual stimuli in the top photograph in Figure 13.1. Young children working in this setting may be overstimulated by the wall clutter. If the photograph had been reproduced in color, you would see that the color scheme contributes to overstimulation by using bright and vibrant reds, blues, and yellows. Examine the textures and surfaces. Where is the softness?

On the other hand, the bottom photograph in Figure 13.1 represents the same room rearranged to create a physical environment supported by research findings—designed to enhance learning, provide comfort, and increase the usability of space. If Figure 13.1 were in color, one obvious change would be the room color; the room has been repainted peach with touches of green, thus giving a balance of warm and cool colors. Study the clear flow of the traffic pattern, the distinct separation of quiet and noisy areas, and the strategic placement of dividers. Take another glance. What can be said about the display of children's work, accessibility of materials, and additional touches of texture?

Compare the rooms presented in Figure 13.1. Is there a difference in coziness and emotional warmth? What growth opportunities for children are promoted by these two room arrangements? What evidence is there that the room at the bottom of Figure 13.1 was planned according to the developmental goals—to encourage children's autonomy, initiative, competence, exploration, discovery, cooperation, and interactions with others?

A well-planned environment is an effective teaching strategy. Many potential problems can be eliminated by room design. Consider possible arrangements that reflect the following management concerns: capturing children's attention, providing smooth transitions, decreasing opportunities for potential quarrels, and minimizing wandering.

Poysner (1983) advises us, "The physical environment of the classroom is a web of micro-variables, which are highly interrelated and in many instances interdependent. Each factor of the classroom environment can and should be examined independently" (p. 36). This chapter discusses three key indoor factors in detail: room arrangement, lighting, and color.

Room Arrangement.   Classrooms come in an assortment of sizes and shapes, and seldom are two arranged exactly alike; classroom organization has no prescribed formula. Instead, certain elements necessitate special consideration. This section of the chapter emphasizes room arrangement (how it is derived from program goals), the placement of interest centers, traffic patterns, and the location of materials and equipment; it also introduces the importance of warmth and texture.

Program Goals	Implications for Classroom Arrangements
To strengthen children's construction of knowledge	Materials are open-ended.
	Children have center choices.
	Items in classroom centers use classification for storage.
To enhance children's autonomy	Furniture is child-size. Drinking fountains, sinks, and toilets are child-height.
	Cubbies are labeled with names and pictures.
	Classroom areas are well defined and labeled.
	Materials are accessible for children's choice. Empty tables or work spaces are available for child-planned activities using self-chosen materials.
To foster children's natural curiosity	Traffic flow takes children past centers of possible interest.
	Center content changes to reflect the children's emerging interests.
	Materials can be manipulated and re-formed.
To support children's active learning through exploration and interaction with other children, adults, and concrete materials	Diverse materials are available, organized, labeled, and accessible to the children.
	There are places and spaces to work alone or with others.
	The arrangement allows for overflow and opportunities for conversations.
To recognize each child's importance and unique-ness. To allow children to develop at their own indi-vidual rates	Bulletin boards and room decorations are at the children's eye level. Wall decorations involve the children and display their work.
	Individual labeled cubbies are provided.
	Various materials and centers based on the children's developmental needs, cultural heritages, interests, and town/city/rural orientation are available.

Figure 13.2.   Foundations of preschool room arrangements.

Unless teachers are fortunate enough to build their own schools, options in room arrangements are restricted by the fixed space—the configuration of the room and the placement of the electrical outlets, plumbing, floor coverings, windows, and doors. Restrictions may also appear in available resources; however, most teachers become masters of the art of scrounging!

GOALS   As we explore program goals, recall the top photograph in Figure 13.1. Did the teacher in this classroom coordinate the design of the room arrangement with developmental principles and program goals? A *setting deprivation* (Weinstein, 1981) occurs when the program plan and the classroom environment

Program Goals	Implications for Classroom Arrangements
To allow children to be physically active	Adequate space is supplied in all areas and traffic paths.
To support whole-language and literacy development through the child's own experiences	Print-rich environment is supplied. Listening, writing, and reading centers; experience stories; dictated stories; poetry charts; typewriters; and computers are visible. Housekeeping includes cookbooks, note pads and pencils, telephone books, etc.
	Varied dramatic play props are provided.
	Centers have enough space for children to converse easily with each other.
To foster children's learning about the world by role playing and engaging in imaginative play	Dramatic play centers are present. Varied and abundant props are changed on the basis of children's interests.
To enhance children's creativity and appreciation of fine arts	Art, music, writing, and dramatic play materials are readily available and accessible.
	Pictures of artists, musicians, authors, and actors/actresses are displayed at child's eye level and frequently changed.
To provide bountiful experiences for children in representation, classification, problem solving, seriation, spatial relations, number associations, and time duration	Every interest center provides materials to stimulate cognitive development.

Figure 13.2.   *(continued).*

are in conflict. In contrast, room arrangements that are backed by developmental principles and congruent with school goals result in conducive learning conditions. Figure 13.2 gives a beginning list of program goals accompanied by implications for preschool classroom planning. While reading through the list, think about what additions, deletions, expansions, or revisions would be necessary for primary grade classrooms (e.g., *Program goal*—To assist children in understanding the meaning, as well as the mechanics of math. *Implication for classroom arrangements*—Variety of math manipulatives available at math center and on the children's resource shelf). If composing the K–3 list, you may want to refer to the Taylor and Vlastos (1988) guidelines for classroom designs.

Within the field of early childhood education, there are many variations in programs. Not all have the same developmental goals. All programs, however, are enhanced when the underlying principles and stated goals work together with the room arrangement; "the physical environment should give maximum support to the program goals" (Osmon, 1971, p. 35). In the next exercise, try your hand at identifying program goals and the corresponding implications for classroom arrangements.

Action Project 13.1

Program Goals and Classroom Implications

Choose two types of schools from the list below:

Private half-day preschool	Campus laboratory schools
Parent cooperative preschool	State-funded preschool
Head Start	All-day child care
Family day care	Montessori
Private primary (K–3)	Public primary (K–3)

Arrange visits to your two selections. Obtain a copy of each school's goals; perhaps an introductory brochure provides this information. Observe one class at each site for approximately 1/2 to 1 hour, and watch for environmental implications of the stated goals. Using the information from your observation, fill in the form below by stating two goals for each school and the corresponding implications.

Example:

School: Growing and Learning: Center for Early Childhood Development

Program type: Parent cooperative preschool

Goals	**Implications for Classroom Arrangements**
1. To provide an anti-bias curriculum	Pictures, books, and materials on walls or shelves reflect diversity and are free of stereotypes.
	Dramatic play areas reflect various sex-role options.

School:

Program type:

Goals	**Implications for Classroom Arrangements**
1.	
2.	

School:

Program type:

Goals	**Implications for Classroom Arrangements**
1.	
2.	

LAYOUT   "Classroom space works best for children who make their own choices when it is divided into distinct work areas" (Hohmann et al., 1979, p. 35). Using the center approach, Greenman (1988) identified three plans for room layouts: the *maze* (defined areas are separate and placed throughout the room—sides, corners, and middle area), the *perimeter strategy* (areas are placed around the outside with the central space left open for traffic access and overflow from centers), and the *central activity area strategy* (areas are grouped together in the center of the room with open space on the outer edges). One layout is not superior to another, and indeed many teachers design their own classroom layouts using modifications of these plans. A well-designed layout, however, will reflect the program goals and maximize the use of the "always too little" classroom space.

After the general layout has been chosen, the designation of specific centers within the classroom should follow "some guiding principle or principles, such as importance, frequency of use, functional relationships, or sequence of use" (McCormick & Ilgen, 1980, p. 355). Examples associated with the principle of functional relationships are shown below.

- Noisy areas are adjacent (e.g., blocks and housekeeping).
- Quiet areas are adjacent (e.g., independent reading and computers or manipulatives).
- Areas that flow into one another are adjacent (e.g., reading and science or writing and independent reading).
- Areas that need access to the sink or electrical outlets are adjacent (e.g., art and science or music and science).
- Areas that serve more than one purpose are placed accordingly (e.g., lunch tables used for manipulatives during free play).

TRAFFIC PATTERNS   Traffic patterns, which are planned concurrently with the location of areas, also affect the room arrangement design. "No matter what the strategy, clear pathways are essential" (Greenman, 1988, p. 142). While looking at the top photograph in Figure 13.1, you thought about examples of how working and communicating in group settings can present potential mobility problems. The skillful teacher plans traffic patterns that are clear to doorways and bathrooms and open to interest centers.

> Children need to know where they are going, how to get through a space, and the quickest way to an activity area. Hard-to-reach areas receive less use; paths that cut through an area interfere with "work in progress" and create distractions; and narrow pathways cause congestion. Therefore, create a network of pathways that connect activity areas. This network should also limit the access to areas; for instance, one entrance to an area. There should be no dead ends. . . . Define the edges of pathways with furniture and changes in floor covering. (Vergeront, 1987, p. 5)

Kudos go to teachers who map out the traffic flow between centers or desk areas and during cleanup and transitions. The final test, however, comes when the teacher bends down to see whether the planned traffic routes and spatial organization are visible from the child's eye level (Loughlin & Suina, 1982).

MATERIAL SELECTION AND EQUIPMENT LOCATION   Also adding to the room arrangement design are the selection and placement of materials within an area. The knowledgeable practitioner selects classroom materials that reflect the program goals, developmental appropriateness, and assessed individual needs and interests. For example, if the teacher wants to develop language and literacy competence, materials for writing and reading (paper and pencils/markers, magazines, cookbooks, typewriters, etc.) must be abundantly available in all areas of the room; visible and accessible materials stored together invite children's use.

In addition, teachers carefully select equitable representations of gender, culture, ethnic backgrounds, and abilities. "What isn't seen can be as powerful a contributor to attitudes as what is seen" (Derman-Sparks & A.B.C. Task Force, 1989). In order to build positive identity and self-esteem, special emphasis is given to classroom materials and equipment that represent the specific classroom population.

> If children come from diverse cultural backgrounds, we would encourage teachers to use graphics and materials reflecting those backgrounds. For instance, parents in the Southwest, with their unique multicultural heritage and architecture, have complained that classrooms and playgrounds there look no different from those in Wisconsin, Los Angeles, New York, or Chicago. In a predominantly black school, the child might better identify with black artists than with Renoir. The schools on Indian reservations should strongly reflect where they are instead of using Anglo-made and Anglo-looking materials. (Taylor & Vlastos, 1975, p. 32)

Ultimately, the selection of materials will determine if and where tables, floor space, or media equipment will be placed within the room arrangement.

Effective room arrangements take into consideration shelving and storage for materials. Children can exercise initiative and creativity when materials are labeled clearly, organized systematically, and accessed easily. Some pieces of equipment and furniture can double as natural dividers or boundaries when thoughtfully placed (see Figure 13.1).

Researchers at the University of Tennessee (De Long, Tegano, Moran III, Brickey, Morrow, & Howser, 1991) offer another dimension to consider in material location. These researchers compared children's attention spans and levels of play in relation to small and large spaces. The data indicated that in smaller places preschool children "enter complex forms of play more quickly, engage in complex play segments of longer duration and tend to spend a slightly greater percentage of their overall play time in complex play" (p. 8). For classrooms that are large and open, this study has serious and important implications. Smaller defined spaces can be created by the use of small rugs within an area; Montessori schools effectively use this principle. Dividers and different colored floor areas are other ways to create smaller spaces within an often overwhelmingly large setting. Figure 13.3 shows some excellent ways to create smaller spaces.

In addition to providing small places within large spaces, effective room arrangements offer private spaces for children to take a break from groups and the stimulation of active rooms or to be alone during emotional regrouping. Privacy can be created in small spaces "simply by stretching a makeshift canopy over an area and putting a pillow or a small rug on the floor" (Cherry, 1981, p. 42). Private spaces include areas just for one; a cardboard barrel with a cutaway

Figure 13.3.   Classroom use of small, defined spaces.

door and a decorated interior just big enough for a single child is a welcome addition to all-day child care settings. Niches under a desk or up in a small loft can serve the same purpose. A special designated private space can be a child's retreat where no one else can enter, not even the teacher.

WARMTH AND TEXTURE   Successful room arrangements depend on the introduction of warmth and textures. Recall the discussion early on in this chapter about comfortable and uncomfortable places. Did you identify two of the essential comfort qualities as variation in textures and softness?

Children applaud softness; it seems to go hand-in-hand with security. Visualize children plopping down on a lap, petting the classroom bunny, or taking their blankets to nap.

> A soft, responsive, physical environment reaches out to children. It helps children feel more secure, enabling them to venture out and explore the world, much like homes provide adults the haven from which they can face an often difficult and heartless world. (Greenman, 1988, p. 74)

In classrooms equipped with colorful, easy-care, durable plastic furniture, softness may be added by introducing a few small rugs, bean bag chairs, oversized floor pillows, cushions on some of the plastic chairs, and valances to windows.

Plants of various sizes can add softness within the early childhood classroom. Many teachers not only integrate plants in the science area but also place them here and there within the room, as we would do in our homes. The use of plants brings living things indoors, enhances the feeling of coziness, and adds an opportunity to experience responsibility. Extreme caution must be exercised when selecting plants for the classroom; some have poisonous leaves, bulbs, or other parts.

In discussions of classroom warmth, an important consideration is children's height in relationship to the ceiling. Tony Torrice, a San Francisco designer who specializes in children's environments, uses dados (a decorative wallpaper or paint border) to visually lower the ceiling to the children's level (Torrice & Logrippo, 1989). "The best way to determine placement of a dado is to estimate the average height of the children occupying the room. The dado should then be placed one adult-hand's measure above that height" (*Center Management* staff, 1990, p. 14).

Another idea in providing psychological warmth and security in the classroom setting is offered by Janina, a primary grade teacher. While doing home visits, she observes and listens attentively. She watches to identify what the child favors in her or his home that can be added to the classroom. This is a golden opportunity to say to the child, "You are special" and to make the child feel more secure. Perhaps she adds a book about the child's new pet or some long sheets of computer paper that the child loves to draw on at home. These simple ideas help create a magnetic ambience.

In summary, positive room arrangement reflects numerous factors. It requires the teacher to deliberate and articulate sound program goals and phi-

Ceilings appear lower and rooms become cozier when dado borders are applied.

losophy. Once that position is clearly defined, the following elements can be thoughtfully woven into the classroom design: center placement, traffic pattern plan, material and equipment location, and warmth and texture.

Lighting. "Lighting? That's not a teacher matter," early childhood educators may say. "Lighting is an architect's job; it's determined before teachers first walk into the classroom." This may be the case, but what if research revealed that lighting affects the learning process? Would it then become an educator's issue? Let's investigate how the amount and types of lighting influence the early childhood classroom.

If all the lights in houses or offices were uniform throughout, giving off the same amount of light no matter what room the occupant was in, visual comfort would not be met. In homes, focused bright lights are used on desks and night stands for doing paperwork and reading whereas a more diffused light can be placed on ceilings. How effectively is lighting used as a tool in the early childhood classroom? Are the lights bright in the areas requiring closeup work, such as the art, manipulative, and language areas? Or are they the same throughout—even in areas where less intensity is required (e.g., cubby, coat storage, or lunch area)?

In the past, school lighting systems supplied invariable bright light. Lighting was basically uniform throughout the entire school. As lighting becomes appreciated as a teaching tool, educators are looking to research to challenge this approach; two important facts have been disclosed. First, the amount of lighting needed for children's and teachers' comfortable vision depends on the number of windows as well as the color of and reflection from the walls, tops of tables, polished surfaces, ceilings, and mirrors (Dorsey, 1980; Greenman, 1988). Second, eye fatigue is reduced when light levels are responsive to the activities within the room and the action required by the activities (Ruud, 1978).

Greenman (1988) and Osmon (1971) propose an innovative idea for varying the classroom light levels. They suggest that children be allowed to participate in controlling the brightness of selected lighting.

> Imagine the sense of power and autonomy, as well as the opportunity for creativity, if some of the lighting were designed to allow children to control raising or lowering the light level or to determine the location of the light. (Greenman, 1988, p. 112)

A team of teachers experimented with this suggestion by adding a few battery-operated portable lamps for children's use in their afternoon preschool program. The lightweight lamps were 8 inches high and made of sturdy plastic; the tiny bulb was not exposed. After the teachers introduced the lamps, they observed how the children used them. Most often, the children toted the lamps inside the fabric tent house; once taken inside the tent house, the lamps stayed there. When the teachers questioned the children about the frequent use of the lamps in the tent, the children quickly explained that they needed light in there because it's so dark! In contrast, the children in the morning class (without access to the lamps), seldom entered the tent.

Design of the Times: Day Care (the report of the National Task Force on Day Care Interior Design, 1992) notes several environmental recommendations; two apply to lighting. "Storytelling in a lower lighting level can settle children down. It also signals to them a new activity is about to occur and renews their attention" (p. 52). The Task Force also recommended varying the lights—for example, adding soft spotlights to specific areas.

Lighting choice can also help create the softness and homeyness described in the section on room arrangement. Try adding a small incandescent lamp (most light bulbs) in the check-in area, entrance hall, or director/principal's office to create a sense of warmth. What about installing dimmer switches for varying the intensity of overhead lighting?

Now let's turn our attention to some new and exciting information on types of classroom lighting. Three kinds of lighting are used in classrooms: natural, incandescent, and fluorescent. Most classrooms are designed with windows to let in sunlight. Some elementary classrooms, however, have no windows; and all early childhood classrooms use some artificial light, even in sunny climates.

An alternative source of artificial light has been developed and is now available for home, school, and work use. It's called full-spectrum lighting and closely simulates natural light, "a major asset towards creating the perfect interior lighted environment" (Duro-Test, 1988, p. 1). Full-spectrum lighting can best be understood by comparing lighting sources using the *color rendering index* (*CRI*). This evaluative measure "was developed to describe how well colors (including the appearances of people) are rendered by artificial light sources compared to natural light" (Mahnke & Mahnke, 1987, p. 41). According to the specifications of the International Commission on Illumination, outdoor sunlight has a perfect CRI of 100, fluorescent full-spectrum light 91, fluorescent cool-white light 62, fluorescent warm-white light 56, and incandescent light about 40.

At the date of this publication, experiments comparing the effects of the various light sources conclude that lighting with a high CRI provides increased visual acuity, less fatigue, improved academic performance, increased attendance, and decreased hyperactivity (Grangaard, 1993; Hathaway, 1982; Hathaway, Hargreaves, Thompson, & Novitsky, 1992; Ott, 1982; Wohlfarth, 1983; Yizhong, 1984). Imagine assisting the learning process simply by changing the light bulb!

The Duro-Test Corporation has been researching full-spectrum lighting to identify more specific benefits for its utilization in educational settings. One of their significant findings is that:

> The ultraviolet spectrum from natural light or a Vita-Lite [a full-spectrum lighting source] causes optical brightener (used in papers and fabrics) to increase black and white contrast and color discrimination. Black and white tasks are more distinct and sharp. Colors appear more vivid. (1988, p. 2)

Ultraviolet light (which is present in full-spectrum lighting and sunlight) plays a key role in visual acuity, but because window glass filters out ultraviolet light (Mahnke & Mahnke, 1987), all classrooms, even ones with large windows, could benefit from full-spectrum lighting. The increased sharpness of black-and-white images has important implications. Print, after all, is black and white. Perhaps full-spectrum lighting may assist literacy development.

Educators can begin by adding full-spectrum lighting to specific rooms or changing the existing fluorescent lights to full-spectrum lights. Frank and Rudolf Mahnke (1987), environmental designers working in Europe and the United States, note that "full-spectrum lighting should be used in classrooms, libraries, and gymnasiums, but it is not particularly necessary in corridors" (p. 55).

Check the schools in your local area. Do they use full-spectrum lighting? If so, a short visit to these schools could provide additional awareness of its importance.

In conclusion, the early childhood educator can promote positive learning conditions by:

- Observing children's vision needs.
- Providing sufficient but not excessive lighting.
- Planning lighting systems with variation.
- Investigating the possible use of full-spectrum lighting.

Color.   Many have studied the psychological effects of color on people and their behavior (Birren, 1978; Grangaard, 1993; Hilbert, 1987; Torrice & Logrippo,

1989; Wohlfarth, 1981). Architects, educators, hospital administrators, surgeons, optometrists, beauticians, industrialists, and military personnel have applied these findings about color effects to their respective occupations. Scores of fascinating studies have been done on this topic; Hathaway (1982) reviewed several and summarized their results as follows:

- Color can alter perception of temperature, room size, weight, and the passage of time.
- Color can influence work speed, moods, pulse rate, blood pressure, muscle reactions, and psychomotor performance.
- Colors affect emotions; cool colors (blues and greens) initially relax whereas warm colors (reds and oranges) initially stimulate.

Wohlfarth (1981) investigated the effects of the combination of color and light on severely handicapped children. In Phase 1 of the study, the lighting was cool white fluorescent, the walls were orange and white, and the room accessories were primarily yellow with one blue table and two peach tables and gray chairs. In Phase 2, the lighting was full spectrum and the room color was relaxing shades of blue. When both phases were compared, the Phase 2 results showed fewer aggressive behaviors, a significant drop in blood pressure, and a decrease in nonattentive behaviors—indicating that children spent more time on task in the psychodynamically prescribed environment.

Derived from the work of Birren (1972, 1978, 1988), Figure 13.4 enables teachers to apply color associations to early childhood classroom environments. The main classroom color choice is the interior color scheme. Many classrooms boast primary colors, assuming that these vivid colors are pleasing to spirited young children. Birren (1972) warns, "when the colors chosen are too bright, the combinations too 'dramatic,' the effect may be wholly out of place, and the observer may actually be distracted from his tasks or made uncomfortable in his environment" (p. 256). Instead, designers and color consultants for young children's classrooms prefer yellow, peach, or pink tints (stimulating colors) for walls with accents in either green or blue shades (calming colors). The balance of warm and cool colors equalizes the emotional climate and avoids a specific mood. Ideally, the classroom colors blend well together and with the room rather than stand out on their own, grabbing the children's attention when they first enter the room. Birren (1972) also warns about neutral white shades for walls.

> Despite the fact that some lighting engineers may freely recommend white and off-white colors for working environments (to gain as much light as possible per watt consumed) the bright environment is quite objectionable. White walls may close the pupil opening, making seeing difficult, and set up annoying distractions. For the sake of 5 or 10 percent increase in lighting efficiency, there may be a drop of 25 percent or more in human efficiency. (pp. 246–247)

Think about visits to early childhood classrooms. Many have several different colors throughout each room as well as many items decorating the walls, sometimes in disarray. Together, these two elements can overstimulate and give a circus appearance, a case of visual pollution. Instead, the goal for interior spaces for

Color	Effect	Implications for Classroom
Red (rose/pink/maroon)	Draws attention, can alarm	Large, red butcher paper on table under new materials or new activity
		Background or letter color on a parent board or notice when a communicable disease or other information needs highlighting
		Background for emergency rules
	Stimulates activity	Motor development equipment, bean bags, and balls
		Light tints on interior walls
Orange (peach/salmon)	Stimulates activity	Motor development equipment
	Appetite appeal	Orange, peach, salmon for tablecloths or placemats
	Cheering	Light tints on interior walls
Brown	Stability	High climbing equipment or lofts; bases painted a deeper shade give appearance of more stability
Yellow	High visibility	The bathroom door or frame around it; yellow line on floor leading to bathroom in two-year-olds' classrooms
		Baskets for completed work in K–3 grades
	Stimulating	Light tints on interior walls
Green (blue-greens)	Reduces muscle tension	Water table, play dough
	Nature/growth	Science area accents
		Room accent color
Blue	Reduces weight perception (if pale in color)	Baskets for picking up blocks; bean bags
	Reduces time perception	Napping cots
	Calms	Water table, play dough
		Rug or cushions in reading corner
		Inside color of a "private space"
		Room accent color
White	Emotionally neutral	Ceiling for nondistraction

Figure 13.4. Color effects and their classroom implications.

Source: From *Color Psychology and Color Therapy* by Faber Birren, 1960. Copyright © 1951, 1960 by Faber Birren. Published by arrangement with Carol Publishing Group. A Citadel Press Book. Adapted by permission.

children is to reflect safety and comfort. This goal becomes increasingly important when you are planning for children who have been exposed to drugs or who have attention deficit disorder.

The influence of color in children's environments is just beginning to receive research attention. Watch for new information in this area. When reading works on the subject of the psychological effects of color, however, be sure to check the author's sources. Some books are not based on research and cannot support their claims.

Outdoor Environments

In some classrooms the teachers perceive their role indoors very differently from their role outdoors. These teachers spend their planning time focused on indoor activities. When they are outside, they act as safety supervisors. To support a child's developmental growth both indoors and outdoors, informed teachers view the outdoor physical setting as an extension of the indoor setting and act accordingly (Taylor & Vlastos, 1975). The following characteristics of the outdoor school environment are important:

- Outdoor arrangements welcome children. Landscaping enhances the developmental processes, such as hills for rolling and dirt or sand for digging. Surfaces are varied in texture and height. Some choices are wood, concrete, sand, grass, dirt, rubber, fabric, brick, or stones.

- Boundaries define specific areas. Traffic patterns are clear, safe, and direct.

- Teachers plan and set up interest areas daily. The areas are based on children's developmental needs and interests, space, staff, and weather conditions.

- Arrangements provide for a variety of interactions. Spaces are designed for playing in small groups, in pairs, or alone.

- Materials are available for different developmental levels. Examples are sandbox tools for emptying, filling, and pouring as well as tools that can be used for representing. On the primary grade playground, climbing bars of varying heights can be available.

The big difference between indoor and outdoor environments is the amount of opportunities, equipment, and planned experiences for children's gross motor development. Motor activities are emphasized in the outdoor environment because of the greater area per child. "For playgrounds to incorporate active motor play, 100 square feet per child is a reasonable playground minimum" (Greenman, 1988, p. 187). In contrast, recommended minimum space indoors is "about 35 square feet of free space per child" (National Association for the Education of Young Children, 1981, p. 1).

Outdoor play yards are usually furnished with permanent pieces of equipment that promote motor development. Preschools and kindergartens generally offer swings, climbers, a sandbox, a hard surface for tricycle riding, an empty table or two, and perhaps a slide. Grades 1 through 3 often have climbers, bars, slides, swings, and open spaces for group games in place of riding toys.

When evaluating the effectiveness of the outdoor environment, Kritchevsky and Prescott, with Walling (1977) suggest considering both the variety and the complexity of the play units. They define variety as "the number of different kinds of units" (p. 12) and complexity as "the extent to which [the play units] contain potential for active manipulation and alteration by children" (p. 11). Think about these two points and inspect the two playgrounds pictured in Figure 13.5.

Figure 13.5. Playgrounds. *Top,* preschool; *bottom,* primary grade.

Figure 13.5 presents photos of outdoor play arenas not yet set up for a particular day. Before bringing out additional activities or equipment, teachers informally assess the play space by considering the following:

- Equipment or space provisions for children to develop and practice the motor skills of running, hopping, jumping, climbing, balancing, throwing, and catching.
- A variety of climbing equipment (e.g., ropes, ladders, platforms, poles, or nets).
- Different levels of difficulty.
- Variations of specific kinds of equipment (e.g., tire swings, rope swings, or swings with seats).
- Enough equipment so children won't have long waits for turns. (Long waits rob children of the very purpose of outdoor time.)

Student Activity 13.1

Outdoor Gross Motor Opportunities

List additional equipment that could be added to the outdoor yards in Figure 13.5, and state a brief justification. Think about furthering children's development of agility, balance, strength, flexibility, and endurance of motor skills.

Example: A tire swing—provides variety and promotes the development of coordination and strength.

1.

2.

3.

4.

When evaluating a play yard, also appraise the open-endedness of the materials. Kritchevsky et al. (1977) define the flexibility of materials using the terms *simple, complex,* and *super.*

A super unit can be likened to a large sponge which soaks up a lot of water; it accommodates the most children at one time and holds their interest the longest. A complex unit is like a smaller sponge and ranks second in degree of interest and number of children it is likely to accommodate at one time. A simple unit is like a paper towel, indispensable but short lived, and ranks third. (p. 12)

Outdoor yards that supply only simple equipment often entice children to seek out the prized equipment (e.g., tricycles) on a preschool play yard. Several children will race to see who gets them first, and unless the teacher intervenes, a few children may spend the entire outside time cruising bike paths on shiny ped-aled vehicles. In this case, the environment limits the child's chance at well-rounded motor development and sets the stage for much quarreling.

In contrast, if the materials are open-ended and always accessible for children's use, children will design their own super units. Available materials that can be moved, manipulated, and changed feed developmental needs. Material flexibility and availability, however, make some teachers very nervous. They worry about safety as the children enthusiastically drag materials and build creations. Certainly, watchful supervision and occasional advisement is necessary as children solve problems and create. On the other hand, teachers must be alert to Greenman's (1988) caution about safety on playgrounds that have only simple play units. "Children will add risk and daring in order to cope with boredom. They will jump off inappropriate equipment like slide ladders, play chicken, and test the limits of people and things" (p. 188).

Outdoor play spaces can furnish children with opportunities to develop motor skills along with imagination, creativity, communication, and investigative skills. Figure 13.6 suggests some ideas to use in planning outdoor spaces that assist in the development of the preschool child. That figure is preceded by Student Activity 13.2, planning outside environments for the primary grade child.

Student Activity 13.2
Outdoor Primary Grade Experiences

Generate some ideas that could be used to augment the traditional K–3 playground. Use Figure 13.6 as a model.

Teacher-planned activities

1.

2.

3.

Available materials for child-initiated activities

1.

2.

3.

Teacher-Planned Activities—Individual or Small-Group Choice

- A sensory table with colored or plain water (Add funnels and sturdy plastic containers of various sizes. Change the contents on other days to flour or cornstarch. Or make the water soapy and bring out the dolls and plastic housekeeping dishes that need washing.)
- Small plastic buckets of water and large paintbrushes for wall or sidewalk painting
- A blanket under a shade tree and a basket of manipulatives or books brought from the inside
- A few buckets of water and child-size plastic shovels and plastic containers in the sandbox
- Supervised construction table with wood scraps and tools for hammering and sawing (Add glue and painting equipment. Add Styrofoam or wood shaving pieces to glue.)
- Easel painting
- Obstacle course
- A garden
- Props—various plastic hats; traffic signs and cones for the bike path; small plastic people, dinosaurs, or animals for the sand area
- Games—follow the leader, jump rope, ring toss

Available Materials for Child-Initiated Activities

- Balls and bean bags
- Riding toys—trikes, two-wheelers, wagons, scooters, taxis
- Large building blocks
- Cardboard boxes or plastic crates of various sizes
- Child-size wheelbarrows
- Sheets or blankets, clothespins, and rope for tent making or imaginative play
- Buckets and containers
- Small shovels and large, sturdy spoons

Figure 13.6. Outdoor preschool experiences—Weather permitting!

This section would not be complete without a discussion of the drinking fountain. Some states have licensing regulations requiring child care centers to have drinking water readily available to young children. Permitting each child to get drinks as needed is preferred to asking the child to wait and then making one long line to get a drink before going inside (recall information on impulse control in Chapter 2). Allowing children free access encourages autonomy and independence as well as good health practices.

Observing the Physical Environment

Up to this point, the details of the major physical elements of the classroom environment have been examined. The importance of various factors in promoting positive learning conditions has been discussed. Now the focus of the chapter shifts to observation strategies.

Rating scales, checklists, tally event sampling, and time samplings are the observational methods most commonly used for environmental assessments. In previous chapters you have read about these methods and have already had some practice assessing environments. Using your experiences and the information in this chapter, think for a moment about possible topics for observation in the physical environment and appropriate methods to use in assessment; then proceed to Student Activity 13.3. Be aware that rating scales and checklists look directly at environmental items whereas tally and time samplings look indirectly at environments, assessing how people use the environment.

Student Activity 13.3
Environmental Observation Topics

This activity has three parts. First, list four possible topics that early childhood teachers could observe either outside or inside. Second, after each topic form a specific observational question. Third, suggest an observational method that could be used to collect information systematically to answer the question.

Topic	**Question**	**Method**
Example:		
Traffic paths	Which traffic paths are used most often and are they congested or free flowing?	Tally event or time sampling

1.

2.

3.

4.

Observational data assist teachers in selecting materials and planning activities.

Preschool Example.   An early childhood art professor enlisted her college students in a variety of class projects. One project, in conjunction with a local preschool, was to construct a checklist of art materials and make recommendations to the school staff for yearly art supply orders and requests for donations.

Five students eagerly chose this project option. The college students responsibly constructed an art checklist utilizing the guidelines in Chapter 6 and the knowledge gained in their college creative art class. As they selected items to put on the list, they were mindful to choose items that were not so small that children could swallow them or put them in their ears or noses. Figure 13.7 is the students' form and the results of their art inventory.

The Cypress Center staff felt fortunate to have the input from the college students. The teachers were, however, surprised to see that they had not considered three-dimensional supplies prior to the inventory check using a designed list. Coincidentally, the school had few materials for three-dimensional art; the teachers were acutely embarrassed to admit that they had overlooked the importance of obtaining and offering three-dimensional materials for the development of spatial relations and increased opportunities for creative expression. The teachers had never had an organized inventory appraisal form. In fact, they had never used systematic observations to look at the physical environment. Instead they had used the "Mother Hubbard" approach: look in and see what is or isn't

Art Materials Inventory

School: Cypress Center
Date: 5/15   Time: 4:00 p.m.
Observers: Star, Lalaynia, Clark, Mihoko, Buffy   Child: N/A

Background Materials:
- ☑ Construction paper
- ☑ Poster board/cardboard
- ☐ Butcher paper
- ☑ Finger paint paper
- ☑ Watercolor paper
- ☑ Newsprint paper
- ☑ Fabric
- ☐ Aluminum foil
- ☐ Paper plates
- ☑ Clear ConTact
- ☑ Tissue paper
- ☑ Tagboard
- ☐ Computer paper*
- ☐ Magazines*

Drawing Materials:
- ☑ Crayons
- ☑ Tempera paints
- ☑ Watercolors
- ☑ Fat chalks
- ☑ Markers
- ☐ Shaving cream
- ☑ Finger paints

Tools for Detaching: *only*
- ☑ Scissors (left- and (right-handed))

Items for Fastening:
- ☑ Glue and paste
- ☑ Hole punch and yarn
- ☑ Tape/Scotch or masking —   *Just for teacher's use*
- ☐ Gummed labels or stickers
- ☐ Pipe cleaners or thin wire
- ☑ Large plastic needles/thin yarn
- ☑ Clear ConTact

Tools for Painting:
- ☑ $\frac{3}{4}$- and 1-inch paintbrushes
- ☑ Watercolor brushes
- ☐ Toothbrushes
- ☑ Dabbers (Cotton wrapped in fabric and attached to tongue depressor and rubber bands)
- ☑ Cotton swabs
- ☑ Feather dusters/feathers
- ☑ Small cars
- ☑ Roll-on deodorant bottles with pop-off lids*
- ☑ Golf balls*

Figure 13.7.   Inventory checklist *(continued on next page).*

Collage Box Items:

- ☑ Fabric pieces*
- ☑ Paper scraps*
- ☑ Corrugated cardboard scraps*
- ☐ Dried flowers*
- ☑ Wallpaper samples*
- ☑ (Ribbons,) yarn, and used gift wrappings*   *only*
- ☐ Lace and leather scraps*
- ☑ Sawdust*
- ☐ Carpet and padding scraps*
- ☑ Assorted donations!*

Three-Dimensional Items:

- ☐ Craft sticks
- ☐ Gummed paper strips
- ☐ Clay and plasticine
- ☐ Wood scraps*
- ☑ Styrofoam pieces (all sizes)*
- ☐ Nature items (branches, pinecones, etc.)*
- ☑ Play dough
- ☐ Cardboard cylinder tubes (all sizes)*
- ☐ Small cardboard boxes*
- ☐ Cotton balls
- ☐ Braid and fabric trims*
- ☐ Wooden or plastic spools (all sizes)*
- ☐ Broom straws/drinking straws*
- ☐ Bottle caps*
- ☐ Wood shavings*
- ☐ Rocks*
- ☐ Empty food or yogurt containers, berry baskets*

Tools for Printing:

- ☑ Gadgets*
- ☑ Sponges*
- ☑ Items of different shapes*
- ☐ Blocks with weather stripping designs

Other:

- ☑ Easels
- ☑ Smocks
- ☑ Drying area or rack

*Donated or free materials

Comments: Organizing the supply cupboard by the categories presented above would expedite restocking. Check the usability of markers. No skin-tone crayons, markers, or paints are available.

Figure 13.7.   Inventory checklist *(continued)*.

left. The teachers were grateful to have a checklist that would ensure a well-rounded collection of art materials that contribute to a comprehensive developmental program.

Primary Grade Example.   It is lunchtime at Dundonald Elementary. Two early childhood teachers are discussing how the classroom setup relates to the teacher's goals. Both of them agree that the classroom arrangement can foster individual initiative in the learning process. After much exchange the teachers seemed satisfied to conclude that the degree to which a student's initiative is fostered varies with the activity.

Viktor returns to his classroom and informally assesses the physical environment; he wonders whether his perception about how and when he supports students' initiative could be confirmed by observational data. He talks to Frank, the principal, about his concern. A few days later Frank shares a rating scale instrument entitled Observable Classroom Climate Profile (Smoot, 1972) he dug out of his file from a college class. Viktor and Frank look over the rating scale (see Figure 13.8) and decide that it will collect the data Viktor seeks. They make some minor changes and choose three applicable components for their instrument. Frank agrees to administer their rating scale (Figure 13.8 and 13.9) during four different class activities.

The results of the three rating scales administered on February 26, 27, and 28 are summarized for data analysis in the spike diagram (Figure 13.10).

When Frank shares with Viktor the collected data and the analysis, Viktor carefully analyzes them and is gratified by the 4's and 5's in work areas and resources. Because of his use of thematic units and cooperative learning groups, his perceptions were accurate in these areas. Viktor is, however, taken aback at the wall usage! After studying the codes he realizes he has been using the wall space as room decoration; he has not thought of it as an opportunity to promote initiative.

On the following day Viktor takes his instrument results back to the lunchroom and brainstorms with other teachers about the use of wall space. He spends a few days thinking about the teachers' suggestions. Then he asks his children for their ideas and shares some of the other teachers' suggestions. Together, he and the class decide to divide the walls into subject areas, using their current theme, *Environmental Awareness*, to tie it all together. The children sign up for groups to work on the three walls. The fourth wall is broken up by a door and windows but left enough space for Viktor to post important announcements. On Friday afternoon Viktor assists each group of children in the design of their wall area. Before leaving school later that day, he reassesses the physical environment. He smiles as he looks at the math wall. That group had diagonally hung a long piece of yellow butcher paper from ceiling to floor with large outlines of various modes of transportation. The caption above it read "PUT YOUR BEST WORK HERE, NEATLY!"

Code Definitions

The following category descriptors are placed on a separate sheet.

Work Areas
1. One assigned desk for each child; child does not leave desk without teacher's permission.
2. General learning centers that children are programmed through; children move at teacher's direction.
3. Desk and work areas; children do daily lessons at an assigned desk and can move to interest centers or chosen task when the daily lesson is finished.
4. Children have a choice as to where they want to sit and work; they can move freely but must do the daily assigned lesson.
5. General work areas and interest centers; children move freely as their chosen task requires.

Wall Usage
1. Everything on the wall is produced and controlled by the teacher.
2. More than half of the material on the wall space is produced and controlled by the teacher.
3. Teacher produces and controls half of material on the wall space; half of the wall space is produced and controlled by the children.
4. More than half of the material on the wall space is produced and controlled by the children.
5. There is evidence that the wall space belongs mostly to the children. At least 80% is produced and controlled by the children.

Supplemental Classroom Resources: dictionaries, math manipulatives, encyclopedias, information books, science tools, art materials, etc.
1. No supplemental resources are supplied by the school for the classroom.
2. Teachers supply supplemental resources if they assess a need for the child.
3. Supplemental classroom resources are available to a child if the child requests specific materials from the teacher.
4. Teacher-selected supplemental resources are supplied for the children's use at specific times of the day.
5. Classroom resource materials are easy to get to and available on a help-yourself basis for each child.

Figure 13.8.   Fostering student initiative through classroom setup: Rating scale definitions.

Revised Observable Classroom-Climate Profile

School: Dundonald Elementary/Second Grade

Dates: 2/26   Times: Language Arts — 9:00 a.m.

                 2/27   Math — 10:00 a.m.

                 2/27   Social Studies — 1:30 p.m.

                 2/28   Science — 1:30 p.m.

Observer: Frank   Teacher: Viktor, Room 9

                                                   Children: 31

Instructions: Rate each item on the scale by circling the appropriate number.

Work Areas

1   2   3   4   5

Wall Usage

1   2   3   4   5

Supplemental Resources

1   2   3   4   5

Figure 13.9.   Fostering student initiative through classroom setup: Classroom profile form.

Revised Classroom-Climate Profile Results

LA = Language Arts   M = Math   SS = Social Studies   S = Science

Figure 13.10.   Rating scale results.

Outdoor Rating Scale

Center or School/Grade:

Date: Time:

Observer: Teachers:

                                               Children:

Playground Rating System (Ages 3–8)

Section I. What does the playground contain?

Rate each item for degree of existence and function on a scale of 0–5 (0 = not existent; 1 = some elements exist but not functional; 2 = poor; 3 = average; 4 = good; 5 = all elements exist, excellent (function).

___ 1. A hard-surfaced area with space for games and a network of paths for wheeled toys.

___ 2. Sand and sand play equipment.

___ 3. Dramatic play structures (playhouse, car or boat with complementary equipment, such as adjacent sand and water and housekeeping equipment).

___ 4. A superstructure with room for many children at a time and with a variety of challenges and exercise options (entries, exits and levels).

___ 5. Mound(s) of earth for climbing and digging.

___ 6. Trees and natural areas for shade, nature study and play.

___ 7. Zoning to provide continuous challenge; linkage of areas, functional physical boundaries, vertical and horizontal treatment (hills and valleys).

___ 8. Water play areas, with fountains, pools and sprinklers.

___ 9. Construction area with junk materials such as tires, crates, planks, boards, bricks and nails; tools should be provided and demolition and construction allowed.

___10. An old (or built) vehicle, airplane, boat, car that has been made safe, but not stripped of its play value (should be changed or relocated after a period of time to renew interest).

Figure 13.11.   Outdoor rating scale.

Source: From Complete Playground Rating System in *Play and Playscapes*, by Joe L. Frost, 1992, Albany, New York: Delmar. Reprinted by permission of Joe L. Frost.

___11. Equipment for active play: a slide with a large platform at the top (slide may be built into side of a hill); swings that can be used safely in a variety of ways (soft material for seats); climbing trees (mature dead trees that are horizontally positioned); climbing nets.

___12. A large soft area (grass, bark mulch, etc.) for organized games.

___13. Small semi-private spaces at the child's own scale: tunnels, niches, play-houses, hiding places.

___14. Fences, gates, walls and windows that provide security for young children and are adaptable for learning/play.

___15. A garden and flowers located so that they are protected from play, but with easy access for children to tend them. Gardening tools are available.

___16. Provisions for the housing of pets. Pets and supplies are available.

___17. A transitional space from outdoors to indoors. This could be a covered play area immediately adjoining the playroom which will protect the children from the sun and rain and extend indoor activities to the outside.

___18. Adequate protected storage for outdoor play equipment, tools for construc-tion and garden areas, and maintenance tools. Storage can be separate: wheeled toys stored near the wheeled vehicle track; sand equipment near the sand enclosure; tools near the construction area. Storage can be in separate structures next to the building or fence. Storage should aid in chil-dren's picking-up and putting equipment away at the end of each play period.

___19. Easy access from outdoor play areas to coats, toilets and drinking foun-tains. Shaded areas and benches for adults and children to sit within the outdoor play area.

___20. Tables and support materials for group activities (art, reading, etc.).

Figure 13.11.   *(continued).*

Action Project 13.2 _____

Outdoor Environment Assessment

Assess the outside yard of a preschool or kindergarten using Section I of the *Playground Rating System* (Frost, 1992) shown in Figure 13.11. Utilizing your observation and the information in this chapter on outdoor environments, make suggestions for improvement. State your rationale for suggestions. (Note: In

Chapter 7, three types of rating scale designs were discussed. This rating scale provides another possible configuration.)

Suggestions: **Rationale:**

1.

2.

3.

4.

Points to Remember

The physical environment may enhance or hinder the learning process. Significant factors to consider, observe, and assess in the indoor classroom setting are room arrangement, color, and lighting. Important outdoor elements are yard arrangement, gross motor development opportunities, and equipment versatility.

Diligent environment planning, based on developmental principles and class goals, is necessary for the outdoor and indoor settings. Various observational methods can assist the teacher in evaluating the physical components. On the basis of data obtained through observations, the teacher can change or rearrange equipment, materials, and centers to best serve the growing needs and interests of children in the classroom.

Think About . . .

In this book, we have covered the following topics: guidelines for observation, highlights of child development, seven observational methods accompanied by classroom examples and corresponding teaching strategies, instrument design and data analysis, and classroom environmental observations. As you now stand before the looking glass, what do you see?

PART V

Observing Clearly

CHAPTER 14

Through the Looking Glass

LISTEN TO THE MUSTN'TS
Listen to the MUSTN'TS, child
Listen to the DON'TS
Listen to the SHOULDN'TS
The IMPOSSIBLES, the WON'TS
Listen to the NEVER HAVES
Then listen close to me—
Anything can happen, child,
ANYTHING can be.[1]

Marian Wright Edelman, a tireless advocate for children, draws on this poem for inspiration: "Focus on what you have, not what you don't have; on what you can do rather than what you cannot do" (1992, p. 102). She urges us all to have confidence that we can make a difference. Let this message ring true for the educators of young children who practice observation in their classroom. Let each teacher strive to be remarkable for all the Annies and Songs and Blancas of the world.

So we come to the end of this book and rely on the final chapter to complete and summarize the journey begun in Chapter 1. Our passage followed the introduction of highlights of development during the preschool and primary grade years, methods to observe the development of individual children, and guidelines to plan effective child portfolios and parent conferences. The route then turned to methods to observe children and teachers at work in early childhood classrooms and included the processes of selecting and designing observational instruments and enriching environments through observation. As you now stand before the observational looking glass, appreciate your sharp and developed vision.

- Your study of developmental growth indicators and observational methods has strengthened your knowledge of *what* to observe in the early childhood classroom and *how* to observe.

- You understand that observational methods are varied and require specific procedures; choice is driven by the purpose of your inquiry. All methods are equally applicable for preschool and primary grade use.

- Your observations of children, teachers, interactions, programs, and environments are recorded as objectively as possible.

- You are prepared to select a portfolio system and plan parent conferences that enrich home/school partnerships.

- Your practical experience has led to proficient applications of the various methods introduced in this text and resulted in satisfying results.

- You understand the processes of designing instruments and analyzing and presenting data that allow teachers to find the answers to specific observational questions.

[1] From *Where the Sidewalk Ends* by Shel Silverstein, 1974, New York: Harper & Row. Copyright © 1974 by Evil Eye Music, Inc. Selection reprinted by permission of HarperCollins Publishers.

- Above all, your practice in applications has prepared you to plan for each child's unique growth based on sound observations.

    Your well-earned observational skills offer a broad perspective of children, teachers, and the early childhood classroom not readily available to the untrained eye. You will enter a preschool or primary grade classroom armed with the ability to recognize and meet each child's individual developmental needs by applying observational methods and planning appropriately. You will be able to examine specific classroom questions and concerns using instruments that you designed. Experience will offer additional practice and further refine and mature your observational skills.

    The greater part of the journey in this text provided an in-depth study of seven different observational methods within the framework of child develop-ment (Chapters 4 through 8, 10, and 11). Now is the time to cement together an overall view of observation in the early childhood classroom by clearly comparing the distinctive features of each method. Figure 14.1 provides the mortar and Student Activity 14.1 some practice.

Student Activity 14.1 _____

Selecting Observational Methods

Read the following scenarios from early childhood classrooms. Write down an appropriate observational method to respond to each.

Scenario: A preschool teacher, Beverly, realizes she thinks about some children in her classroom more than others and worries that she does not support their growth equally. She asks her director to plan an observation to answer the question, "How often does Beverly interact with each child during a preschool session?"

Method:

Scenario: A child has just arrived in Costa's child care program in the middle of the year and is having difficulty adjusting. Costa wants to begin observing this.

Method:

Scenario: An early childhood education student, Lida, would like to begin to learn about classroom management techniques. She plans to observe several different classrooms in order to answer the question, "How do teachers deal with children's conflicts?"

Method:

Method	Subjects	Purpose	Data Produced	Frequency of Use
Running records	Individual children	Observe and document developmental growth; gain overall picture	Qualitative	As necessary
Anecdotes	Individual children	Document developmental growth and significant incidents	Qualitative	Daily
Checklists	Individual children or teachers, programs, and environments	Assess presence or absence of specific characteristics; assess changes over time	Qualitative*	Periodically
Rating scales	Individual children or teachers, programs, and environments	Assess strengths of specific characteristics; assess changes over time	Qualitative*	Periodically
ABC event sampling	Individual children	Observe specific problems and developmental growth in context	Qualitative	As necessary
Tally event sampling	Individual children or teachers and groups; programs and environments indirectly	Study frequencies of predetermined events	Quantitative	As necessary
Time sampling	Individual children or teachers and groups; programs and environments indirectly	Study time sampling of predetermined categories	Quantitative	As necessary

*This text only discussed the qualitative analysis of checklist and rating scale data. Occasionally you might see quantitative data produced and analyzed when using checklists and rating scales.

Figure 14.1. Comparison of observational methods for early childhood classrooms.

The Teacher's Commitment to Observation

> The ability to understand children through observation might be compared to the ability to judge fine art. We all respond to art—positively, negatively, indifferently—but the person with experience and training can better assess the aesthetic value of a work of art. Similarly, we all form impressions of children, but for the inexperienced observer, the impression may be inaccurate, biased, or limited in scope. (Phinney, 1982, pp. 23–24)

To best serve the education of all children in a classroom, the teacher demonstrates an active commitment to observation. The wheels of observation do not turn alone. They require the leadership of a teacher willing to plan observations of each child, the program, and the environment. Observation is a process; to successfully integrate observation into the classroom, the teacher builds time into the daily schedule.

Although based on the teacher's commitment and leadership, observation need not be a solitary activity. Teachers will find support by sharing efforts with directors, principals, colleagues, aides, parents, child study teams, and college students. Burdens of scheduling and time allocations are eased by involving the energies of others. The rewards of observation justify the commitment and follow-through of remarkable teachers.

The Benefits of Observation in the Early Childhood Classroom

The benefits of observation in preschool and primary grade classrooms are plentiful and have been noted throughout this book. Observation serves individual children by providing their teachers with information to chart their developmental growth, plan appropriate activities to support continued growth, uncover the roots of problems, and prepare useful feedback to their parents. Multiple observational methods offer the teacher a realistic view of the whole child. Observation renews the energies of teachers, who can monitor their own effectiveness and make productive adjustments. Observation helps teachers evaluate programs and environments to improve the quality of education offered children.

In closing, the benefits of observation return to children. All children are unique with their strengths and emerging interests and aspirations. The headwaters that nourish a vital commitment to a life's work might hardly be noticed during early childhood but, nonetheless, may contribute to later choices. Corey, a young graduate student in Spanish literature, traces his interest in the subject to his experience in a bilingual kindergarten program. Early childhood is a time for initial exploring and experimenting with possible areas of enjoyment and interest. Look beyond the young child for a moment. A complex society such as ours requires the diverse talents of its citizens to function and progress; fostering and supporting individual abilities thus serves society as well as the individual.

How can early childhood educators advance the development of each child? You know:

- By understanding each child as an individual within the context of a family and culture.

And how can these educators learn about each child? You know so well:

- By watching and listening to what each child does and says.
- By using the information gathered to plan developmentally appropriate experiences and to adjust the program and environment.
- By keeping child portfolios that bear witness to individuality and sharing treasures and concerns with parents.
- By observing through the looking glass with affection, competence, and commitment.

May your vision always be clear as you observe through the looking glass in an early childhood classroom.

Think About . . .

T.G.I.F., Friday already, and three best friends and fellow recent graduates with degrees in early childhood education share a monthly dinner. Maliha is teaching young 5-year-olds in a classroom on an elementary school campus. Clay has remained with his beloved parent participation program and is now a teacher, rather than an aide, in the 3- and 4-year-old classroom. Heather is reeling from the exhaustion and exhilaration of adjusting to teaching in an employer-related child care program after doing her student teaching in a laboratory school.

The three friends catch up, and inevitably, the conversation turns to their classrooms and the people who bring them to life. Maliha describes a child angry and resentful that she is not in kindergarten with her next-door neighbor and the ABC narrative event sampling results that helped Maliha identify which activities and interactions with other children supported the child's self-esteem. Clay relates the uncomfortable entry of a new child with limited English and the exciting program plans that resulted from a timely parent conference and that benefitted all children. Heather shares her feelings of jubilation that her aide now engages in activities with children ever since she videotaped him in the classroom and they viewed the results together. Think about these remarkable teachers and the role observation plays in their success.

Glossary

ABC narrative event sampling

an observational method used to explore the antecedents and consequences of individual children's behaviors within their naturally occurring contexts. Four columns on the recording sheet are labeled *Time*, *Antecedent Event*, *Behavior*, and *Consequence*.

Anecdotal record

an observational method used to summarize a single developmental incident after it occurs. The summary recounts *who*, *what*, *how*, and sometimes *when* and/or *where*. This method documents events involving individual children.

Anti-bias curriculum

a proactive approach using materials, experiences, teacher attitudes and interventions that works toward freeing children of prejudice and stereotypes regarding gender roles, race, culture, handicaps, and social class. It empowers children to like themselves and to respect and appreciate diversity.

Assessment

an appraisal based on observations or other measurements.

Autonomy

an ability to act independently.

Category rating scale

a specific type of rating scale design used to appraise selected characteristics; the observer assesses each item by choosing one of the possible designations listed under each item.

Category system

an approach used for selecting the types of items to be observed (e.g., in tally event or time sampling). In this approach all categories must be mutually exclusive, each category must be distinct and separate from the others, and the categories must be exhaustive.

Cephalocaudal
>   the physical growth pattern characterized by development from head to tail.

Checklist
>   an observational method providing a register of items that, if present, the observer marks
>   off. This observational method is used to assess the current characteristics of a child,
>   teacher, curriculum, or environment; to track changes in these characteristics over time;
>   and to support program planning.

Classification
>   the sorting of objects into classes and subclasses according to similarities and differences.

Closed question
>   an interrogative that has a single correct answer.

Cognitive development
>   the changing and expanding intellectual processes of human beings.

Collaborative apprenticeship
>   the process of peer teaching.

Color coding
>   the use of an assigned color to specify a particular category.

Conference form
>   the written framework for reporting a child's development and arriving at joint
>   parent/teacher goals.

Conservation
>   the concept that something remains the same if nothing is added or taken away.

Cooperative learning group
>   an assigned number of children who are given a task to complete together.

Creativity
>   the process of self-expression as it relates to unique ideas in art, music, movement, drama,
>   and thinking. According to Fabun, expression is creative if it is new to the individual; oth-
>   ers may have expressed the same or similar ideas independently.

Cultural diversity
>   a variety of ethnic and social groups.

Developmentally appropriate
>   refers to age appropriateness (framework for experiences and environment are planned
>   based on the universal sequence of development) and individual appropriateness (experi-
>   ences are consistent with each individual child's interests, abilities, and knowledge).

Divergent thinking
>   an approach that is open to new alternatives, exploring possibilities, and evaluating infor-
>   mation from many perspectives.

Educational practitioner

a trained adult who teaches in a setting for learning.

Egocentrism

the inability to distinguish one's own from others' points of view.

Error of central tendency

the inclination for an observer to rate in the middle when using an odd number of descriptors.

Event

an identified behavior or incident.

Fine motor development

the maturing of small muscles (e.g., fingers).

Fluorescent lighting

an artificial light source in a glass tube that gives off light through the interaction of mercury vapor and electrons.

Full-spectrum lighting

fluorescent lighting that has a range of colors similar to that of sunlight.

Gender identity

knowing one's own gender.

Graphic rating scale

a specific type of rating scale design used to appraise selected characteristics; the observer assigns each item a value on a given horizontal or vertical continuum.

Grid

the graphed box that is formed by a horizontal axis of categories intersecting with a vertical axis of categories.

Gross motor development

the maturing of large muscles (e.g., upper arms).

Growth indicators

the manifestations of development that denote advancement. They are generally the focus of observations.

Halo effect

the susceptibility of an observer to be influenced by preconceived ideas or impressions.

Hand dominance

a preference for the use of the left or the right hand for one-hand tasks.

Help-yourself art shelf

an organized, categorized, and designated low cabinet filled with materials for creating. Children may use these materials at their own discretion during free-choice times.

Hostile aggression
>   aggression in which the intent is to hurt or dominate another.

Incandescent lighting
>   an artificial light source in a vacuum bulb.

Individual Education Plan (IEP)
>   a team-written instructional program designed for a specific handicapped child and based on the child's unique needs, interests, impairment, and abilities. The team usually includes a diagnostic specialist, the teacher, the parent(s), other specified professionals, and the child (if appropriate).

Individual Family Services Plan (IFSP)
>   a multidisciplinary team-written program for the optimum development of a specific handicapped infant, toddler, or preschool child. The program includes support, instruction, and counseling for the family and a comprehensive program for the child.

Information-processing view of cognitive development
>   mental activities viewed as analogous to the working procedures of a computer; focuses on the processes of cognition, not just the outcomes.

Initiation (teacher)
>   when a teacher asks a question, provides needed materials and experiences for individuals or groups, or seizes treasured teaching moments to model.

Instrumental aggression
>   aggression in which the intent is not to hurt but to gain possession of an object, territory, or privilege.

Integrated curriculum approach
>   a program design that incorporates all subjects or disciplines around a central topic or theme.

Interest centers
>   areas of the room set up around an organizational feature (e.g., housekeeping, manipulatives, and blocks).

Inter-rater reliability
>   a measure between two or more observers resulting in a percentage that indicates the amount of agreement; exact agreement is 100%.

Maturation
>   the process of physical development involving the central nervous system.

Metamemory
>   knowledge about memory including knowledge about people as rememberers, varying difficulty of memory tasks, and appropriate memory strategies.

Motor development
>   the maturing of small and large muscles (fine and gross motor development, respectively); this maturing is characterized by fluid movements.

Numerical rating scale

> a specific type of rating scale design used to appraise selected characteristics; the observer assesses each characteristic by choosing one of the given number values for each item.

Objective observations

> recordings based on facts and occurring events.

Observation

> watching and recording significant behaviors, characteristics, situations, events, or surroundings.

Observational instrument

> the form on which an observer records the data. The instrument includes a heading, space for data, and other pertinent information (e.g., instructions, definitions, or codes).

Observational question

> an educational problem or concern to be studied that is stated as an interrogatory.

Observational records

> entries of accounts that have been witnessed and noted.

Observer bias

> a prejudice or judgment based on the feelings or impressions of the one who is assessing or recording.

One-to-one correspondence

> the ability to count objects in sequence, labeling each object with the correct number.

Open question

> an interrogative that has many possible answers and allows the respondent an opportunity to expand and explain.

Operationally defined

> a description based on the function of the item.

Overt

> observable and apparent.

Parent conference

> an arranged meeting between a teacher and a child's parent(s) for the purpose of establishing a partnership in the child's education.

Pilot testing

> the process of trying out an observational instrument to assess its workability.

Portfolio

> a collection of observational records and work samples for one child, usually kept for a period of one year.

Power words
> child-spoken profanity or words that stretch the limits within a school environment.

Preclassification skills
> the abilities that precede classification (e.g., sorting in graphic collections or identifying attributes).

Preschematic art stage
> a period when children (generally 4 to 7 years old) draw their first representations. This term also denotes drawn or painted pictures that have space distortions and disorganized, disproportionate, or omitted objects.

Preschool
> planned learning experiences in a developmental environment for children 2 to 5 years old. Usually scheduled for $2^1/_2$ hours in the morning or afternoon.

Primary grade school
> kindergarten through third grade.

Private spaces
> designed areas in a classroom big enough for a single child and used as a child-chosen retreat.

Process approach to creativity
> a belief that creativity is the result of possessing abilities and having conditions that allow for practice and improvement.

Prosocial behavior
> positive demonstrations of moral development.

Proximodistal
> physical growth pattern characterized by development from the center of the body to the outside.

Psychosocial development
> the changes in human beings involving emotions, personality, and social relationships.

Qualitative data
> information that yields narrative results.

Quantitative data
> information that yields numerical results.

Rating scale
> an observational method in which the observer, using a predesigned instrument, selects a value for each of the listed characteristics. This method is used to evaluate specific characteristics of a child, teacher, curriculum, or environment and monitor changes over time; information gathered from these recordings can be used to plan developmentally appropriate activities and effective teacher strategies.

Recall memory
> remembering without a cue being present.

Recognition memory
> remembering by recognizing something familiar.

Recording form
> a document used to collect observational data (e.g., running records or ABC narrative event sampling).

Record-keeping system
> an organizational method used for systematically storing observations.

Representational thought
> the cognitive ability to allow a mental symbol, word, or object stand for something else (e.g., a child's drawing may represent a house).

Running record
> an observational method used to explore the development of individual children; the observer writes a detailed, objective, sequential narrative of events in progress and adds a brief summary conclusion at the end.

Sampling
> the process of collecting a subset of data to represent the behaviors or events under investigation.

Schematic art stage
> a period of time when a child (generally 7 to 9 years old) develops a form concept. This period denotes drawings and paintings that have schemata, baselines, and two-dimensional organization.

Self-concept
> the psychological construct of the self; this construct is nourished by expanding cognitive and social maturity.

Self-esteem
> the evaluative component of the sense of self; this component derives from the warmth, acceptance, and respectful treatment given a child and from the child's success in selected areas of interest.

Semantic differential arrangement
> a variation of a graphic rating scale in which each line contains segmented boxes with opposite adjectives at each end (e.g., talkative/quiet).

Sensory table
> a large container or a specially designed piece of equipment used for mixing, pouring, feeling, and experiencing items of various textures (e.g., water, sand, or Styrofoam bits).

Seriation

arranging objects in order along one characteristic (e.g., arranging four pieces of sandpaper from fine to coarse).

Sign system

an approach used for selecting the types of items to be observed (e.g., in tally event or time sampling). In this approach all categories must be mutually exclusive and each category must be distinct and separate from the others.

Stage view of cognitive development

mental structures of children change qualitatively because of individual rates of maturation and active experience in the world.

Subjective observations

recordings based on personal impressions and feelings.

Systematized

organized in an orderly fashion.

Tally event sampling

an observational method used to systematically record the frequency of occurrence for an identified behavior or situation within a designated period. This method collects quantitative data primarily about children, teachers, or groups.

Thematic units

a curriculum approach that integrates all content areas by organizing instructional objectives, materials, and activities around a specific topic or theme.

Three-dimensional materials

items that have depth (e.g., cardboard cylinders or wood blocks).

Time sampling

an observational method used for methodical investigation of behaviors that occur in rapid succession. Predetermined units of time and a recording grid guide the observer's collection of quantitative data primarily about children, teachers, and groups.

Traffic patterns

the pathways used to get from one area to another. They can be inside or outside.

Trait approach to creativity

a belief that creativity is innate and unfolds naturally.

Zone of proximal development

the distance between the level of children's independent functioning and the level of their functioning with adult help.

References

ADLER, J. WITH WINGERT, P., WRIGHT, L., HOUSTON, P., MANLY, H., & COHEN, A. (1992, February 17). Hey, I'm terrific. *Newsweek*, pp. 46–51.

ANDREWS, I. (1992). Conference form. San Juan Capistrano, CA: St. Margaret's Preschool.

BARATTA-LORTON, M. (1976). *Mathematics their way*. Menlo Park, CA: Addison-Wesley.

BEATY, J. J. (1990). *Observing development of the young child* (2nd ed.). New York: Merrill/Macmillan.

BEILIN, H. (1992). Piaget's enduring contribution to developmental psychology. *Developmental Psychology, 28*, 191–204.

BELL, D. R., & LOW, R. M. (1977). *Observing and recording children's behavior*. Richland, WA: Performance Associates.

BEM, S. (1989). Genital knowledge and gender constancy in preschool children. *Child Development, 60*, 649–662.

BERGER, K. S. (1991). *The developing person through childhood and adolescence* (2nd ed.). New York: Worth.

BIGELOW, B. J. (1977). Children's friendship expectations: A cognitive-developmental study. *Child Development, 48*, 246–253.

BIRREN, F. (1972). *Color psychology and color therapy*. New York: University Books.

BIRREN, F. (1978). *Color and human response*. New York: Van Nostrand Reinhold.

BIRREN, F. (1988). *Light, color, and the environment*. West Chester, PA: Schiffer.

BLACK, J., PUCKETT, M., & BELL, M. (1992). *The young child: Development from prebirth through age eight*. New York: Macmillan.

BLOOM, B. S. (Ed.). (1985a). *Developing talent in young people*. New York: Ballantine Books.

BLOOM, B. S. (Ed.). (1985b). *Taxonomy of educational objectives. Handbook I: Cognitive domain*. New York: Longman.

BOEHM, A. L., & WEINBERG, R. A. (1987). *The classroom observer: Developing observation skills in early childhood settings* (2nd ed.). New York: Teachers College Press.

BORG, W. R. (1987). *Applying educational research: A practical guide for teachers* (2nd. ed.). New York: Longman.

BRAUSE, R. S., & MAYHER, J. S. (1991). Collecting and analyzing classroom data in theory and in practice. In R. S. Brause & J. S. Mayher (Eds.), *Search and re-search: What the inquiring teacher needs to know* (pp. 131–156). Bristol, PA: Falmer Press.

BRAZELTON, T. B. (1984). *To listen to a child*. Reading, MA: Addison-Wesley.

BREDEKAMP, S. (Ed.). (1987). *Developmentally appropriate practice in early childhood programs serving children from birth through age 8*. Washington, DC: National Association for the Education of Young Children.

BREDEKAMP, S. (1992). What is "developmentally appropriate" and why is it important? *Journal of Physical Education, Recreation, and Dance, 63*, 31–32.

BUELL, L. H. (1984). *Understanding the refugee Vietnamese*. San Diego: Los Amigos Research Associates.

BURTS, D. C., HART, C. H., CHARLESWORTH, R., FLEEGE, P. O., MOSLEY, J., & THOMASSON, R. H. (1992). Observed activities and stress behaviors of children in developmentally appropriate and inappropriate kindergarten classrooms. *Early Childhood Research Quarterly, 7*, 1–17.

CALKINS, L. (1986). *The art of teaching writing*. Portsmouth, NH: Heinemann Educational Books.

CARBO, M. (1983). *The reading style inventory*. Roslyn Heights, NY: National Reading Styles Institute.

CARLSON, K., & CUNNINGHAM, J. L. (1990). Effect of pencil diameter on the graphomotor skill of preschoolers. *Early Childhood Research Quarterly, 5*, 279–293.

CAZDEN, C. B. (1972). Suggestions from studies of early language acquisition. In C. B. Cazden (Ed.), *Language in early childhood education* (pp. 3–8). Washington, DC: National Association for the Education of Young Children.

CAZDEN, C. B. (1988). *Classroom discourse*. Portsmouth, NH: Heinemann Educational Books.

CENTER MANAGEMENT STAFF. (1990, September/October). Design: Keep the kids in mind. *Center Management*, pp. 10, 12, 14–15.

CHERRY, C. (1981). *Think of something quiet*. Belmont, CA: David S. Lake.

CHERRY, C. (1990). *Creative art for the developing child* (2nd ed.). San Bernadino, CA: David S. Lake.

CHI, M. H. T. (1978). Knowledge structures and memory development. In. R. S. Siegler (Ed.), *Children's thinking: What develops?* (pp. 73–96). Hillsdale, NJ: Erlbaum.

CLARK, J. E., & PHILLIPS, S. J. (1985). A developmental sequence of the standing long jump. In J. E. Clark & J. H. Humphrey (Eds.), *Motor development: Current selected research* (pp. 73–85). Princeton, NJ: Princeton Book Company.

COOPERSMITH, S. (1967). *The antecedents of self-esteem*. San Francisco: W. H. Freeman.

CORBIN, C. B. (1980). *A textbook of motor development*. Dubuque, IA: William C. Brown.

CRATTY, B. J. (1986). *Perceptual and motor development in infants and children* (3rd ed.). Englewood Cliffs, NJ: Prentice-Hall.

CROSSWHITE, L. (1991). *A guide to a shared reading experience*. Jacksonville, IL: Perma-bound.

CUTTING, B. (1989). *Getting started in whole language*. San Diego, CA: Wright Group, the United States Publisher.

DE LONG, A. J., TEGANO, D. W., MORAN, J. D., III, BRICKEY, J., MORROW, D., & HOUSER, T. L. (1991). Effects of spatial scale on cognitive play in preschool children. *ASID Report*, July/August, 8–9.

DERMAN-SPARKS, L., & A.B.C. TASK FORCE (1989). *Anti-bias curriculum: Tools for empowering young children*. Washington, DC: National Association for the Education of Young Children.

DOOLEY, D. (1990). *Social research methods* (2nd ed.). Englewood Cliffs, NJ: Prentice-Hall.

DORSEY, R. T. (1980). How to get the most from your present lighting system. *American School and University, 52*, 32–33, 34, 36.

DU RANDT, R. (1985). Ball catching proficiency among 4-, 6-, and 8-year-old girls. In J. E. Clark & J. H. Humphrey (Eds.), *Motor development: Current selected research* (pp. 35–43). Princeton, NJ: Princeton Book Company.

DURO-TEST (1988). *A guide for simulating natural light in interior environments to maximize the quality of working life*. Fairfield, NJ: Duro-Test.

EDELMAN, M. W. (1992, May). Letter to my sons. *Parents*, pp. 98–102.

EDEN, R. A. (1990). Uncovering young children's psychological selves: Individual and developmental differences. *Child Development, 61*, 849–863.

ELKIND, D. (1988). *The hurried child* (rev. ed.). Reading, MA: Addison-Wesley.

EVERTSON, C. M., & GREEN, J. L. (1986). Observation as inquiry and method. In M. C. Wittrock (Ed.), *Handbook of research on teaching* (3rd ed.) (pp. 162–213). New York: Macmillan.

FABUN, D. (1968). *You and creativity*. Beverly Hills, CA: Glencoe Press.

FAMILY HOME ENTERTAINMENT. (1986). *The working parent, daycare, separation and your child's development* [Videotape]. Quincy, IL: Tomorrow Entertainment, Inc.

FASSNACHT, G. (1982). *Theory and practice of observing behaviour*. London: Academic Press.

FEENEY, S., CHRISTENSEN, D., & MORAVCIK, E. (1991). *Who am I in the lives of young children?: An introduction to teaching young children* (4th ed.). New York: Merrill/Macmillan.

FELDMAN, D. H. (1980). *Beyond universals in cognitive development*. Norwood, NJ: Ablex.

FLAVELL, J. H., MILLER, P. H., & MILLER, S. A. (1993). *Cognitive development* (3rd ed.). Englewood Cliffs, NJ: Prentice-Hall

FLAVELL, J. H., SHIPSTEAD, S. G., & CROFT, K. (1978). Young children's knowledge about visual perception: Hiding objects from others. *Child Development, 49*, 1208–1211.

FLAVELL, J. H., SHIPSTEAD, S. G., & CROFT, K. (1980). What young children think you see when their eyes are closed. *Cognition, 8*, 369–387.

FOLLMI, O. (1989, December). Journey to knowledge. *Life*, pp. 109–116.

FROST, J. L. (1992). *Play and playscapes*. Albany, NY: Delmar.

GALLAHUE, D. L. (1982). *Developmental movement experiences for children*. New York: Macmillan.

GELMAN, R. (1972). Logical capacity of very young children: Number invariance rules. *Child Development, 43*, 75–90.

GELMAN, R., & BAILLARGEON, R. (1983). A review of some Piagetian concepts. In J. H. Flavell & E. M. Markman (Eds.), *Handbook of child psychology* (Vol. III, 4th ed., pp. 167–230). New York: John Wiley & Sons.

GENISHI, C. (1982). Observational research methods for early childhood education. In B. Spodek (Ed.), *Handbook of research in early childhood education* (pp. 564–591). New York: Free Press.

GETTY CENTER FOR EDUCATION IN THE ARTS. (1985). *Beyond creativity: The place for art in America's schools*. Los Angeles: The J. Paul Getty Trust.

GINSBURG, H. (1989). *Children's arithmetic: How they learn it and how you teach it* (2nd ed.). Austin, TX: Pro-Ed, Inc.

GINSBURG, H., & OPPER, S. (1988). *Piaget's theory of intellectual development* (3rd ed.). Englewood Cliffs, NJ: Prentice-Hall.

GOODWIN, W. L., & DRISCOLL, L. A. (1980). *Handbook for measurement and evaluation in early childhood education*. San Francisco: Jossey-Bass.

GORDON, A. M., & BROWNE, K. W. (1993). *Beginnings and beyond* (3rd ed). Albany, NY: Delmar.

GRANGAARD, E. (1993). *Effects of color and light on selected elementary students.* Unpublished doctoral dissertation, University of Nevada, Las Vegas.

GREENMAN, J. (1988). *Caring spaces, learning places: Children's environments that work.* Redmond, WA: Exchange Press.

GUNDERSON, L. (1989). *A whole language primer.* Ontario, Canada: Scholastic TAB.

HARMS, T. A., & CLIFFORD, R. M. (1980). *Early childhood environment rating scale.* New York: Teachers College Press.

HARTUP, W. W., LAURSEN, B., STEWART, M. I., & EASTENSON, A. (1988). Conflict and the friendship relations of young children. *Child Development, 59,* 1590–1600.

HARTUP, W. W., & MOORE, S. G. (1990). Early peer relations: Developmental significance and prognostic implications. *Early Childhood Research Quarterly, 5,* 1–17.

HATHAWAY, W. E. (1982, September). *Lights, window, color: Elements of the school environment.* Paper presented at the Council of Educational Facility Planners 59th annual conference, Columbus, OH.

HATHAWAY, W. E., HARGREAVES, J. A., THOMPSON, G. W., & NOVITSKY, D. (1992). *A study into the effects of light on children of elementary school age—A case of daylight robbery.* Unpublished manuscript, Planning and Information Services Division, Edmonton, Alberta, Canada.

HEIDEMANN, S., & HEWITT, D. (1992). *Pathways to play.* St. Paul, MN: Redleaf Press.

HENDRICK, J. (1990). *Total learning: Developmental curriculum for the young child* (3rd ed.). New York: Macmillan.

HENDRICK, J. (1992). *The whole child: Developmental education for the early years* (5th ed.). New York: Macmillan.

HERBERHOLZ, B., & HANSON, L. (1990). *Early childhood art.* Dubuque, IA: William C. Brown.

HIGH/SCOPE EDUCATIONAL RESEARCH FOUNDATION. (1976). *Thinking and reasoning in preschool children* [Videotape]. Ypsilanti, MI: High/Scope.

HIGH/SCOPE EDUCATIONAL RESEARCH FOUNDATION. (1992a). *High/Scope child observation record for ages $2^1/_2$–6.* Ypsilanti, MI: High/Scope Press.

HIGH/SCOPE EDUCATIONAL RESEARCH FOUNDATION. (1992b). *Teacher's manual of the COR.* Ypsilanti, MI: High/Scope Press.

HILBERT, D. R. (1987). *Color and color perception: A study in anthropocentric realism.* Stanford, CA: Center for the Study of Language and Information.

HIRSCH, E. S. (Ed.). (1990). *The block book.* Washington, DC: National Association for the Education of Young Children.

HOHMANN, M., BANET, B., & WEIKART, D. P. (1979). *Young children in action.* Ypsilanti, MI: High/Scope Press.

HOUGHTON MIFFLIN. (1989). *Houghton Mifflin literary readers: Selection plans and instructional support. Book 1. Teacher's guide.* Boston: Houghton Mifflin.

HUTT, S. J., & HUTT, C. (1970). *Direct observation and measurement of behavior.* Springfield, IL: C. C. Thomas.

KAPEL, D. E., GIFFORD, C. S., & KAPEL, M. B. (1991). *American educators' encyclopedia.* New York: Greenwood Press.

KAPLAN, P. S. (1991). *A child's odyssey: Child and adolescent development* (2nd ed.). St. Paul, MN: West.

KATZ, P., & ZIGLER, E. (1967). Self-image disparity: A developmental approach. *Journal of Personality and Social Psychology, 5,* 186–195.

KELLOGG, R. (1970). *Analyzing children's art.* Palo Alto, CA: Mayfield.

KERLINGER, F. N. (1986). *Foundations of behavioral research* (3rd ed.). New York: Holt, Rinehart & Winston.

KERR, R. (1985). Fitts' law and motor control in children. In J. E. Clark & J. H. Humphrey (Eds.), *Motor development: Current selected research* (pp. 45–53). Princeton, NJ: Princeton Book Company.

KONNER, M. (1991). *Childhood*. Boston: Little, Brown.

KREUTZER, M. A., LEONARD, C., & FLAVELL, J. H. (1975). An interview study of children's knowledge about memory. *Monographs of the Society for Research in Child Development, 40*(1, Serial No. 159).

KRITCHEVSKY, S. & PRESCOTT, E. WITH WALLING, L. (1977). *Planning environments for young children: Physical space*. Washington, DC: National Association for the Education of Young Children.

LAWLER, S. D. (1991). *Parent-teacher conferencing in early childhood education*. Washington, DC: National Education Association of the United States.

LEAVITT, R. L., & EHEART, B. K. (1985). *Toddler day care: A guide to responsive caregiving*. Lexington, MA: Lexington Books, D. C. Heath.

LEAVITT, R. L., & EHEART, B. K. (1991). Assessment in early childhood programs. *Young Children, 46*, 4–9.

LINDERMAN, M. G. (1990). *Art in the elementary school: Drawing, painting, & creating for the classroom* (4th ed.). Dubuque, IA: William C. Brown.

LINDGREN, K. (1992, February 16). Sex bias in class? Few teachers raise hands. *Los Angeles Times*, pp. B1, B5–6.

LOUGHLIN, C. E., & SUINA, J. H. (1982). *Learning environment: An instructional strategy*. New York: Teachers College Press.

LOVETT, S. B., & FLAVELL, J. H. (1990). Understanding and remembering: Children's knowledge about the differential effects of strategy and task variables on comprehension and memorization. *Child Development, 61*, 1842–1858.

LOWENFELD, V., & BRITTAIN, W. L. (1987). *Creative and mental growth* (8th ed.). New York: Macmillan.

LUSCHER (1969). *The Luscher color test*. New York: Random House.

MACCOBY, E. E. (1980). *Social development*. New York: Harcourt Brace Jovanovich.

MACCOBY, E. E. (1990). Gender and relationships: A developmental account. *American Psychologist, 45*, 513–520.

MAHNKE, F. H., & MAHNKE, R. H. (1987). *Color and light in man-made environments*. New York: Van Nostrand Reinhold.

MANN, J., TEN HAVE, T., PLUNKETT, J. W., & MEISELS, S. J. (1991). Time sampling: A methodological critique. *Child Development, 62*, 227–241.

MARSH, H. W., BYRNE, B. M., & SHAVELSON, R. J. (1988). A multifaceted academic self-concept: Its hierarchical structure and its relation to academic achievement. *Journal of Educational Psychology, 80*, 366–380.

MASLOW, A. H. (1970). *Motivation and personality* (2nd ed.). New York: Harper & Row.

McCORMICK, E. J., & ILGEN, D. (1980). *Industrial psychology*. Englewood Cliffs, NJ: Prentice Hall.

McCUTCHEON, G. (1981). On the interpretation of classroom observations. *Educational Researcher, 10*(5), 5–10.

McKERNAN, J. (1991). *Curriculum action research*. New York: St. Martin's Press.

MEDINNUS, G. (1976). *Child study and observation guide*. New York: Wiley.

MEDLEY, D. M., & MITZEL, H. E. (1963). Measuring classroom behavior by systematic observation. In N. L. Gage (Ed.), *Handbook of research on teaching* (pp. 247–328). Chicago: Rand McNally.

NATIONAL ACADEMY OF EARLY CHILDHOOD PROGRAMS. (1991). *Guide to accreditation* (rev. ed.). Washington, DC: National Association for the Education of Young Children.

NATIONAL ASSOCIATION FOR THE EDUCATION OF YOUNG CHILDREN. (1981). *Some ways of distinguishing a good early childhood program*. Washington, DC: National Association for the Education of Young Children.

NATIONAL ASSOCIATION FOR THE EDUCATION OF YOUNG CHILDREN & NATIONAL ASSOCIATION OF EARLY CHILDHOOD SPECIALISTS IN STATE DEPARTMENTS OF EDUCATION. (1991). Guidelines for appropriate curriculum content and assessment in programs serving children age 3 through 8, a joint position statement. *Young Children, 46*, 21–38.

NATIONAL TASK FORCE ON DAY CARE INTERIOR DESIGN. (1992). *Design of the times: Day care*. Seattle, WA: Dan B. Spinelli.

OSGOOD, C. E., SUCI, G. J., & TANNEBAUM, P. H. (1957). *The meaning of measurement*. Urbana, IL: University of Illinois Press.

OSMON, F. (1971). *Patterns for designing children's centers*. New York: Educational Facilities Laboratory.

OSTLING, R. N. (1992, February 24). Is school unfair to girls? *Time*, p. 62.

OTT, J. N. (1982). *Light, radiation, & you*. Old Greenwich, CT: Devin-Adair.

PAGE, R. M., FREY, J., TALBERT, R., & FALK, C. (1992). Children's feelings of loneliness and social dissatisfaction: Relationship to measures of physical fitness and activity. *Journal of Teaching in Physical Education, 11*(3), 211–219.

PALEY, V. G. (1986). *Mollie is three*. Chicago: University of Chicago Press.

PARTEN, M. B. (1932). Social participation among pre-school children. *Journal of Abnormal and Social Psychology, 27*, 243–269.

PFLAUM, S. W. (1986). *The development of language and literacy in young children* (3rd ed.). Columbus, OH: Merrill.

PHINNEY, J. S. (1982). Observing children: Ideas for teachers. *Young Children, 37*, 16–24.

PIAGET, J. (1963). *The origins of intelligence in children*. New York: W. W. Norton.

PIAGET, J., & INHELDER, B. (1967). *The child's conception of space*. New York: W. W. Norton.

PIAGET, J., & INHELDER, B. (1969). *The psychology of the child*. New York: Basic Books.

POEST, C. A., WILLIAMS, J. R., WITT, D. D., & ATWOOD, M. (1990). Challenge me to move: Large muscle development in young children. *Young Children, 45*, 4–9.

POYSNER, L. R. (1983). *An examination of the classroom physical environment*. Unpublished research paper. Indiana University, South Bend.

REMMERS, H. H. (1963). Rating methods in research on teaching. In N. L. Gage (Ed.), *Handbook on research on teaching* (pp. 329–378). Chicago: Rand McNally.

RHODES, L., & NATHENSON-MEJIA, S. (1992). Anecdotal records: A powerful tool for ongoing literacy assessment. *Reading Teacher, 45*, 502–509.

ROGERS, C. S., & SAWYERS, J. K. (1988). *Play in the lives of children*. Washington, DC: National Association for the Education of Young Children.

RUUD, A. (1978). What to look for in classroom lighting. *American School and University, 51*, 45, 48.

SCARR, S., WEINBERG, R. A., & LEVINE, A. (1986). *Understanding children*. San Diego: Harcourt Brace Jovanovich.

SCHIRRMACHER, R. (1988). *Art and creative development for young children*. Albany, NY: Delmar.

SCHNEIDER, W., & PRESSLEY, M. (1989). *Memory development between 2 and 20*. New York: Springer-Verlag.

SCHWARTZ, S., & POLLISHUKE, M. (1991). *Creating the child-centered classroom*. Katonah, NY: Richard C. Owen.

SCHWEINHART, L., & McNAIR, J. (1991, Fall). The NEW child observation record. *High/Scope ReSource*, pp. 4–9.

SHAFFER, D. R. (1993). *Developmental psychology: Childhood and adolescence* (3rd ed.). Pacific Grove, CA: Brooks/Cole.

SILVERSTEIN, S. (1974). *Where the sidewalk ends*. New York: Harper & Row.

SMOOT, S. A. (1972). *A comparative study of teacher attitudes toward open education and their actual classroom climates*. Unpublished master's thesis, Arizona State University, Tempe, Arizona.

STANFORD CENTER FOR THE STUDY OF FAMILIES, CHILDREN AND YOUTH. (1991). *The Stanford studies of homeless families, children and youth*. Stanford, CA: Stanford University.

STODDART, T., & TURIEL, E. (1985). Children's concepts of cross-gender activities. *Child Development, 56,* 1241–1252.

TAYLOR, A. P., & VLASTOS, G. (1975). *Learning environments for children*. New York: Van Nostrand Reinhold.

TAYLOR, A. P., & VLASTOS, G. (1988). *Guidelines for classroom designs*. Corrales, NM: School Zone.

TAYLOR, B. J. (1991). *A child goes forth: A curriculum guide for preschool children* (7th ed.). New York: Macmillan.

THOMAS, R. M. (1992). *Comparing theories of child development* (3rd ed.). Belmont, CA: Wadsworth.

TORRANCE, E. P. (1976). Education and creativity. In A. Rothenberg & C. R. Hausman (Eds.), *The creativity question* (pp. 217–227). Durham, NC: Duke University Press.

TORRANCE, E. P. (1977). *Creativity in the classroom*. Washington, DC: National Education Association.

TORRICE, A. F., & LOGRIPPO, R. (1989). *In my room*. New York: Fawcett Columbine.

VERGERONT, J. (1987). *Places and spaces for preschool and primary (indoors)*. Washington, DC: National Association for the Education of Young Children.

VYGOTSKY, L. (1978). *Mind in society: The development of higher psychological processes*. Cambridge, MA: Harvard University Press.

WATSON, D. L., OMARK, D. R., GROUELL, S. L., & HELLER, B. (1981). *Nondiscriminatory assessment. Volume I. Practitioner's guide*. San Diego, CA: Los Amigos Research Associates.

WAY, L. (1992). Fall conference form. Laguna Niguel, CA: Pacific Preschool.

WEINSTEIN, C. S. (1981). Classroom design as an external condition for learning. *Educational Technology, 21,* 12–19.

WELLMAN, H. M. (1990). *The child's theory of mind*. Cambridge, MA: MIT Press.

WERNER, E. E., & SMITH, R. S. (1982). *Vulnerable but invincible: A study of resilient children*. New York: McGraw-Hill.

WITT, J., HEFFER, R., & PHEIFFER, J. (1990). Structured rating scales: A review of self-report and informant rating processes, procedures, and issues. In C. R. Reynolds & R. W. Kamphaus (Eds.), *Handbook of psychological and educational assessment of children: Personality, behavior, and content* (2, pp. 364–394). New York: Guilford Press.

WOHLFARTH, K. (1981). *The effects of color/light changes on severely handicapped children*. Unpublished paper, University of Edmonton, Alberta, Canada: Alberta Education.

WOHLFARTH, K. (1983). *The effects of a color psychodynamically designed environment upon mental performance, scholastic performance, and physiological reaction of elementary school students*. University of Edmonton, Alberta, Canada: Alberta Education.

WOLFGANG, C., MACKENDER, M., & WOLFGANG, M. (1981). *Growing and learning through play*. Paoli, PA: Instructo-McGraw Hill.

WRIGHT, C., & FESLER, L. (1987). Nurturing creative potential: A model early childhood program. *The Creative Child and Adult Quarterly, 12*, 152–161.

WRIGHT, H. (1960). Observational child study. In P. Mussen (Ed.), *Handbook of research methods in child development* (pp. 71–139). New York: John Wiley.

YIZHONG, Z. (1984). Effects of color rendering properties of light sources on visual acuity. *Acta Psychologic Sinica, 16*(2), 193–203.

YORK, S. (1991). *Roots and wings: Affirming culture in early childhood programs*. St. Paul, MN: Redleaf Press.

Index

ISBN 0-02-387491-0